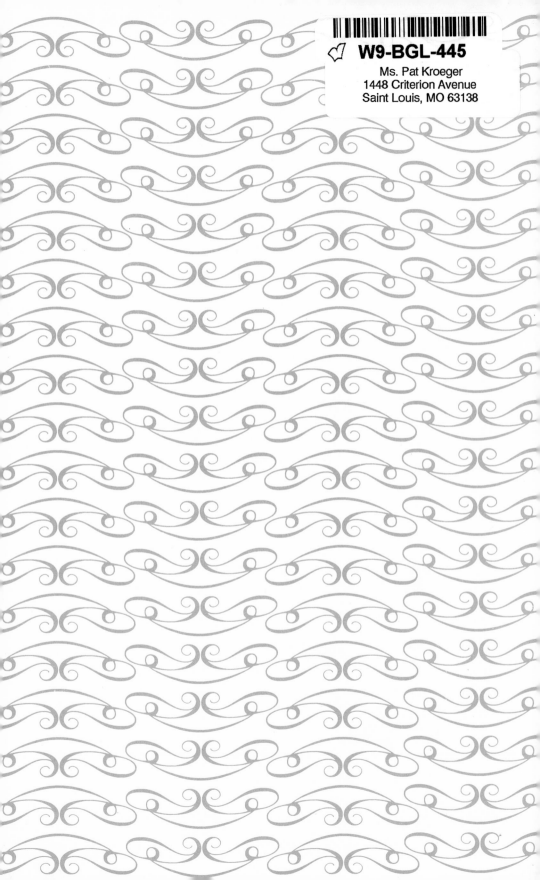

Back Talk

Back Talk

TEACHING LOST SELVES TO SPEAK

Joan Weimer

RANDOM HOUSE

NEW YORK

Some names and identifying details have been changed. If the people mentioned here were to write their own accounts, they would probably be quite different from mine. To the best of my ability, I have tried to describe truthfully how it felt to be me.

All rights reserved under International and Pan-American Copyright Conventions. Published in the United States by Random House, Inc., New York, and simultaneously in Canada by Random House of Canada Limited, Toronto.

Grateful acknowledgment is made to the following to use both published and unpublished material:
CPP/Belwin, Inc., and Songwriters Guild of America: Excerpt from "Honey," by Seymour Simons, Haven Gillespie, and Richard A. Whiting. Copyright © 1928 (renewed 1956) by EMI Feist Catalog Inc. All rights reserved. Reprinted by permission of CPP/Belwin, Inc., Miami, Florida, and Songwriters Guild of America.
Western Reserve Historical Society: Excerpts from the Mather Family Papers housed at the Western Reserve Historical Society, Cleveland, Ohio. Used by permission.

Library of Congress Cataloging-in-Publication Data
Weimer, Joan Myers.
Back talk : teaching lost selves to speak / by Joan Weimer.
p. cm.
ISBN 0-679-41546-7
1. Weimer, Joan Myers.   2. English teachers—United States—Biography.   3. Spinal cord—Wounds and injuries—Patients—United States—Biography.   4. Women teachers—United States—Biography.
I. Title.
PE64.W55A3   1994   820.9—dc20   93-44742
[B]

Manufactured in the United States of America on acid-free paper
Book design by Tanya M. Pérez
2   4   6   8   9   7   5   3
First Edition

For David
and
In memory of my mother

If I could go into a convent, (where I didn't have to confess, nor rise before daylight for icy matins), I think I could write three or four novels better than any I have yet done. But there are no worldly convents. So I'll write my new effusions on another star, and send them back to you by telepathy.

—Letter written shortly before her death
by Constance Fenimore Woolson

CONTENTS

	Prologue	3
1	Taking Advantage	10
2	Informed Consent	31
3	Learning to Walk	45
4	Credentials	56
5	Buried Goddesses	75
6	The Proud Salmon of the Pond	89
7	Sisters of Charity	111
8	Maternal Mirrors	130
9	Brass Horse, High Horse	150
10	Spirits from the Vasty Deep	167
11	Not All of Them Will Love You	186
12	Why Literary Women Break Down	206
13	The Healthiest Woman in New Jersey	226
14	Meeting Miss Grief	242
15	Nightmare Doubles	255
16	Not Everything Can Open	274
	Epilogue	287
	Acknowledgments	293
	Notes	297

Back Talk

PROLOGUE:

Stopped in My Tracks

On my mother's doorstep I pause to take in her view. In the wide inlet of the Charles River, black-and-white Canada geese are nudging their goslings into the water. I envy their swim; the June day is humid. Before I can touch the bell, the door opens and my mother peers anxiously up at me. My husband she ignores.

"You poor kid, come in, come in. Wait—wipe your feet. The goddamn geese—did you pick up any of their calling cards?" I twist to check the soles of my feet and my new back brace cuts off my breath. David refuses to look at his shoes. I drop my bag on the tightly upholstered sofa and my mother moves it to a table. "Can I give you a cold drink?" she asks.

"We can only stay a minute."

"So? What did they tell you?"

I tell her. Straight. She's eighty-six years old, less than five feet tall and much less than a hundred pounds, but she says herself she's a tough old bird. She can take it.

She shakes her head. "Well, I always say surgery is clean."

She knows better. "This surgery would be pretty grim," I tell her. "I'm going to try to avoid it by wearing this brace."

I pull up my shirt. If a Merry Widow corset were made out of rigid white plastic instead of black lace, reinforced with steel stays instead of whalebone, fastened with Velcro strips instead of sexy red laces and pierced with a few air holes, it would be a Boston Overlap Brace. If my grandmother had wheels she'd be a Ford.

"You have to wear that all the time? That's awful!"

"But it lets me go about my business."

"Don't take advantage, Joan." Her voice is gravelly from radiation for a tumor on her vocal cords, but her familiar words hit my ears in the voice she had fifty years ago. Don't badger me, don't talk back—

"Take advantage of what, Frances?" David's baritone bounces off my mother's walls. To me her meaning's obvious: if the doctor told me I could walk in this brace, she thinks I'll try to play tennis in it.

"Poor David," my mother says, "having to take care of you."

David looks at her in amazement. For the first five years of our marriage, my mother never used his name. But she nursed my father for thirty years, and now David's going to suffer the way she did.

"Never mind," she goes on. "You don't have a thing to worry about. I'll put money in the *pushkie* for you every day."

"It couldn't hurt," I say.

"What's a *pushkie*?" David asks. Standing next to my mother, he looks vastly tall, male, and Aryan.

I bring him the Jewish National Fund's blue tin from my mother's kitchen counter. Her own mother stuck coins in it to bargain with God. My mother knows better.

I phone my sister. We came to Boston to see the surgeon who fixed her husband's spine. "What a rotten shame," Ruth says.

4

"Look, if you do have to have the operation, I hope you'll have it done in Boston. You and David can stay at my house as long as you need to."

She means it. She really would take on an invalid and her husband for months. I thank her but I know I won't accept. If I have to go through this surgery, I'll need to be the grown-up person I am in New Jersey, not the adolescent I always am in Boston.

I phone my brother. "It doesn't sound like much fun," Richard says, "but if you have to do it, you'll get the best and the latest at the Brigham."

I hug my mother good-bye. The top of her head fits under my chin. Her thin gray hair is stiff with lacquer.

David helps me lie down in the back seat of the car. I haven't figured out yet how to sit in the brace without strangling myself. "She's just like my mother," he says.

"She's nothing like your mother!"

He buckles his seat belt, looks back over his shoulder at me. "The first time I walked into that apartment, I thought I was walking into my mother's house." He means his adoptive mother. "The immaculate wall-to-wall carpeting, every object in its place. They even look alike—tiny little women, always frowning."

"*My* mother is smart and funny and—"

It takes more breath than the brace allows to argue over the hum of the air conditioner. David turns onto the Massachusetts Turnpike. All I can see are leafy treetops and clouds. All I can do is wonder how a woman like me landed in this fix.

March. That's when the trouble started. Hiking in the woods or chasing down a tennis lob, pain stabbed my left leg. My chiropractor's x rays showed one vertebra sticking out from the rest of my spine like a bucktooth.

"That's spondylolisthesis," Kim said. "Your old x rays don't show a vertebra out of line. What happened?"

"To my spine? Nothing."

"You didn't have a fall, or an accident?"

"Nothing I remember. Besides, my back feels fine. It's my leg that's a nuisance."

"It's more than a nuisance," Kim said. "It's a serious condition. You have to rest."

"But it's the middle of the semester!"

I went back to work. One morning I was hurrying across the Drew campus to my ten-o'clock class. The sun was brilliant, the wind icy. It whipped light snow around the gray stone building that houses the English Department, tickling the gargoyles that look down from the roof. I got as far as the library before fire seared my leg. Come on, I told the leg, we'll be late for class. The next step stopped me in my tracks. I rubbed my calf and foot through my leather boot. Another step, another stop. The pain squeezed tears from my eyes. They ran down my face and froze in the wind. I limped across the courtyard of the classroom building. The big clock in the tower showed I was eight minutes late.

"Sorry," I told my students. I pulled out my battered copy of *Moby-Dick*. "Let's look at Ishmael in the Try-Works. What's puzzling about that scene?" They shuffled through their books while I shuffled out of my purple down coat.

"All that hellfire," said a lanky young man at the far end of the front row. Normally I sit with students in a circle, but that room was too small, so I strolled around it while I taught. I was walking toward the student who had spoken when hellfire broke out in my leg. There was an empty chair in the front row. I perched on the arm. Then I walked up and down the rows of students. Then I leaned against the blackboard. Then I tried the

6

chair again. Every time my leg forced me to move, I dropped a stitch of the fabric I was trying to knit out of the text and the students' responses. The students were sharp and engaged but the pain was sharper.

After class I stopped in the media center to tape an installment of a cable TV series I'd been moderating, called *Women in the Center and Why They Belong There*. I squirmed so much in my chair the cameraman stopped filming to ask me to sit still. Back in my office I shoehorned myself through the narrow space between my big scarred desk and the chair where students sit. I was taking the lid off the coffee yogurt that was going to be my lunch when a graduate student poked her head in the door.

"Can you see me any time today? I've written myself into a corner."

A half-read chapter of her dissertation was sitting on my desk, on top of forty ungraded midterms. I could finish it that afternoon after I checked on the medical supplies my Friendship City group was shipping to Nicaragua that weekend. "Come by around four," I told her, thanking God that spring vacation would start the next week.

I placed a call to the archivist at Rollins College in Florida. She'd thrown herself into my search for records of the life of Constance Fenimore Woolson because she was as indignant as I about the neglect of this remarkable nineteenth-century writer.

"Still no sign of Woolson's notebooks or journals?" I asked.

"Not yet," Kate said, "but I'm still sleuthing. I did find her diamond ring."

"What was Woolson doing with a diamond ring? She was never engaged, and she was always strapped for cash."

"I have no idea, but I'm wearing it right now." I wondered if Kate's fingers would match her German accent. I looked at my own stubby fingers. Would the ring fit me? "I'll meet your plane Sunday night," Kate went on. "How will I recognize you?"

I laughed. "I'll be the short one with reddish-brown hair and a limp. I've done something funny to my leg."

That evening I met two friends for dinner at a Mandarin Chinese restaurant. Shiny red dragons guarded the cash register. Ilona's high heels clicked as she walked ahead of me to our table, moving so fast I had to remind myself she was nearly seventy. Sharon slid smoothly into the booth next to me. Her halo of blond hair and her white wool dress gave her an angelic look, but her pointed chin sent the same resolute message as my square one. My leg was burning, but I wouldn't cancel this dinner. For months I'd wanted these friends to meet. By the time we'd finished the hot-and-sour soup, they were talking frankly.

"But don't you think psychotherapy encourages narcissism?" Ilona asked Sharon, who's a therapist. "People who stay in therapy for years get so terribly wrapped up in themselves." Ilona's French accent gave glamour to everything she said. "Now you, Joan, you're the least self-absorbed person I know."

"Am I? I never thought about it." They laughed. I heard what I'd said and joined in. "My self just doesn't give me much trouble."

"Joan is the only person I know who has never been depressed," Sharon told Ilona. "Try to tell her about it and she just doesn't get it."

"It keeps me high," I said, "seeing how many balls I can keep in the air at once."

"I wonder who you'd be if you weren't juggling." Sharon put her hand on my arm. "Joan, do you think you might have lost track of your other selves?"

"Other selves?" I laid down my spoon. "What other selves?"

The waitress brought shrimp with cashews, broccoli dotted with garlic. We piled our plates.

"I see a lot of women who've built careers and raised families wondering if they've buried other parts of themselves," Sharon said.

"Some artistic or spiritual capacity they never developed?" asked Ilona.

"Developing this muscle," I said, "I suppose you might neglect that one, like a person spending all her time on one Nautilus machine."

Running in my head was Thoreau's remark that he had lost long ago a hound, a bay horse, and a turtle dove, and was still on their trail. I'd always seen *Walden* as the record of Thoreau's search for these mysterious missing parts of himself. I had never thought I'd need to make a search like that. I've always known who I am. I am what I do. The person who does what I do is me. It's a circus, doing what I do, being who I am. Much more fun than living deliberately, which is what Thoreau says he went to Walden Pond to do. To drive life into a corner and find out for himself if it was mean or sublime. To wedge his feet down through the mud and slush of appearance until he hit the hard rocky bottom of reality. Not to live what was not life.

I thought then that what I was living *was* life—life at its best, with banners flapping and trumpets blaring. I didn't want to live deliberately. As things would turn out, I would have to learn. The pain in my leg would prove to be serious. The treatment would be protracted and the prognosis poor. No one could tell me if I would ever again be able to do the things that had told me who I was. The woman juggling her glittering balls would be no use to me. I'd need a different self. I suspected I'd had one once, maybe more than one. Probably I'd had good reasons for shoving them into a cage and hiding it in a dark corner. But now I'd need to release those ghostly selves, to brush aside the cobwebs and open that cage. To my astonishment, I'd find the key to its rusted lock in the hands of Constance Fenimore Woolson.

1

Taking Advantage

*M*y first morning in Florida it's raining hard.

"Not a very good morning," I say to the elderly black doorman at my motel.

"Any day I wake up and find I'm still moving, *that*'s a good morning," he says.

I'm still moving, but not fast. It takes me fifteen minutes to walk the four short blocks to the low stucco building marked Woolson House. Kate's waiting for me there. I'd expected someone heavier in every way than the gray-haired woman in size-eight jeans who met me last night at the airport. Today, under her big umbrella, she's elegant in navy silk—"for a big meeting this afternoon."

"Woolson's ring would look great with that dress."

"Didn't I tell you? When I found out it was worth five thousand dollars, I put it back in the vault in a hurry! Where do you suppose she could have gotten such a ring? It was hardly worn. Maybe she didn't like it."

I've never liked diamonds. So why am I so disappointed that I won't get to try on the ring? Kate unlocks the wrought-iron gate that closes off a small alcove filled with Woolson's belongings, given to Rollins College in the 1930s by her niece. I've seen an inventory so I know what to look for—the deeply carved Italian chairs, the silver inkwell, the painted carvings of an old man and old woman. I make notes, unmoved. Nothing here brings this dead author to life. "Where are her books?"

"In my office. I've gathered everything there for you."

The library is near Woolson House, but not near enough for my leg. We take the elevator to the archives. Kate has cleared a large table for me a few feet from the shelves where she's arranged Woolson's own books. "But before you get down to work, I thought you'd like to see these."

She pulls out a folder of ten drawings labeled " 'Pictures for Plum' by Constance Fenimore Woolson. Returning Calls in Asheville: Grandma and Aunt Connie."

"Drawings? I never knew she did any."

"Do you know who Plum was?" Kate asked.

"That was her niece, Clare Benedict."

"Clare died before I came here," said Kate, "but I understand that darling little Plum turned into a very annoying old lady. She gave us Woolson House for classes in writing, because Connie had written so lovingly about Florida. She gave us Connie's books and pictures and furniture—and then she kept sending us lists of things she wanted back."

"I wish she'd left you the originals of the journals and letters she expurgated." In her biography of her aunt, Clare puts in three maddening little dots every time a letter gets really interesting.

"Well, these cartoons don't look expurgated."

I leaf through them. There's no date, but I know Woolson stayed in Asheville, North Carolina, a couple of times in the 1870s. She was in her thirties then, wandering the South to find a climate that would help her mother's rheumatism. I've read

letters she wrote from Asheville and from smaller towns—
Goshen, Virginia, and Hibernia, Florida, and Cleveland
Springs, North Carolina, from which she'd walked two miles to
the nearest post office. Letters from a woman raised in Cleveland and educated in New York and starving for opera and theater and new books.

Kate hands me a drawing titled "The Pavements of Asheville." Two women wearing hats with veils and carrying para-
sols are leaping from rock to rock over craters of rubble. "Look
at those elegant ladies slumming."

"It wasn't long after the Civil War. They could stay at boardinghouses for next to nothing—which is what they had."

"What do you think of her mother?" Kate asks, looking over
my shoulder. I spread out all the drawings. There's Hannah
fussing with her voluminous skirts and shawls, determined to
look like a lady in a mud puddle, while her trim daughter says,
"Oh, *do* hurry, Mother." Woolson fords streams over stepping-
stones, calling back to her mother, "You are getting your dress
wet!" while Hannah mutters, "Don't *speak* to me!" Woolson
climbs lightly up a cliff, saying, "Lovely view up here," while
her mother crawls behind, gasping, "Is there?" and then collapses, bedraggled with mud, on the hostess's front steps.
Woolson thrusts her parasol like a bayonet at cows and frogs
(neatly labeled in case Plum couldn't recognize them), saying
"Get out! Shu! Shu!" while her mother waves her handkerchief
and moans, "*How* much further?" Woolson is overcome only
when she returns to the hotel and a maid shows her a tray full
of visiting cards "left for you this afternoon."

"That's just how I've always imagined them," I tell Kate.
"The energetic daughter, capable and impatient. The fussy, dis-
gruntled mother. Don't you think Woolson knew her niece
would laugh at these cartoons because she'd recognize how her
Grandma and her aunt Connie really did behave?"

"But isn't there a letter somewhere," Kate says, "about how

wonderful Hannah was to Connie when she was finishing her first novel? Didn't say 'don't,' didn't make her do things she didn't want to do—"

"Which means that all the time she *wasn't* finishing a book, Hannah *did* say 'don't' and *did* make her do things she didn't want to do."

The italics in my voice surprise me. What's Hannah to me?

Kate sets me up with her electric kettle, tea bags, and snacks so that I won't have to go out in the rain if I don't want to. I don't want to. I want to stay right here with Woolson's books. She lugged trunks of them around the world, possessions much more intimate than those lumpy Italian chairs of hers in Woolson House, more intimate even than the hundreds of letters I've transcribed. Letters just passed through her hands on their way to other people. These books I'm holding now, she held in her hands for hours and hours. What she wrote in them was for her eyes only. And mine.

This flash of possessiveness makes me laugh. You'd think she'd accepted that diamond ring from me and run off with someone else! The Dean's Council didn't pay my way to Florida so I could moon around here like a jealous lover. I'm here to research my book. I'm going to call it *Gendered Genres*. It will show how Woolson's fiction exposed the assumptions about women and men that lurk inside the fiction of more famous writers like her great-uncle James Fenimore Cooper and her intimate friend Henry James.

I discovered Woolson three years ago when I was looking for a reason to live in Italy. David and I had spent our last sabbatical in Florence—dropping in on Michelangelo's *David* on our way home from our Italian lessons, buying our typing paper in a Renaissance *palazzo* from a woman whose ancestors sold stationery to the Medicis. I needed a reason to go back. So I started looking for a nineteenth-century American woman writer—my academic specialty—who'd lived in Italy. Margaret Fuller was the obvious choice, but I couldn't stand her prose. Finally, in a book about Americans in Italy, I found a chapter, a whole chapter, praising a woman writer I'd never heard of. Miss Woolson's mind, said Van Wyck Brooks, was "astute, realistic and witty." In the 1870s and '80s she wrote "stories too good to be forgotten" which sometimes "rivalled Henry James's." The Drew library had one of her five novels, two of her four volumes of short stories. I read one story and knew she was my passport to Italy.

Soon I saw she was much more than that. She could make a sentence sing or wail or burn. She wrote complex, realistic stories about women stranded in remote places, about women struggling to paint or write. Critics called her George Eliot's successor. Readers clamored for more stories and novels and poems than she could produce. So why had I never heard of her? She deserved a revival. I wanted to be the one to revive her.

Woolson's life excited me too. She'd lived in Florence and Rome, London and Oxford—the very cities David and I have chosen for our sabbaticals. Woolson lived there all alone—an independent woman supporting herself by her writing. I was impressed. I chased down her letters at Harvard and Princeton and Columbia, at Cleveland and Cooperstown. I was fascinated. Now, three years after I first read her name, I have to admit I'm obsessed.

She occupies most of the space in my imagination. She hums at the back of my consciousness even when I'm thinking about other things, refusing to let me go about my business unaccompanied. In the cities we both love she's most persistent. When I stood on the hillside outside Florence where she lived for several years in the 1880s, looking down past the cypress trees and vineyards to the red towers and domes of the city, I felt her standing beside me in the boots she wore for her six-mile walks, pointing out the landmarks with the parasol she carried like any other Victorian lady. Near the Pantheon, I looked for a woman with Woolson's erect, graceful carriage walking through Rome's piazzas. I've met her walking through Kensington Gardens and listening to trumpet concerts in the chapel at Christ Church in Oxford. Most often, whether I'm in Italy or England, New Jersey or Florida, I see her framed for long moments in her Venice window before she falls in horrible slow motion to her death.

When I wake in the night I lie wondering what it was like to be her. To have your five older sisters die before you were twelve. To spend your twenties consumed by the national passion of the Civil War, your thirties in the postwar South, your forties living and writing in Europe. I wonder how it would be to have an intimate and maddening friendship like hers with Henry James. To have her literary success, her freedom to live wherever she pleased for as long as she pleased. To suffer her terrible loneliness. To long for death for years before you finally fell—or leapt—from your balcony in Venice when you were fifty-three years old.

This year I'll turn fifty-three. Soon I'll be the same age Woolson was when she died. I've never wanted to die. All I want is enough hours to do all the things I want to do. It drives me wild that a woman whose tastes were so much like mine and whose successes were so much greater could want to destroy herself when she had lived no longer than I have.

But I didn't come to Florida to worry about her death any more than to try on her diamond ring. It's her literary relations I'm researching. I shove myself back to work. Woolson bought all Ruskin's books as they came out, I note. That's a surprise. She says in one of her letters that she's about to "enrage myself over Ruskin. I hate him, and hate's very enlivening." She found Matthew Arnold enlivening too—she's peppered him with question marks. But here she's marked with pairs of double lines a passage about Thoreau's solitude. And here she's turned back the corner of a page where Mérimée is longing for death.

Here's a volume inscribed by Henry James. I hold it to my

face, trying to catch her scent, or his, through the smell of leather and old paper. I fail. Here's a suspiciously slim copy of *Leaves of Grass*. This book isn't just abridged, it's expurgated so violently that the editor begs serious readers to buy Whitman's complete poems. Woolson was a serious reader if there ever was one. What was she doing with a volume like this?

I need a modern edition of *Leaves of Grass* to check what Woolson had missed. It's a long walk through an unfamiliar library to find it. My leg, which was cool enough while I was sitting and reading, is burning now. Back at my table I stand with one foot on my chair, rubbing my calf and foot while I compare the texts. No "Song of Myself"? Outrageous! No "Children of Adam"? Not surprising. She hadn't missed much there. But did she miss it on purpose? Was she a shrinking Victorian lady? I don't believe it. Not the woman who climbed mountains and used her parasol to drive away cows and frogs. Some prude must have given her the book as a gift. But there's no mitigating inscription inside the cover—no "To Connie with love, Christmas 1886, from Cousin Georgiana"—only a list of the poems she liked best. The Civil War poems, naturally. She called herself a red-hot abolitionist, called the war years the most intense of her life. Some of her women characters nurse delirious soldiers in isolated farmhouses and ride like demons on horseback to warn troops of attacks, but all she managed to do herself, as far as I can tell, was raise money for field hospitals.

But Whitman actually worked in those hospitals. That must be why she marked his lines about a church turned into a hospital, hellishly lit by great torches, echoing with screams, reeking with ether and blood. I know exactly how she felt when she read those lines. Fascinated. Appalled. Most of all excluded. Cut off from the great event of her time. That's how I felt when other people went to Mississippi as Freedom Riders and I couldn't ask my mother to take care of my three young children so I could get beaten up and sent to jail.

Of course Woolson marked Whitman's great ode to Lincoln. My stomach clenches as it always does when Whitman makes me see "the debris and debris of all the slain soldiers of the war." My arms get bumpy at "the fragrant pines and the cedars dusk and dim" where the poet retreats with his grief. Some unnameable part of me shivers at his "praise! praise! praise! For the sure-enwinding arms of cool-enfolding death." When Woolson held this book in her hands, was she already longing for "cool-enfolding death"? Or was she thinking of the war dead and of Lincoln? The shock of Lincoln's death would have been as fresh to her after twenty years as the shock of Kennedy's assassination still is to me. Everyone remembers where they were when they heard the news. I was sitting in a green upholstered chair nursing Leslie, gazing out the window at the last leaves clinging to a maple tree, when the radio concert was interrupted by the news from Dallas. That poor baby wailed for days until I realized that the shock had dried up my milk and she was starving. What was Woolson doing when she heard about Lincoln's shooting?

I do some quick subtraction on the corner of my notepad. I was twenty-seven and Woolson had just turned twenty-five when our presidents were shot. I had a new master's degree in English and three small children and no idea how I'd ever put those two passions together. She was teaching herself to write and telling herself her passion for Colonel Spaulding wasn't love but just the glamour of the war. I watched Kennedy's funeral on television while I gave Leslie her bottle and tried to explain to Dave and Mark why there were no cartoons for them to watch and why I was crying. Could Woolson possibly have seen Lincoln's funeral train making the slow journey Whitman describes? I open the modern, annotated edition of the *Leaves*. Sure enough, on its way from Washington to Springfield, Illinois, the funeral train passed through Cleveland.

My arms tingle. I gaze out the window at palm fronds thrash-

ing in the rain and see Woolson standing among the "crape-
veil'd women" Whitman says waited at the depots. I see her
standing tall and slim amid "the countless torches" and the
"tolling tolling bells' perpetual clang." She'd have gone with
her father and stood at the station holding his arm and singing
"dirges through the night" in her fine contralto voice. Her
mother and sister would have stayed home. They detested
crowds of common people. She'd have had her father all to herself that day.

Kate comes back at five. "You can stay till the library closes at
eleven, if you don't mind being alone here with Connie."

It jars me every time Kate calls Woolson "Connie." No one
knows Woolson better than I do, and I've never allowed myself
that liberty. I don't feel entitled to the intimacy of first names.
Who am I to call her Connie the way her father did, or Aunt
Connie as Clare did, or Constance as her mother did? And I'd
never call her Fenimore, the way Henry James did behind her
back.

"I think we'll be all right," I tell Kate. It's the first time I've
said "we."

Kate shows me how to lock up the archives when I leave, and
turns out all the lights except the ones where I'm working.
When the door clicks behind her, my room becomes a lighthouse in a storm. Never in my life have I worked so long with
such unbroken concentration and so little restlessness. I leave
my chair only to go to the shelf that holds Woolson's books, to
the tea kettle, the toilet, and the window, where I stand with
one leg on a chair, absentmindedly rubbing it while I watch the
rain lash the windows and the sky clear and then darken and
then brighten with moonlight. I see Woolson as a middle-aged
spinster studying ferns under her cheap microscope in cheap
boardinghouses in Goshen and Hibernia and Shelby in the
1870s. As a glamorous expatriate living in the Villa Brichieri
overlooking Florence in the 1880s, then in the Casa Biondetti

overlooking Venice's Grand Canal in the early 1890s. As a bundle of white nightclothes falling from an arched window in the Casa Semitecolo late on the night of January 24 in 1894.

It always comes back to that. It's not the witty author, the intrepid traveler, the affectionate correspondent I hold on to. The woman I can't let go of, the woman who won't let go of me, is Miss Grief. That's what she calls a defeated woman of genius in one of her best stories. It's Miss Grief that Richard Greenough sculpted. His fine white bust of Woolson stands in a corner of the next room. I looked at it this morning. Now I limp around the file cabinets and tables, finding my way by light from the street and the moon, and stand before her again. The strength and repose of her mouth and chin draw me toward her. The reserve Greenough captured so well in her downcast eyes pushes me back.

What I really want to write is her life. I know I can't. Her notebooks have vanished. Her most intimate correspondents destroyed her letters. Too much has been lost. You'd think there was a conspiracy to erase her history. If it's someone's life I want to write, I should find a different subject. But I don't want a different subject. I want her.

She looks less forbidding now in the moonlight than she did this morning under fluorescent light. Less remote, but somehow sadder. I want to touch her. Slowly I run my fingers down the short curls on her forehead and around her ears. Her long hair had been cut during a fever. I'm glad she couldn't braid it into the low bun she usually wore. I can caress the fine curve of the back of her head, stroke the nape of her neck. My own neck quivers. My cheeks are hot.

Her eyes seem to rest on the little book I absentmindedly carried with me, her copy of *The Teaching of Epictetus*. I turn on a small lamp and page through the book, looking for her markings. Here's a passage she's marked with those wavy double lines in both margins. She looks down at the words she'd framed so firmly:

> And when, it may be, that the necessary things are no longer supplied, that is the signal for retreat: the door is opened, and God saith to thee, *Depart.*

Proof she killed herself? No. She doesn't say she agrees with Epictetus that God himself opens the door to death when life becomes intolerable. Here's another set of her firm pencil marks. The editor is explaining that Epictetus often pointed to "the open door," the editor explains, when arguing "that it is unmanly to complain of a life which he can at any time relinquish. . . ." Unwomanly, too, I correct the ancient sexist. "Self-destruction was . . . permissible" when a person had suffered "some disaster or affliction which rendered a natural and wholesome life impossible."

I try to look through the blanks Greenough carved for her eyes. "Had you suffered some disastrous affliction, Connie?" I ask. "Was your Venice window the open door?"

My voice echoes through the dark, silent rooms. For long minutes I gaze at her. She keeps her silence. I can't call it her peace.

It's nearly eleven. I pack up the pages and pages of notes I've taken and lock the archives. The rain has stopped. I walk back to the motel under dripping trees. Tonight the five-minute walk takes me half an hour.

Back in New Jersey I tell my chiropractor, "I need one of your magic bullets."

"No magic," Kim says. "Just rest. Yes, Joan, I mean *you!*"

Okay. Classes don't start for three days. Since my pain is gone the minute I lie down, I figure three days on my back will fix what's wrong with me. I've never taken my own physical pain seriously because it's always temporary. Headaches and cramps, broken bones and childbirth always run their course. I get up and go back to Drew. Week by week it takes longer to walk to class. I pull out my appointment book, a messy mosaic of blue and black and red ink, and cancel everything but my classes. When I get to class, I'm distracted by pain that gets hotter day by day.

I call Dr. Frederick. He's an orthopedist who did artistic operations on a torn cartilage in my knee and an unhealed crack in my foot, who repaired my children's fractures—Dave's collarbone, Leslie's shin, Mark's knee. While we always argue about his conservative politics, I like his conservative way of practicing medicine. He's grown another chin since I saw him last, but his hands are as knowing and gentle as ever.

"I'm going to draw a pin up your right leg," he says after checking a dozen other things. "Does it feel any different when I do it on your left leg?"

I'll say it does. My left leg feels like there's a thick sock between my skin and the pin. I hadn't realized it was numb.

"You've got a herniated disc next to L5," he says. "Here, I'll show you." And he finds in a book a picture showing the pattern of pain you get when a disk bulges next to the fifth lumbar vertebra. Red circles are drawn on the calf and foot exactly where mine are burning.

"That's it!" I'm delighted by the precision of the diagnosis. So that's all that's wrong with me.

"Total rest," he says. "Otherwise the disk could rupture and you'll need major surgery."

"Okay."

"I mean total rest," he says firmly. "You get up only to go to the toilet. You'll take an anti-inflammatory drug, and Valium. With eight weeks of total rest, maybe less, ninety-five percent of discs like yours go quietly back where they belong."

It sounds wonderful, so wonderful I feel guilty. Now that the general himself has taken me off active duty, I realize I'm exhausted. Fighting pain consumes astonishing amounts of energy. I never knew that. "I don't need a tranquilizer," I tell him.

"The Valium's to relax your muscles. They're in spasm, putting pressure on your disk." He thinks I need to be doped up to stay down. Maybe he's right. He's known me for years.

I go home and break the news to David. He puts his arms around me. "*Now* will you take care of yourself?"

"That's the problem. I can't. You're going to have to do everything."

Already he does the shopping, the laundry, the dishes, because his teaching load is lighter than mine. He doesn't care if I never iron his shirts, but he says he married me for my cooking as much as my legs. He hates to cook. It's his orphanage syndrome, I tell him, this longing to have a woman cook for him since his mother died when he was three.

"I can buy frozen dinners," he says.

"If you can find any without sugar." Hypoglycemia sends David into a near-coma if he eats sugar or drinks alcohol. He's going to have to cook. And he still has two more weeks of teaching and hundreds of papers to grade.

"We'll manage. It's worth it if you can avoid surgery. Do you have to hold perfectly still?"

"Just keep off my feet."

"What about making love?"

"Dr. Frederick didn't say. And I was careful not to ask. I figure anything I can do horizontally is legal."

Cheerfully, David heads for the kitchen.

I settle down on the sofa and the pain turns off like a light switch. I must be goldbricking. While colleagues are teaching my classes and David is burning the fish, I'm reading all the way through *The New York Times* every morning, even the "Science" and "Home" sections. I'm listening to Mahler and

Vaughan Williams, to *All Things Considered,* to friends who call and visit. I could learn to like this life if I didn't have to ask David for everything I want. I try to ration my requests so he won't get fed up with me before my eight weeks are over. I won't ask him for a cup of tea. I'll read another of my students' final essays. It's bad. I haven't taught anyone anything. I really want a cup of tea. I can put on the kettle on my way to the toilet. I bring the tea back to the sofa and go on writing comments on ninety final exams and ninety final essays. This is the worst part of my job, but doing it now makes me feel like a professional instead of a parasite. I parcel out the papers, so many a day. When I've done my stint I indulge myself in the detective novels Ilona brings me.

"You don't have to return them," she says.

"Who else would read them in this condition?" The pages of her paperbacks are always wavy because she reads them in the bathtub and drops them in the water when she falls asleep. "For your next birthday," I tell her, "I'm going to get you one of those trays you suspend across the tub."

"Don't! If the splash of the book didn't wake me up, I'd drown. Besides, I read my serious books sitting up. It's just mysteries I read horizontally. Did you know they used to call the great French courtesans *'les grandes horizontales'*? You might think of yourself as a *'petite horizontale.'* "

I wonder what it would be like to read Woolson horizontally. I know how to read with my mind and I know how to read mindlessly to put myself to sleep. But what if I could read with some other part of myself, with my heart, maybe, or my soul, if I have such a thing? Would I feel that strange shimmering connection with Connie that came over me in the dark archives at Rollins? Reading in that unprofessional way I know is heresy that merits excommunication from scholarly ranks. But I'm off duty. No one will know. I imagine myself coaxing Connie's sad statue to respond to me, but the minute I try to read something more demanding than the newspaper or Ilona's wavy-paged mysteries, the Valium puts me to sleep.

Six weeks after Dr. Frederick sent me to bed, my leg isn't numb any more. That must mean the disk isn't bulging any more. I throw the Valium in the wastebasket and walk outside. The deer have gorged on my tulips but turned up their noses at the hyacinths. I bend down to smell their fierce perfume, stand up to take in the blaze of the forsythia. I walk around the yard, inhaling the soft, scented air, sniffing my freedom. No pain at all in my left leg!

Then my right leg buckles. Something stabs me in the groin. I go back in the house and rest awhile. Then I try walking up the street. Fists clutch at the back of my knees. I turn back. I get to the mailbox and the knife stabs me again. I didn't have any of these symptoms six weeks ago! Dr. Frederick tells me to go back to bed for a day and then try walking again. No better. He sends me back to bed, telling me to call him every day, including weekends and holidays, to report my progress. On Memorial Day he calls me back at eleven at night, when he's finally finished operating on people who've shattered various bones in holiday accidents.

"I'd hate to be your wife," I tell him, "but it's a privilege to be your patient."

"We'll see how much of a privilege it is when we figure out what's wrong with you. It's time for you to have an MRI."

This expensive kind of x ray shows some narrowing of the bony channels the spinal nerves pass through on their way to the legs. That could explain my pain, Dr. Frederick says. The next step is much more invasive—injecting radioactive dye into my spinal cord to get accurate pictures of the nerves themselves. If the myelogram confirms that bone growth is squashing my nerves, he'll keep me in the hospital and operate immediately.

24

No, he won't. What for? My pain is a nuisance, but that's all it is. I want a second opinion. My internist gives me names of neurosurgeons in New York and New Jersey. None of them can see me for six weeks. I can't sleep. I lie in bed obsessing about what to do, who should do it, where, when. During the day I torture David with the same questions.

"The worst of it," I tell my sister Ruth when she calls, "is not being able to think about anything else."

"Would you come to Boston if Sam's surgeon could see you right away?"

I would. He can. David and I drive to Boston. The surgeon looks too young to practice medicine, but he has a big reputation. My symptoms puzzle him. He sends me for a C-T scan. It doesn't match my x rays. My fifth lumbar vertebra seems to drop back into line when I lie down and slip forward when I stand up. That's bad. He sends me for the myelogram. Lying on a tilted table, watching my own insides on a TV monitor, I can see for myself where the nerves get narrow. That's spinal stenosis, the neuroradiologist tells me. That's very bad.

The surgeon comes to the hospital room where I'm lying flat because you can't lift your head for twenty-four hours after a myelogram. "You need some pretty complicated surgery," he says. I don't believe him. Two months ago I was playing tennis. David believes him. He's looking at me with enormous concern. My chest starts to throb. The doctor explains that I've somehow broken the joints that connect my fifth lumbar vertebra to my spine. That's the spondylolisthesis Kim diagnosed months ago. Normally, detached vertebrae stabilize somewhere. Mine doesn't. It slides back and forth every time I move. My body has produced masses of bone spurs in a misguided effort to stabilize itself. Now the bone spurs are crushing my nerves. That's what's causing my pain.

He's saying *my* body has all these things wrong with it? I'm too angry to understand the diagnosis. He has to explain it all

25

over again. "But I just spent six weeks on my back, and all the pain in my leg went away!"

"The spondylo caused a disk to herniate. Bed rest fixed the disk. It didn't fix the problem."

Seeping into my brain is the news that I have a very big problem. Several problems. A detached vertebra. Bone spurs. Compressed nerves. I need a triple-barreled operation, the doctor says. First he'd decompress my spinal nerves by removing the bone spurs that are crushing them. Then he'd carve matchsticks of bone from my hip and layer them on my lumbar vertebrae. To pull my detached vertebra back where it belongs, he'd screw everything together with a metal plate that might have to be removed in a second operation.

At least I'd be asleep while he was doing all this carpentry on my body. But when I woke up I'd find myself in a plaster body cast from my ribs to one ankle. My spine would have to be totally immobilized. Eventually I'd be strong enough to get to the bathroom and back on crutches, though I wouldn't be able to sit upright. After three months of that he'd saw off the cast and promote me to a body brace. If the bone graft didn't fuse within nine months, he'd do the whole thing again.

Oh no he wouldn't. Incarcerate my whole torso for a whole year? Or even two? A woman whose theme song has always been "Don't Fence Me In"? He should know that it takes all my self-control to sit quietly for ten minutes with my head confined by the crook of a dentist's arm. I'd tell him so if there weren't a baseball stuck in my throat.

"How many of your patients fuse the first time?" I finally manage to say. Eighty-five percent. "And are they good as new?" Almost everyone feels better after a successful fusion. "How much better?" Some people—he can't say how many—are completely free of pain, while some just have less pain than before. He can't say how much less. A lot depends on whether the nerves are already scarred. Ten percent are no better after surgery. Five percent are worse. My prognosis? Well, the spinal stenosis suggests the nerves may be scarred. My history of fractures that don't heal well worsens the odds of fusing. He can't say how much.

He's telling me I could be crippled. Even if I go through that nightmare he's just described, I could still be crippled. He's crazy. David's looking glazed. Medical talk bewilders him. He was raised a Christian Scientist.

"But—but—it seems crazy to go through all that, when I have so little pain."

"Consider yourself lucky."

"How about physical therapy?"

"Exercise would just make things worse. Mobility is the problem. It's the motion of your vertebra that produces more bone spurs and it's bone spurs that scar. What you need is stability." I hate stability. "I know it's a shocking piece of news. If you're not ready to face the surgery, I suppose you could spend three months in a Boston Overlap Brace. It's the same brace kids wear to correct curvatures of the spine."

"In bed?"

"Oh no. You could go about your business." A thin current of air seeps into the sealed box in my chest.

"Would she just be postponing the inevitable?" David asks.

"Well, there's an outside chance that the brace might stabilize the vertebra. Of course she'd still have the bone spurs."

"Would it do any harm to wait?" David asks.

"I think you could risk it."

"I'll do it!"

"Wait till you see the brace before you decide. It's pretty drastic. I'll call down to the brace shop and make you an appointment. You can ride there on a gurney."

"Can't I walk?"

"How's your head?"

"Fine!" Myelograms can produce phenomenal headaches, but not in me.

"Okay." He shakes David's hand, then mine. "Good luck."

When he's gone, I turn to David. My eyes fill. He takes me in his arms. "Oh sweetheart, I'm so sorry—"

I bury my face in his neck. "What a mess! All our plans—" The tears spill. I dry them on David's shirt. "Let's go see that brace."

A technician has me lie down on a table in the white plastic body suit. He pulls the straps so tight I gasp.

"It has to be that tight to stabilize your spine," he says. "If you wear it any looser, you might as well carry it around in your hand." I try to sit up but nothing flexes between my breasts and my crotch. "Roll onto your side," he says, and catches me neatly before I fall on the floor.

Babies are wailing all around me and I want to join the chorus. The brace shop for the Brigham and Women's Hospital is in the Children's Hospital. On the table next to mine, having his leg braces adjusted, is a year-old child whose skull is so distorted I can't locate his left eye. Behind me, a technician is comforting a two-year-old. "It's rough, honey," he says, "breaking your leg just a week after you got out of your last cast." Thirty years ago one of my babies wore a cast from his armpits to his ankles. My arms and chest can still feel the thick plaster that kept Dave's flesh away from mine for a year. My flesh creeps now with the horror of entering the world of the abnormal. Dave's hips still aren't right, but they're good enough for him to ride his bicycle from Los Angeles to Anchorage. I hope to hell the babies howling all around me do as well. I hope I do.

My ribs and hipbones rasp against the rigid plastic of my brace. I need a deep breath but the brace won't allow it. Look at these babies, I tell myself, fighting panic. Look how lucky you are. You've had fifty-two years of normal life. These kids never got to run at all before they were strapped into braces and mummified in casts. It doesn't help. It just piles their misery and their parents' misery on top of mine.

You're not in such a bad way, I tell myself. You can control your pain just by lying down. You don't have crippling arthritis like Mary's, something that just gets worse and can't be treated. You don't have a damaged heart or breast cancer or a brain tumor. You're not going to die of this. Where's your sense of perspective? Even if this business with your spine is as serious as the doctor thinks it is, it's not tragic.

The brace shop at the Children's Hospital does brace you against self-pity. Even if three months in this hideous brace don't stabilize my spine, even if I do need that drastic operation, my body's strong. I'll heal fast. All right, my bones break, but when was I last sick? Or even tired? Sometimes David asks me if I'm tired. The question always surprises me. Well, now that he mentions it, I suppose I might be grouchy because I'm tired. I hadn't noticed. "You're fine," he says with a mixture of admiration and exasperation. "Always fine."

I walk out of the brace shop and pull up my shirt to show him the brace. He reaches out for me and I walk into his arms. The brace jostles and I pull away, blinking back tears. We walk slowly through the maze of antiseptic corridors. For once I know I'm sick and tired. And wet. I didn't even feel my bladder open. The brace must have compressed it. I turn to stride back into the hospital and confront the technician who fitted me to the brace, but my wet pants bunch up between my legs. I can only hobble. Outraged, I stuff my underpants into the trash can in the ladies' room and persuade the technician to cut the brace shorter in the front.

The corridors are full of people sitting in wheelchairs and pushing walkers and hobbling along in leg braces. I could be one of these people. Not one of the professionals whizzing importantly past us, but a person who moves slowly and painfully and awkwardly. If I can wet my pants I can turn into a person like my mother, a person who needs help.

"Maybe you'll do better than they think," David says. "Doctors always prepare you for the worst. Then they look like heroes when things go well." He puts his arm around my shoulders. Even this is impossible. The brace digs into my hip-bones, scrapes against my ribs. I shake my head and move away. I imagine a summer looking at David's gloomy face looking at my gloomy face. It gives me an idea.

"As long as I'm not having surgery this summer, why shouldn't we go to London?" Every spring, as soon as David turns in his final grades at Rutgers and I turn in mine at Drew, we rent our house and go somewhere cooler and less familiar than New Jersey to do our summer research and writing. Since all our children have been on their own, it's been London. Our Newark–Heathrow tickets are sitting in my desk drawer.

David looks at me. "You think you could manage?"

"Why not? I may not be able to do much, but at least we'll be cool there."

He gives me the lopsided grin I love. "Of course! We've got a reprieve!"

In five days we find a tenant to rent our house, locate a flat in London, pack a few clothes and folders of notes, and make our escape. If I pull the brace tight enough, my leg doesn't buckle. The clawing behind my knees I can ignore.

2

Informed Consent

*E*vasive action this may be, but even though I'm allowed out of my brace only to sleep and swim, it feels like liberty. In a health club near our Kensington apartment, every morning for twenty-four laps my body feels strong and light. Then I have a hot buttered scone and Earl Grey tea at the Muffin Man tea shop. Then I take the tube to the British Library. I love sitting under the huge blue dome, but I hate the stuff I'm reading. I need to build a theoretical scaffolding for my book on Woolson's literary relationships, but my mind keeps skidding off the abstractions on the page and goes hunting for something solid and human. The only book that excites me would excite nothing but ridicule from the scholars who wrote the volumes piled on my desk. It's a book Connie recommended to a friend just six months before her death. She said it offered "the only working hypothesis I have ever seen as regards the strange facts of telepathy, hypnotism, etc. I don't know whether you are interested in such subjects. (I am.) The book is *The Law of Psychic Phenomena* by the American T. J. Hudson.''

My interest in such subjects is very mild. Still, after weeks of dozing off and jolting awake when my Iron Maiden cuts off my breath, any diversion will do. Besides, I'm in one of the few places on earth where I can get the obscure old book that impressed Connie so much. Not that getting it will be easy. For books as old as Hudson's, the British Library doesn't condescend to anything so vulgar as a card catalog, much less a computer. It lists them on little paper slips pasted into huge, thick volumes shelved in concentric circles at the center of the spiderweb of desks that fills the Reading Room. My Iron Maiden holds my back straight as a flagpole. I bend at the knees and drag out the twenty-pound volume that lists authors whose names begin with "H," stand up and catch my breath. I copy down the citation, walk stiffly to the center of the web to drop off my request for the book, and since I'm in motion, keep walking, out the door where the guards inspect my bag to make sure I haven't stolen anything, through the vast foyer of the British Museum, past the queue of orderly Japanese and tidy African and anarchic Italian tourists waiting to get into the Museum, and across Great Russell Street for a sandwich of Camembert and sliced apple on granary bread.

When I get back from lunch, legs aching, Hudson's book is waiting on my desk. I want to hide it, as if it were pornography. Silently I defend myself to the bearded man sitting next to me, picking at the frayed cuff of his navy pinstriped suit while he reads up on the law of Hammurabi. Doesn't he know that serious psychologists like Freud and Jung and William James went to seances and wrote scholarly papers about ghostly apparitions? If they could prove that mediums were not frauds but were really transmitting messages from the dead, then they'd know that the immortality of the soul was not just a pious hope but a scientific fact.

That's what all those table rappings were really about. Death and immortality. That's why Connie was reading the proceedings of the Society for Psychical Research during the last three years of her life, and reading T. J. Hudson's book on psychic phenomena in the last months of her life, and asking her friend Dr. Baldwin just six months before her death what he thought about it all. She must have wanted to know what would become of her if she threw herself out the window.

That image haunts me. It's not Connie haunting me. I don't believe in ghosts any more than I believe in polka-dotted elephants. It's just that Connie has overcome my scholarly training in detachment to make a place for herself in my inner life. If I shivered when I read her letters in the Western Reserve Historical Society in Cleveland, or when I gazed at her sculpted face in the library at Rollins, or when I stood in Cooperstown in her grandparents' drafty stone house or in the snowy churchyard where many of her relatives were buried, that wasn't her ghost breathing down my neck. It was just my hyperactive imagination.

I think this spiritualist stuff is all nonsense. But what did Connie think? I pick up *The Law of Psychic Phenomena,* a neat little blue volume. I should have known Connie wouldn't recommend a silly book. Hudson is interested in the part of the self that's subject to the power of suggestion, which he calls the subjective mind. Subjective minds communicate by telepathy. Dying people can send particularly strong telepathic messages. What we call haunting, Hudson says, is really a kind of telepathy that lingers.

All right, what if it is? I sit up straighter in my chair, trying to relieve the pressure of the brace on my ribs without increasing it on my hipbones. Let's pretend that the images of Connie filling my mind are telepathic messages that have hung around for almost a century looking for a receiver. For a kindred spirit. I do have a little psychic power, enough to make my daughter Leslie call me when I can't reach her. My mother often phones me just as I'm picking up the phone to call her. I always knew when my sister Ruth went into labor; I'd wake up with contractions. Maybe I'm a "sensitive." Or maybe I'm nuts.

Hudson seems sane enough. He understands how the power of suggestion can make your body sick. I jot down a quick list of Connie's illnesses—the aches and spasms in her writing arm and neck and back, the terrible pain in her ears when she tried artificial eardrums for her deafness, the exhaustions and the breakdowns and the rest cures, the bouts of influenza that preceded her death. Of course she was excited when she read that the same power of suggestion that made her sick could make her well. Hudson understands autosuggestion. "Deny the power of disease to obtain the mastery," he says. Isn't that what I've done, coming to London, sitting here in the British Library? I squirm to shift the brace off a raw spot on my hip. It's not helping as much as it did at first. As I walked back from lunch I had that stabbing in my groin. I should have started self-hypnosis sooner. Denying the power of disease may not be enough to reverse the progress of this illness.

I slide my hand under my shirt and loosen the Velcro strips of my brace—slowly, so the noise won't attract the attention of the Hammurabi scholar. I take a guilty breath. Even loosened, the brace won't let my ribs expand enough for a deep breath. Now Hudson is defending hypnosis. It needed defense. The subject's subjection to the hypnotist horrified Connie's idol Hawthorne, nauseated her friend Henry James. Hudson admits that the subject could be made to "feel pain or pleasure, joy or sorrow—all at the caprice of the man in whose power he has placed himself." But no hypnotist could make an upright person kill or steal, he insists, or perform or permit acts of "sexual outrage." Hypnosis can't override morality or the instinct of self-preservation. It can't instigate suicide.

I'm reading with Connie's eyes. I'm thinking her thoughts. A chill goes up my spine under the sweaty plastic of my brace. What if a person's desire for death is stronger than her instinct to preserve her life? If she couldn't heal herself, could she think herself dead? If Hudson's right that the subjective mind "does not depend for its existence upon the continued life of the body," then after death, Connie would have thought, her subjective mind would meet the subjective minds of all the people she'd loved. Death would end only her loneliness.

I take the bus home. Every week it's taking me longer to walk from the British Library to the Underground station at Tottenham Court Road. The bus is slower than the Underground, but it saves me six blocks. And it passes DeVere Gardens, just off Hyde Park, where Henry James lived for years. I like to imagine Connie walking down that street to visit him. Just beyond Kensington Gardens the bus passes Argyll Road, where Henry's sister Alice lived during the last year of her life. Connie visited Alice and her companion Katharine Loring there. Over tea they'd talk about one's right to kill oneself when pain and terror become too much. Forty-one Argyll Road may have been the one place in London in 1892 where you could talk about such subjects with perfect frankness. I wish I'd been there.

I get off the bus one stop after Argyll Road, one stop before Holland Park. Stopping to buy raspberries from the woman who sells fruit on the corner—the only food that's cheaper in London than in New Jersey—I let myself into our one-bedroom flat on the fifth floor of a huge block of flats that rents to transients like David and me. It's empty. David is still at the Goethe Institute, reading about postwar Germany for his novel. I rip off my brace with a screech of Velcro. The undershirt I wear under the brace is soaked with sweat. It turns to ice as the air hits it. I pull it off and crawl under the quilted bedspread, stuffing a pillow under my throbbing legs. It's the middle of August. When I started wearing the Iron Maiden in June, I was walking easily from the flat to the tube station, from the tube station to the British Museum. My mind skids away from the truth like a needle over a phonograph record. I force it back. The brace isn't working. My vertebra is still wandering. My bones are still producing spurs. They're crushing my nerves. Fear hums in my throat.

David's key turns in the lock. He comes into the bedroom carrying a bunch of dark-red roses. I take them, inhale them, smile up at him. It's not a very good smile. "What's wrong?" he asks. "Too much literary theory?"

"I read other stuff today. One more day of theory and I was going to have a tantrum right there in the British Library."

"You'd get a fantastic echo under that dome."

"I'm fed up with London. Let's get out of town for a few days."

"I've been saying that for weeks!" He brings a pile of maps and guidebooks to the bed and we choose Chester. It has Roman ruins for David and a Norman cathedral with misericords for me and a nearly complete ring of ancient walls around the whole city. "You can even walk on top of the walls," David says.

"I think Connie walked on them with Henry James. Remember the scene at the beginning of *The Ambassadors* where Lambert Strether's walking around the walls of Chester with an American woman? She's Connie to the teeth." I've been rereading James's great novel. I take the plastic-bound library copy off the night table and find the page. "Listen to this. Strether's saying that this woman he's just met 'knows things he didn't . . . intimate things about him that he hadn't yet told her and perhaps never would.' They go strolling on the wall—James calls it 'the tortuous wall . . . pausing here and there for a dismantled gate or a bridged gap, with rises and drops, steps up and steps down, queer twists, queer contacts.' Isn't that good? Then the woman says, 'You've recognized me—which is rather beautiful and rare. You see what I am.'"

My voice breaks. That's how it felt to meet David. That's how it felt for him to meet me. He takes the book out of my hand and slides under the bedspread beside me. "I hope I'm going to be able to walk around the walls at Chester," I tell him. "Walking was bad today. When I think what it'll be like for you if I have to go through that surgery—"

He pulls me toward him, strokes my hair. "It doesn't matter."

For the next half hour it doesn't matter. Then it matters all over again.

So we take the train to Chester. We stand in front of the enormous Town Hall, gaping and laughing at the turrets and pinnacles shooting off in all directions. "I don't know how to break this news to you," David says, "but I'm actually starting to like Victorian Gothic."

The guidebook says it's only two miles around the walls. That's two horizontal miles. If you count all the stairs you have to climb at gates and gaps—in some places the wall is forty feet high—it's maybe two miles and a half. Every fifty yards or so I pause to admire a half-timbered almshouse, a tower named Thimbleby, a pub called the Bear and Billet. Pause to look out across the River Dee to Wales. Pause. Sit. Pause.

David's leaning against the high stone barrier that keeps you from falling off the walls. I'm sitting on a cold stone bench. "You know who I feel for?" he asks. "The Roman legionnaires. Can you imagine how the winters here felt after Rome?" His fine blond hair is blown into spikes. The wind from Wales is cold even on this sunny August day. "Just think how those civilized Romans would have loathed the Welsh."

David likes the Romans. I like the Welsh. I always side with rebels. "Those uncivilized Welsh beat back the English right here at Chester," I tell him. I've been reading the guidebook. "Owen Glendower led them."

"That crazy Welshman was real? I always thought Shakespeare made him up."

I love Glendower's boast that he can "call spirits from the vasty deep," and Hotspur's retort: "Why, so can I, or so can any man. But will they come when you do call for them?" This is why we come to England—to call spirits from the vasty deep of history, to walk along the top of ancient red sandstone walls and admire an extravagant Elizabethan building, with its cock-eyed windows and doors, its bulges and sags, its black wood cornices carved with impossible beasts. To imagine Connie and Henry James walking arm in arm around the city. To imagine the people shot down on these walls.

Today I'm one of those casualties. In spite of three months of living in the Iron Maiden, the backs of my legs are fiery fists.

"How far do you think we are from our hotel?"

"About half a mile," David says. His eyes search my face. He knows I want to see the misericords in the cathedral that's just below us. "Why don't you rest here and I'll find a taxi."

I don't want to stay here by myself with nothing to distract me from the picture forming behind my eyes. It's a cartoon of a man lying in a hospital bed completely encased in plaster, with one leg hanging in traction. I know it's funny but I can't remember the caption.

"I can manage half a mile, if we do it in installments." I hate to waste money on taxis almost as much as I hate to admit there's anything wrong with me. Usually David protests my stinginess. Today he doesn't argue with me. He puts his arm around my shoulders and we walk slowly through the town. At one of our many stops, I see our reflection in a shop window. What is that athletic-looking man doing with that stiff-bodied woman with the grim face?

At the hotel I lie on the bed with pillows under my knees. The burning in my legs doesn't stop when I lie down. I know the only choice I have left is the choice of surgeons.

British Rail lets you break your return journey, so the next morning David and I get off the train at Coventry as we'd planned. Why not? I'm in no hurry to face what's ahead of me. David finds a taxi to take us to the cathedral. Today I don't give him any argument. When the driver stops, we think he's made a mistake. The huge building in front of us with its slitted lines of windows looks like a bunker dressed up as an office building.

"Is 'modern cathedral' an oxymoron?" I ask David as we walk around the new pink sandstone walls looking for the ruins of the ancient church.

We decide it's not. If the survivors of the Nazi raid on Coventry had restored their cathedral or razed its ruins, they'd have erased the memory of what happened here. We stand in the shell of the ancient cathedral, its Gothic windows naked to the sky. On the stone altar stands a cross made of roof beams charred by Nazi fire bombs. Behind the cross is carved "Father Forgive." If God existed, we would need to forgive him.

How absurd to stamp my foot at a God I don't believe in! It's idiotic to reject a world of pain that is the only world we have. When Carlyle heard that Margaret Fuller had decided to accept the universe, he's supposed to have snorted, "By God, she'd better!" To me he'd say the same.

David and I love to explore the intricacies of cathedrals together. I can forget I'm a Jew in a Christian sanctuary and admire clustered columns that branch into arches and frame windows that hum with color. But in Coventry's modern sanctuary, severe concrete columns hold up a ceiling of relentless concrete diamonds above plain plastered walls. A wrought-iron screen is both a crown of thorns and a wall of barbed wire—a microcosm of all wars, a monument to all loss. I am overwhelmed by the mountain of the world's pain of which mine is a morsel of dust.

On our way out of Coventry, David and I stop only long enough to buy some intensely fragrant late-August strawberries that we wash in a street fountain and eat sitting on its rim. On the long train ride from Coventry back to London, I rehearse with him the same choices that gave me insomnia in New Jersey. Should I go back to the Boston surgeon who wants to put a metal plate in my back and me in a body cast? Should I spend six weeks waiting for an appointment with a New York neurosurgeon? Should I look for a spine surgeon in New Jersey, or go back to Dr. Frederick, even though he's a general orthopedic surgeon? Maybe I should just jump out the window.

Past the grimy glass unroll the green hills of Shakespeare's Warwickshire. I wonder if they'd feel as soft as they look. For the first time in my life I can imagine how someone could stare at the days stretching ahead and decide to skip the whole thing, thank you very much. I reach under my shirt to loosen my brace. Three months in this cage of plastic and steel for nothing! Three months of not being able to take a deep breath. I rip open the Velcro and tear off the brace. The polite British passengers pretend not to notice. I'd love to heave it out the window and scare the daylights out of some sheep, but I know I'll have to wear it again after some surgeon reconstructs my spine. I park the brace on the empty seat next to me. It sits like a passenger with her head and limbs lopped off. David, sitting opposite, pulls out his clamshell camera and takes our picture. I'm damned if I'll smile for the birdie.

Back at our Kensington flat, I phone Leslie at her medical school in Cleveland to ask what she thinks of having Dr. Frederick operate on my back.

"You know he's a superb surgeon," Leslie says. "And you

know you can trust his integrity. If he says he can do your back, I'd believe him."

I phone Mark, who's at chiropractic school in Iowa, expecting to hear surgery condemned.

"One of my professors was carried out of his classroom into surgery last week," he tells me. "Kim did everything for you that a chiropractor can do. I don't see that you have any choice."

I call Dr. Frederick. He's studied the myelogram films sent from Boston. It's clear to him that much of my pain comes from the bone spurs. He's sure I'll feel a lot better once they're gone. And he thinks I'll do as well if he fuses my vagrant vertebra in its present bucktoothed position as if he tried to pull it back into line by screwing it to its neighbors with a metal plate. He doesn't like those metal plates. Often they break, he says, and you need a second operation to take them out. I won't need a second operation to remove an electronic stimulator, either, because now there's one that can be worn externally, and though it's still experimental, it's showing good results. Either of these gadgets should boost the odds of my bones fusing on the first try. How much? At least a few percentage points.

"I'd like still better odds," I tell him, "but I much prefer your opinion to the second opinion I got in Boston." What I like best about Dr. Frederick's view is that he thinks a body cast is unnecessary, and that because my injury is near the base of my spine, I can convalesce in a shorter brace than the suffocating Iron Maiden. That news relieves me the way a convict would be relieved to hear he was only going to be hanged, not drawn and quartered. I ask him to schedule the operation as soon as possible. If I have to put my life in someone else's hands—which is the thing I hate most about this surgery—I want to do it now, and I want the hands to be his.

. . .

We round the tree-lined curve to our New Jersey house, David driving the car we rented at the airport. I stiffen, bracing myself to find our house a charred hulk like Coventry Cathedral. It's not a wholly neurotic fear. The first time we rented our house, our tenants burned up our kitchen. For the last ten years, though, we've always found our house standing pretty much the way we left it. Just a few books in the wrong bookcases and waist-high weeds in the pachysandra.

We call all the relatives to give them the news. Each of David's three children promises to pray for me. They mean well but they make me squirm. "I've never been comfortable being prayed over," I tell Mark when he calls. "How did you used to feel when one of David's children would ask grace at our table 'in Jesus' name'?"

"I knew Jesus made you nervous, though I didn't really know why. But I'm always glad when someone prays for me. You never know, it might do some good."

My son's openmindedness chastens me. When our friend Habu phones from Cairo without knowing of my condition, and promises to pray for my recovery, I praise his intuition and thank him. "With Allah alerted as well as Jesus and the God of Israel," I tell him, "I've got all bases covered."

But the efficacy of prayer is about as convincing to me as the use of spunk-water to remove warts. I get a lot more reassurance from the example of my friend Vicki. She had a successful spinal fusion six years ago. "The anticipation was the worst part," she remembers as we sit drinking iced tea on her patio. "Next worse was the shaking for three days after surgery." But a week after that, she walked around the block. "I nearly fainted," she says, tossing her short gray curls. "It was idiotic. But I had to know I could do it."

Now she can ride her bicycle over eleven Colorado mountain passes in thirteen days, when she's not dancing around in her gorilla suit or her chicken costume for her singing-telegram business. Before that she was a chemist, and she still has a scientist's thoroughness.

"I've saved a pile of articles I gathered when I was researching my own spine surgery. You're welcome to them, though some of the stuff's kind of graphic."

I always want to see what I'm getting myself in for. After I study the photographs and drawings I wish I hadn't. It's not just my bones that are going under the knife. It's my whole nervous system. The bone spurs Dr. Frederick's going to carve away are pushing against my spinal cord.

"This is crazy," I tell David. "This operation could paralyze me. Why should I go through it? My back doesn't hurt at all. My legs don't hurt all that much."

"Not as long as you're lying down."

David hates to hear things more than once, and he's heard all this much more than once. I just can't stop circling like a prisoner looking for a chink in the cell walls. Every night I wake up soaked with sweat from dreams that the surgery paralyzes or cripples or kills me.

When I finally enter the hospital and read the Informed Consent form, I find my nightmares spelled out as real possibilities, along with things I haven't thought of, like strokes and heart attacks. Who in their right mind would consent to a procedure where such things could happen? Maybe it's not too late to change my mind. It's ten at night. Surgery's scheduled for seven tomorrow morning. A nurse comes into my room. "Has anyone ever told you you look just like Shirley MacLaine?" she asks. Everyone does. "Have you signed the form?" Not yet. While she shaves my back from neck to heels, I seriously consider taking this last chance to opt out. Dr. Frederick comes in. He never goes home.

"Do all these gruesome things really happen?" I ask him.

"They have happened. Never to me."

"Tell me the very worst things you think could really happen to me."

"The bone graft might not fuse. Your nerves might be scarred. Scar tissue might stick to your bones. If it does, the adhesions could limit your mobility."

I guess that wouldn't leave me much worse than I am now. I sign the form. A nurse brings me a sleeping pill and I swallow it. A chaplain drops in and offers to pray with me. I'm actually tempted, that's how scared I am, but I thank him and refuse. I buried God when I was nineteen. I haven't seen any reason to dig him up since. Just because I'm frightened doesn't mean that God exists. If he did he ought to be paying attention to people suffering from the *Contra* war and the Salvadoran death squads and the Ethiopian drought, not to one middle-aged middle-class woman who doesn't appreciate how lucky she is to be able to have the complicated operation she needs to reconstruct her spine and let her live a normal life. If all the things that can go wrong don't.

3

Learning to Walk

I hear someone calling, "Joan. Joan. Can you hear me? It's all over. You're fine."

I'm not dead. But for six long hours, my temperature has been lowered close to the temperature of a corpse, and I don't feel much warmer or more lifelike now.

"You're in the recovery room," says the friendly voice. That sounds all right. I open my eyes and see bright lights and nurses rushing around and bodies lying on beds. I close them again.

"See if you can move your toes," says the voice. Evidently I don't do it, because it asks again, "Can you move your toes?"

I try to concentrate. Toes. How do you move your toes?

I'm trying to figure it out when the voice says, "Terrific!"

"They moved?"

"Absolutely. Do it again. Beautiful!"

If my toes wiggle, I'm not paralyzed. Dr. Frederick didn't

spear my spinal cord while he was carving away my bone spurs. I tremble with relief and with cold. My body is a frozen mummy lying precariously on a narrow shelf. The nurse piles on blankets and when I get warm enough I go back to sleep.

I wake up to feel my bed in motion. Through a window I see the night sky. It was barely daylight when they trundled me off to surgery. David is waiting in my room. When he takes my hand, tears come. Now I really know I'm alive.

"My toes move," I say. "Did they tell you?" It's a shock hearing my voice. It sounds so ordinary for someone who's just come back from the dead.

"No one told me anything," he says. His voice is shaking. "You're all right?"

"I guess so." I can't feel anything below my neck. Maybe that's normal. "Are you?"

"I will be now." He grips my hand. I look at his long pianist's fingers, his heavy gold wedding band. "Dr. Frederick told me you'd be back from surgery early this afternoon." His voice still trembles.

"What time is it?"

"Ten at night. I kept calling the hospital, and all they'd tell me was that you were still in the recovery room. I couldn't reach Frederick. The hospital finally called a half hour ago to tell me you were coming up from recovery, but no one told me what was wrong." Deep creases run from his nose to his chin. Behind his glasses his eyes are wet. I reach out to touch his face, my hand trailing tubes. So my arms work. The rest of me must be here somewhere. Those peaks in the sheets must be my feet.

A private-duty nurse is checking the plastic sacks on the IV poles on both sides of my bed. She seems to know what to do for this foreign object that's displaced my body. She pulls up my chart from the foot of my bed. "They kept you in recovery because your blood pressure wouldn't come up. Finally they gave you a blood transfusion."

46

"Whose blood do you think I got?" Before surgery I called dozens of people till I found four with blood like mine and lives I thought put them at the lowest imaginable risk for AIDS. It was bad enough having to trust my spinal cord to Dr. Frederick. I didn't want to trust my life to a blood-screening program.

David doesn't answer. He's asleep in his chair, exhausted from all those hours watching the clock, trying not to think that something had gone terribly wrong and wrecked our life together. I was luckier, asleep all day. My eyes close. David's grip loosens. His hand falls to the bed and wakes him. "Go get some sleep," I tell him. He kisses me, lightly but long. I watch him leave.

The nurse shows me a little button attached to my bedside. Any time I'm in pain I can tap it and get some morphine. The gadget also limits how much I can give myself in an hour. "Most patients take less than the limit," she says, "and much less than you'd need if you'd been waiting four hours for a shot." The fact that Overlook Hospital offers this Patient Controlled Analgesia, while most New York and Boston hospitals do not, helped me decide to stay with the local talent. It's good to feel in control of my pain, since I can't control anything else but my arms and head.

Maybe Dr. Frederick changed his mind and put me in a body cast after all. I touch my stomach. Nothing there but me. My hand recognizes the contours of my body but it feels as if I'm touching someone else. Then the nurse turns me from my back to my side. Half an hour later she turns me back onto my back. In another half hour she turns me onto my other side. Each time she does it the shock tells me there's something alive down there to hurt and that it does belong to me.

The next evening David is sitting in the chair trying to stay awake. He's taught three classes on three hours of sleep and is working so hard at being a supportive spouse that I wish he'd go home. I'm about to tell him so when the door opens and my son Dave appears. It's a shock to see him wearing a tie, and above it his dark bushy beard and mustache trimmed into a dashing Vandyke. He's come straight from work at the small publishing company where he's now senior editor after a year of lightning promotions. As soon as he learns his job, he says, they promote him to the next level of his incompetence. But his boss is smart, I think, to keep Dave too busy to get bored. This is the longest he's ever stayed in one job. My mother says, "Dave has sand in his shoes, but you can't stop him."

"I don't want to stop him," I've told her. "I'd like to join him!" Join him tracking bear and smoking salmon in Alaska, join him reporting in Nicaragua, join him riding his bicycle across the Rockies.

The two Davids manage a few minutes of polite conversation before the older one leaves. "I'll let you catch up on each other," he says. David looks so exhausted that I feel I ought to get out of bed and let him lie down. I should help him reach the feelings under his fatigue. I should direct the emotional traffic between him and Dave. Only now that I don't have the energy to do it can I feel what hard work that is.

Dave puts down the handsome plant he's brought me. "It's seven o'clock," he says. "Want to watch your old quiz show?" He's been addicted to *Jeopardy* since he was in kindergarten and watched me win some money on the show. No one else's mother was on television. It gave him clout.

"Sure, turn it on," I say. "You'll skunk me."

I skunk him. I'm amazed. After Dr. Frederick operated on my foot my brain was full of oatmeal for three months. This time it's racing, though I was under anesthesia three times as long.

"If we could just get you to the studio tonight," Dave says, "you'd make a fortune." The phone rings and he answers. "Lezelfish!" he exclaims. "How's Dr. Killpatient?" I listen to a few rounds of sibling banter before reaching for the phone.

48

"How are you feeling, Mom?"

"Not bad. Dave can tell you my brain works. I've been imagining you working in a hospital like this one."

"I hate hospitals," Leslie says. "I don't want to work with such sick people. I'm pretty sure I'm going to do family medicine."

"Should be ideal for someone as easily bored as you are." She'll be able to do obstetrics and pediatrics and geriatrics, internal medicine and even minor surgery. My baby.

"My mother's daughter," she says.

"Except that your mother couldn't get through the first week of medical school."

"Why do you think I went into medicine?" she says. "I had to find something you couldn't do."

"And you thought that was hard?"

"I'll come see you as soon as my pediatrics rotation ends. Talk to you tomorrow."

Dave leaves and I find myself weeping hard. I seem to be crying because I love him so much. It makes no sense. Maybe it's because he's the only one of my children living within a thousand miles, the only one I can touch with my hands. I am literally awash with gratitude that they love me in spite of what I've done to them—shushing them so I could study, leaving their father, marrying David.

But the crying makes me angry and ashamed. When I'm crying I can't speak. I need words to present myself as a reasonable person whose requests deserve respect. Without them I'm a blubbering baby who can be ignored.

It's not pain that's making me cry. The pain isn't nearly as bad as I thought it would be. When it threatens to get serious I head it off by tapping a button. I'm not weeping from fear, either. I can move my toes and remind myself I'm not paralyzed. But I cry when the florist delivers roses and carnations and lilies, when nurses bring me piles of get-well cards, when friends call and visit. Why should I cry when I'm feeling loved? I hate crying. I can see why I don't do it more than a couple of times a decade.

Sharon arrives wearing a purple T-shirt with silhouetted women dancing in a circle under the moon and stars. I ask her about this crying. "Makes sense to me," she says. "I've been welling up all week. I've just realized I've never been able to accept nurturance, only to give it."

"Just like David. I'm feasting on my friends' attention and he's starving to death. Friends keep offering to feed him but he won't eat." The tubes running into my arms from the intravenous poles on each side of me are a web of friendship holding me safe. Love drips into my veins, into my bloodstream, into my tear ducts.

Mark calls and I tell him about this web. "Sounds to me like an image of that higher intelligence that flows through everyone," he says.

"Is that the same wisdom that tells you what's wrong with a patient?"

"Sometimes I just feel a connection running through my hands to someone's body even if I haven't asked the Maker and Source to be present."

"You don't ask the Maker out loud, do you? Your patients might think you're a witch doctor."

Mark's son Brendon is clamoring in the background. He's almost two, and looks like the painted cherubs in Italian churches. I don't feel up to a phone conversation with him; they usually consist of my singing "I Love You a Bushel and a Peck"—the song my mother sang to my babies—while he giggles. I'd like someone to sing to me.

The private-duty nurses Dr. Frederick said I should have for the first three days would probably do even that if I asked them to. Perfect mothers is what they are. They have nothing in the world to do at any time of the day or night except take care of me. I can ask any time for anything at all—not that my requests are particularly exotic: a drink of water, a pillow under my knees, a cool washcloth, a dry nightgown. Now I know how a perfectly tended infant feels. Blissful.

On the fourth day I lose my private nurses and my magic morphine button. Now I have to ask for medication when my spine howls or my legs ache or my head throbs because the orthopedic ward is so damned noisy. I have to ask for a bedpan now that the catheter is gone. I have to wait till one of the overworked floor nurses has time to answer my call. I'm furious, like a baby whose mother is too busy with her other children to come the minute she calls. I bawl.

Then I progress into toddlerhood. A second blood transfusion finally pumps up my blood pressure enough so I won't keel over if I stand up. It's time to learn to walk. Nancy, the kindest of the nurses, shows me how to use the metal trapeze over my bed. I grab it, pull myself up, inch my legs over the side of the bed. I sit there, sweaty and chilled, amazed by verticality. When the nausea and dizziness and pain subside, Nancy shows me how to transfer myself from the bed to a walker. She holds my arm firmly while I figure out how to balance myself on my feet. Then she helps me back into bed. I collapse into sleep.

That afternoon a woman comes to mold a piece of plastic to my back. It's not much bigger than a piece of typing paper, though a lot thicker. She shows me how it slips into a slot in the back of an elastic brace. No plastic in the front, nothing to squeeze my ribs. It looks like a short wraparound girdle, almost frivolous after the steel-ribbed plastic cage of the Iron Maiden.

"That'll be fantastic!" I say. "But not yet."

"You can't walk until you're fitted to the brace."

"Are you sure Dr. Frederick said I was supposed to wear it now? Today?"

She shows me his order. I believe the written word. While I try to remember how to get out of bed, she warms the plastic on a little hot tray to make it flexible. Then she helps me out of bed and leans me up against the wall like a captured bandit. Before she touches me I start to shake. She pushes and presses the softened plastic against my raw spine. Then she helps me back into bed. "When you get the bandages off," she says, "you'll come into the store and I'll remold it."

That's what she thinks. I shake with terror at the very idea of letting anyone touch my spine ever again. The tears don't spill until after she's left, and by the time Nancy comes back to teach me to walk, I'm just sniffling. This time I'm pretty good at getting to a sitting position. My arms are strong. They should be, I was swimming all summer. Nancy places the rigid plastic part of the brace against my back, and starts wrapping the elastic around my stomach. I grab the ends from her hands. If it has to be done I'll do it. I'm pretty thin after four days of a liquid diet, and I can close the Velcro with a respectable overlap without pulling the brace very hard against my back. But when I pull myself up onto the walker, Nancy notices how loose the brace is. My hands are holding tight to the walker and I can't stop her from ripping open the Velcro and rewrapping it, tight. I've never fainted in my life, but I'm thinking about doing it now. I sink back on the bed, cursing the tears that threaten to disgrace and silence me.

"Can we compromise?" I finally manage to say. She lets me make the brace a little looser. Then she helps me pull myself up and get balanced on the walker.

"Now move your right leg forward."

I try but nothing happens. I look down at my foot. Move, please. Nothing happens. Come on, move. Move, damn you! Sweat drips onto my foot. There must be some terrible neurological damage. Nancy bends down and moves my right foot forward a few inches.

"Now put your weight on it," she says, gripping my elbow. Figuring out how to do that is the hardest mental task I've ever performed.

"I can't tell if my weight's on it or not."

"It is." She moves the walker a few inches forward. "Now move your left foot."

It's just as stupid as the right one. Nancy crouches and moves it for me. My foot registers the touch of her hands, but it doesn't seem to be attached either to my trunk or to my brain. I don't understand why it's bearing my weight. Nancy walks my right foot backward one step, and then my left foot, and sits me down on the bed again.

"You did fine," she lies. "Take a rest. No, leave the brace on," she says as I start to tug on the Velcro. "We'll try again in a little while."

I'm too exhausted to argue. I don't even try to stop the tears from running down my cheeks and into my neck. But when Nancy comes back and stands me up again and moves my right foot and then my left foot and then my right foot, my legs begin to catch on. I take a step by myself. It's wobbly, but it's definitely a step. So is the next one. Nancy shows me how to move the walker first, then walk up to it. "Do you want to walk to the toilet?"

I estimate twelve steps from here to the bathroom. Too many. Then I remember how it feels to lift my hips onto a bedpan. Nancy teaches me how to lower myself onto the toilet. Two weeks ago these trembling legs swam twenty-four laps in fifteen minutes at the Kensington Health Club. She helps me back to bed and the minute she's gone I'm wailing.

I walked. Why am I not ecstatic? A crabby adolescent has booted out the toddler. I am incapable of gratitude, outraged that my strong body has been reduced to hobbling and trembling, furious at having to strap a rigid brace over raw flesh and bone and maneuver on a clunky walker.

David comes and I cry some more. "It's not serious," I tell him, snuffling into his shoulder. "You don't have to deal with it. I'm just flushing some emotional toilet."

"Go ahead and enjoy it," he says. I actually do enjoy it.

I begin to enjoy weeping when I'm wakened in the middle of the night by a sweat that soaks my sheets, or by dreams that storm through my room every night. The tears tap vats of feeling sealed off for ages. One day my eyes stay dry. That night I go to sleep almost afraid I won't wake up weeping. I dream that David and I are driving up to my parents' house. It's raining, and my father comes to the door to meet us with an umbrella. He opens the car door and holds the umbrella over my head. He's laughing. I wake up very happy. This is what I always wanted from my father—just an umbrella to keep off the rain, not a fortress to protect me from danger. And a laugh that says it doesn't really matter if we get wet, it's only a little rain, he's so happy to see me happy with the husband I love.

I remember what Alice Walker says would have happened if her embittered father had lived to see what she made of her life:

> *He would have grown*
> *to admire*
> *the woman I've become.*

Would this have happened if my father hadn't died when I was twenty-two? No. My father has been dead for thirty years. I have never mourned for him. I hated him for hurting my mother. Now for the first time I weep for the ways he hurt himself.

When my mother phones I tell her I've been crying a lot, though I don't say why.

"Just don't lose your self-esteem," she says.

"It doesn't feel like shame. More like cleaning out clogged drains."

"I hope you won't introspect too much," she says. "That's how your father made himself miserable, scrutinizing himself all the time."

I am enough her daughter to distrust introspection too. Why live with your eyes on your navel and your fingers on your pulse? A good healthy self doesn't need a lot of tending. It gets on with its work in the world. "I've been thinking about all the running around I used to do," I say.

"You were busy," she says. "That was good."

"I'm not so sure."

I hang up and lie back on my pillows. What's happening to the woman who is what she does—the woman who works to free political prisoners, who interviews women in the Third World, who works up new college courses every year, who cooks *pasta puttanesca* for her friends? If the things Dr. Frederick said could go wrong do go wrong, if I can't do the things that have defined me, who am I? An invalid? David's wife? My children's mother? My mother?

Sharon phones. "Something's pulling me in new directions," I tell her.

"Good! Can I come too?"

"I'm not sure you'd want to. Sometimes I think I'm moving toward a deep mountain lake. Other times it looks like a minefield."

4

Credentials

The red brick wall of the hospital parking garage is my chief incentive to get out of bed. Beyond the baskets and bowls of flowers that fill the windowsill and spill onto the floor, that blank wall is all I can see from my bed. I'm getting desperate to see the sky. Gripping the trapeze that hangs over my bed, I pull myself upright, strap on my brace, balance myself on my walker and shuffle off to the other side of the orthopedic ward where the rooms do look out on sky and trees, although the colors are clouded by the gray tint of the glass. The patients who have these rooms seem too dulled by pain or hopelessness or age to watch the light and seasons change outside their windows, but I study those shifts as if they were x rays of changes inside myself.

A week after surgery, I'm fed up with nurses who wake me in the middle of the night to ask how I'm feeling. I ask Dr. Frederick when I can go home.

"Maybe Friday," he says.

That's four days away. I sag. "How about Wednesday?"

"Too soon."

"Do I have to stay here until my sutures come out?" I can't wait to get rid of the metal staples that dig into me when I lie on them.

"No, I'll take them out in my office. You'll have a beautiful scar, just a thin white line. It's your drug allergies and low blood pressure I'm concerned about." I suspect he's really keeping me here because he thinks the way my mother does— that I'll "take advantage" of freedom and do too much too soon.

"I feel all right," I tell him, "and Wednesday would be convenient for David. He has no classes that day."

Dr. Frederick peers down at me. "All right, Wednesday." I don't tell him David has no classes on Friday, either.

David drives me home at fifteen miles an hour, but my back still registers every bump and curve. The tears that wash my face don't come from pain. They're from bliss. The sunlight dazzles me. The air I draw deep into my lungs smells of fresh-cut grass. I'm stunned to find the world still here. Just a few leaves have fallen, just a few more have turned yellow and orange and red. I'm not too late for the deep blue skies and clear air of October that hone my awareness of every newly sharpened outline.

At our front door I pause. "I can't go inside," I say. David brings cushions and I lie on a lounge chair in the yard. Patches of sun flicker through the trees' deep shade, patterning the grass with a giraffe's spots. I can tell that some part of me had died because I feel it now coming back to life. Leaves and grass, clouds and sky, penetrate my pores. I think I never really looked at the world before today. Until now I never had the leisure to see. If my back would let me, I'd stay out here all night. It won't. It won't even tolerate our king-sized bed until David unrolls on my side the blue rubber mattress pad, contoured like an egg carton, that Nancy insisted I take home with me from the hospital. I think of the quarts of my sweat that pad soaked up and look at it with pure loathing. I want to hose it off, but I can't wait for it to dry. I need to sleep.

David turns in his sleep to take my hand. Tears come because he seems to love me even when he's unconscious. Still, I felt less alone in my hospital bed than I do now holding David's hand. He's as far from me in his uncomprehending sleep as I was from him during the long day's night of anesthesia. I miss the private room where I could bawl as much as I liked without bothering anyone.

When David goes off to Rutgers in the morning I expand into the solitude like a dry sponge in water. After ten days of staring at brick walls, I want to be alone with the faded Chinese rug and tarnished Egyptian brass table and worn leather chairs of a room I've lived in for twenty-nine years. After the racket of the hospital, all I want to hear is silence. All I want to do is gaze out the windows at the enormous maple tree across the street whose leaves are edged with red and gold, and at the giant oaks turning copper in our back yard. Lying on the sofa, I see them through the sudden blur that bliss brings these days.

The painting over the mantel models the golds and reds with shadows of gray and purple. I follow the brush strokes, wandering over the peaks and into the dark hollows of the Spanish mountains my friend Jean painted. That was before the tumor invaded her brain. Every time she came out of the hospital she'd lost another piece of herself. I began to *find* missing pieces of myself in the hospital.

The shapes and colors of Jean's canvas enter my body like

shafts of light. I have to keep these new channels open. In the hospital I rode these strange floods of memory and feeling by writing them down. To brace my resolve to keep on doing that, I've brought Joan Didion's essay "On Keeping a Notebook" to the sofa. *"Remember what it was to be me,"* she says; "that is always the point." Then she gives me a shock:

> I think we are well advised to keep on nodding terms with the people we used to be, whether we find them attractive company or not. Otherwise they turn up unannounced and surprise us, come hammering on the mind's door at 4 A.M. of a bad night and demand to know who deserted them, who betrayed them, who is going to make amends.

All my life I've done my damnedest to desert and abandon the people I used to be. Like Cinderella fleeing from the scullery to the palace, I've fled from loneliness to love, from confinement to freedom. I've stripped off the dirty rags of the past. But I went too far. I snapped off the people I used to be from my present self the same way I broke off a vertebra from my spine. I lie perfectly still, staring at Jean's mountains. I don't need a surgeon to tell me my bones won't fuse and my nerves won't heal unless I fuse "what it was to be me" with the woman I've become. I know it in my bones.

But I don't know how to do it. I don't remember where I left the people I used to be. Every leaf drifting down from the maple tree pulls an invisible string in my chest.

"It's refreshing to know where to find you," David says when he comes home from teaching. "I've always thought it would be nice to have you a little more dependent on me."

"Not *this* dependent!"

This morning he had to tape plastic wrap over my dressing—

an invention of mine not sanctioned by Dr. Frederick but one that lets me take a shower without wetting my incision. He had to hang around to make sure I didn't faint in the shower. Then he had to remove the wet plastic and the old dressing; sponge drippy brown antiseptic around the metal clamps because I'm allergic to the tidier antibiotic ointments; tape on a fresh dressing. Since I can't reach my feet, he had to put on my socks and shoes and stick my feet in the legs of my pants. Now he'll cook dinner and do the laundry.

"I hate being so helpless!" I say.

"It's not your fault." His voice is weary, weary. He goes back to the car for bags of groceries.

When he's put them all on the kitchen counter, "How about a hug?" I ask. Though he held my hand in his sleep, awake he hasn't voluntarily touched me.

"Can your back stand it?"

"Let's see." It can stand only a grip around the shoulders. I feel like a Foreign Legionnaire who's just gotten a medal from General de Gaulle. This is not our usual style. We've been wrapping ourselves around each other for seventeen years. Our children grumbled that it was never safe to walk into the kitchen when we were both at home. The younger ones would let us take them into our hug, and we'd explain that you can't store up affection any more than you can store vitamin C. It's true. I can feel scurvy coming on right now.

"Daniel and Henry called to see when you could have lunch," I say. He's admitted he's jealous of all the attention I've been getting.

"I can't see people." His voice shakes. "It's just too much of an effort right now."

"They don't expect you to entertain them. Let them take care of you for a change."

"You forget we're different," David snaps back. "You feed on company. It drains me."

"And you're already depleted."

"Jammed up is more like it. Or frozen."

"Tell me about it." This is the closest we've come to a real talk since my surgery.

"You're not interested." He starts to walk away.

"Whoa!" I grab his hand. He stops, but stands at arm's length.

"You talk all the time," he says, "but you're either talking to someone on the phone or you're talking at me. A monologue isn't conversation."

It's true I'm spending a lot of time on the phone. It's true I'm talking nonstop. Leslie tells me it's good for me, a natural response to trauma. But it's also true that David's had his own trauma, one he hasn't been able to talk about.

Our friend Daniel calls. "I'm all right," David says. "Just tired. How are *you*? Yes, we're managing all right. How are your classes this semester?"

He hangs up. "Parrying comes naturally to you," I say. "No wonder you were captain of the Oberlin fencing team." I mean to be flirtatious. He knows I love his powerful fencer's legs. But he's too weary for a riposte. I see him backed up against a wall, saber lying useless on the ground, while three musketeers hold their swords' points to his throat. Athos: his anger that I have so many needs. Porthos: his refusal to be angry with such a needy creature. D'Artagnan: his terror that I might have died. But I'm in no shape to knock those swords away.

The next afternoon Sharon phones between patients. She hears tears in my voice. "Congratulations on feeling what you feel," she says.

"A highly overrated condition."

"What are you sad about?"

"You have enough patients to listen to without me."

"Just tell me."

Words tumble out of me. "I'm sad because I was absorbed in my work when my children were little, and wrapped up in David when they were older. I'm sad because David isn't as perfect as I'd thought. And I'm sad because my body has betrayed me. Sad for other people with damaged bodies." Two weeks ago I didn't know I was sad about any of those things.

"You know what I don't hear on your list of things you're sad about?" Sharon asks. "Not being able to work."

"You're right! I'm not the least bit sad about that. In fact, I feel like a kid who wakes up and sees it's snowed a foot and a half in the night, so she can build snow forts instead of going to school." The University is letting me postpone my sabbatical until I'm well enough to use it. Disability insurance is paying my full salary for six months. I have a whole year off at full pay, a huge gift of leisure to take in the world with this strange new intensity.

But Sharon's question startles me. I love my work. How can I be so relieved at putting down the profession for which I sacrificed so much of my children's early years? At least that's what my mother used to say. I'd snap back that most mothers spent more time shopping at the mall than I spent going to graduate school. Was she right? If I really did march relentlessly on to my Ph.D., children wailing behind me, how come it took me thirteen years to get my degree? Sharon hears her next patient arrive, and I lie staring at the cracks in the ceiling trying to remember how many courses I took the semester after Mark was born, and how old Leslie would have been when I was studying for comprehensive exams. But my memory has too many gaps. They're like the gaps in the record of Connie's life that drive me wild. At least she left documents I can work from—stories and novels, letters and reviews, marked copies of her books. My eyes drift along the shelves of books by the fireplace, most of them marked in David's handwriting or mine or both. If I ever had a biographer, what would she make of my marginal notes?

In my file drawers, next to my notes on Woolson's marginalia and my typed copies of her letters, there are carbons of some of my letters to my children, along with their letters to me. I never kept a journal, but I kept some papers I wrote in college and graduate school. My cheeks catch fire. These days my body registers every strong feeling before I know what it is. I can use these documents the same way I used Connie's! Even if I can't remember the selves I've deserted, still I can reconstruct what it was to be me as if I were my own biographer.

I roll off the sofa—without a metal trapeze I can't sit myself up—strap on my brace, and walk unsteadily into my study. It's a small corner room with two large windows looking out on the back yard. The birds have emptied the feeder that hangs from the lilac tree just outside one window. From the other window I can see the hemlocks stripped of needles to the exact height a deer can reach. Though I've been away from this room for less than two weeks, in its unnatural neatness, without its familiar piles of student papers and stacks of library books, announcements of conferences and meetings, it doesn't look like mine. I look curiously at the bright flowered curtains I made myself, the comfortable desk chair I reupholstered myself, the teak shelves David hung for me and the tall bookcase he built to replace the bricks and boards I'd been using when we met.

When we got married, David insisted I buy this walnut desk. I run my fingers absently along its grain. It was the first thing we bought together. God knows how we paid for it. We were broke from paying lawyers and child support for David's children. But he'd been appalled when he'd seen my study in the cellar: a huge secondhand secretary's desk, an old bridge chair, an ancient gooseneck lamp, and a rusty metal file cabinet in a low-ceilinged room with two small, high windows and ribbons of yellow paint peeling from the damp walls. He asked me why

I hadn't used this sunny guest room for my study. I told him I liked working in the basement, and I did. I liked its cool temperature in hot weather, and I loved its distance from family traffic.

But when I looked at my study with David's eyes, I could see that I wasn't just hiding from my family so I could work. I was trying to hide my work from my family. Not only to protect my private world of thought, but to protect my children from the sight of their mother's naked ambitions. Just last week my son Dave remembered how furious he'd get when I'd spread note-cards across the kitchen counters and tell him not to touch them. I didn't remember doing that. But I do remember the day Leslie came home from kindergarten, the first year I was teaching full-time, and told me, "I've decided what to be when I grow up!" Her curly ponytails bounced with excitement. I waited to hear her tell me she was going to be an astronaut or president of the United States.

"I'm going to be a mommy like Mrs. Knight," she said, "and stay home and wait for my children to come home from school."

How could such a small child turn such a big knife?

For years I've told myself and my mother that the only thing that would have been worse for my children than working when they were small would have been not working. I'd have managed them to death. Now I look through our backyard at the house where Betsy Knight waited at home for her son, Paul, where she taught him and Leslie to go outside and punch the oak trees instead of hitting each other. Then they grew up and Paul fell off a mountain, and not long after she lost her only child and her only career, Betsy lost her life to cancer.

She taught me how to shape lapels and collars by hand-stitching them to canvas interfacing. Betsy sewed, beautifully, as a hobby. I sewed—coats and jackets and pants for myself, overalls and dresses for the children—to save money. Why did

I do that? I was plenty busy with three kids and graduate school and the Civil Rights movement. Howard had a good income. He never made me feel the money was his and not ours. But I hated to spend money I hadn't earned. Maybe that's why I bought secondhand furniture for my study in the basement.

I watch a sparrow hopefully inspecting the ground under the empty feeder. It wasn't just money that didn't belong to me. If money belonged to Howard, time belonged to my children. When I took courses, when I taught classes, I was stealing time from them. That's why I thought going to work was taking time off. That's why I never took time off just for myself. What would I have done with it, anyway?

Now I have time off. I can't work. The months stretching ahead of me look like a huge shiny white box elaborately tied with satin ribbons. I know there's nothing inside but smaller boxes. The extravagant gift I've been given is nothing but the time to untie all the ribbons and open each box and notice how it feels to do that. I'm amazed to discover that it's the only present I want.

I remember how I learned to be ashamed of spending time or money on myself. My father taught me. Before he'd give us our weekly allowances—each child getting a different number of coins according to age, our mother getting a big stack of bills because she was the oldest—we had to show him our "Accounts." After "Income" we had to itemize "Outgo," and not more than five cents could go under "Miscellaneous." Was it fiscal responsibility he was teaching us, as he peered down through his bifocals at our accounts? Or submission? That ritual felt like a fact of life to me as I was growing up. Now it makes me shudder. The only way to evade my father's desperate need to control was to lie. When I bought candy I'd say I'd given money to the Red Cross.

The sparrow unearths an ancient sunflower seed. All he's going to get for his earnest pecking is a shrivelled kernel. My father didn't want me to take money from anyone but him. When he found out I was waiting on tables in my college dorm, he was furious. He was spending too much on my tuition for me to waste my time like that, he said, but I think what bothered him was that I was earning money I could spend as I pleased, without asking his approval in advance or accounting for it afterwards. He wasn't stingy. He was happy to pay for whatever he approved of. He wanted to buy me a fur coat when I got married. What was I going to do with a fur coat? What I needed was a thousand dollars to pay for my first year of graduate school. But it was the coat or nothing. A fur coat was what a good Jewish father gave his daughter. A Ph.D. was not.

I see myself, twenty-one years old, married six months. It's 1957. My arms are covered with weeping sores from a mysterious skin disease. I'm sitting on a hard black vinyl sofa in a drafty furnished apartment, reading a letter from Harvard. If I can finance my first year of graduate work myself, they'll provide fellowships after that. I take the letter to my father. He's disappointed in my "poor reasoning and faulty standards" for thinking a married woman can pursue a career. He tells me for the thousandth time that he won't pay for what he doesn't approve of. At that moment he makes absolutely certain that I will eventually get the credentials to earn my own money and spend it on things he disapproves of.

I accepted the offer of a lesser university to pay my tuition and a salary for teaching two courses. "I just hope you won't put your career ahead of your husband's," my mother said.

"I would never do such a thing!" I said. Not ahead of his, I thought. But certainly alongside it.

"I had to sell my share of my millinery business when I married your father," she reminded me, "even though he was out of work. He would have felt like nothing if he had to be supported by a woman." She was not endorsing masculine pride. She was just telling me the facts of life.

I've never forgotten that it was my father's fault that I had to study first at a university so inferior it paid me to attend, and then at Rutgers, which charged state residents only thirteen dollars a credit, instead of at Harvard. But somehow my familiar anger doesn't rise today. I lean against my desk and notice that the sparrow gave up and left. I might not have done well at Harvard. Women graduate students there were often ignored or treated with contempt. A lot of them dropped out. Harvard's contempt would have finished me, but my father's fired me up. Without it, I might not have persisted for thirteen years to get the degree that got me the job I wanted.

Why did I think I was absolutely dependent on my father's approval? I could have gone to a bank and asked for a loan. I never thought of doing that. Why not? I stare at the empty bird feeder. I thought I'd fooled my college professors into giving me the grades and recommendations that had fooled Harvard into admitting me. And I wouldn't ask my husband to go into debt to invest in my career because at the bottom of my heart I didn't believe I would ever actually become a college professor who would earn enough to pay back a loan. I had just one woman professor at Tufts, I'd have just one more at Rutgers. I had no reason to think I could be another such exception. To be fair, though, my father never said that I couldn't become a college professor. He just said I shouldn't.

My legs know I've been standing too long. Why did I come in here, anyway? To dig out documents for my biographer. My back won't bend enough to let me open the file drawer of my desk. Sitting on my desk chair gets me no closer to the drawer. I drop to my knees and tug the heavy drawer toward me. Blue plastic tabs mark the files in the front: CFW Bibliography, CFW Family, CFW and Henry James, CFW Letters. Way at the back is a creased manila folder marked "JW Credentials." It's full of university transcripts, diplomas, newspaper clippings, old versions of my curriculum vitae. My father was hardly the only man who thought women shouldn't have credentials like these. There was a psychiatrist—. Heat floods my face. I mop my neck with my shirttail. Hot flash? No. Rage.

Howard asked me to see a psychiatrist when I asked him for a divorce. I agreed, positive I could show them both how sane I was. What was that doctor's name? I've repressed it. But I'll never forget what he said: my neurotic striving for a doctorate showed I suffered from penis envy. I was flabbergasted. It was 1970. Feminists had been critiquing Freud for years. Maybe this doctor was just trying to break down my defenses. I'd show him women could be rational.

"It may have been very neurotic for me to marry at twenty and have three children by the time I was twenty-seven," I told him. Fighting with my father had taught me how to sound calm when I was shaking with fury. "But I don't think the brain is a masculine organ, and I don't think taking courses is a neurotic symptom."

"Taking courses is not earning a Ph.D.," the doctor said.

"You think it's more neurotic for me to work for a doctorate than it was for you or Howard?"

"As men, we needed to support our families."

"Plenty of men support their families without doctorates," I pointed out. "And plenty of women have to support themselves, and their families."

"But you don't have to," the doctor said. "Couldn't you have waited until your children were grown?" Had he been talking to my mother?

"And then start to qualify for a job as a college professor?"

"You have to have prestige and an independent income?" He made them sound like crimes or diseases.

"Yes. Don't you?"

"And how do you think that makes your husband feel?"

"I never thought his manhood was so fragile that it depended on my dependency. He supported my work."

"And you're so grateful that you're leaving him?"

I sat silent. I saw exactly where he'd twisted the logic of the argument, but I knew if I said another word I'd start to cry, and he'd read my tears as capitulation. I didn't cry. Not until I was sitting in my car. Yes, damn it, I'd been grateful, tremendously grateful, when Howard took the children off to the park on a Sunday morning so I could write a paper about parents and children in the plays of Eugene O'Neill. I hadn't seen any irony in the situation. Certainly I hadn't expected any gratitude for taking charge of the children so he could go to work or play golf on his day off. My work was self-indulgence. His was necessary. I was so profoundly grateful that he "let me" go to graduate school—as my father would not have done—that for fourteen years I told myself it didn't matter that we had no intimacy. I didn't know any couples who did.

My face is as hot as the backs of my knees. I lean on the file drawer, push myself back to my feet. When we got married and decided to live in my house, I wanted David to have this sunny room looking out on lilacs and hemlocks for his study, but he insisted I take it. At thirty-four, I was just starting my career, he said. At forty-three, his was established. He set up his desk in a corner of our bedroom. I moved up from the basement. My desire to work was only one desire he helped me move upstairs.

I stumble down the hall to the bathroom, swallow a Percocet, splash cold water on my red face. When I left that psychiatrist's office I sobbed the way I sobbed when my mother told me I was selfish to study when my children were small, when she told me I'd ruin their lives by divorcing their father. I cried but I kept on going. I finished my doctorate. I got a full-time job teaching at Drew. I divorced Howard. I married David. At each great turn in my life I imagined my mother's voice saying, "You got what you wanted, didn't you?" That was the worst crime a woman could commit. But the last time I saw her she surprised me.

"If I were a young woman today," she said, "I'd have kept

working after I got married. I'd have hung on to my millinery business."

I pull off my brace and collapse on the sofa. I "took advantage" of my freedom this morning and I'm paying. Percocet works fast. Soon I can open my eyes and look through the file I've brought from my study. At the back is a Rutgers transcript that begins in the fall of 1958. Dave was six weeks old and my breasts leaking milk when I managed to button an old skirt and drive to New Brunswick once a week for a course in Greek drama. The transcript ends in the spring of 1970. Dave would have been twelve, Mark ten, and Leslie seven. These papers ought to show me if my work was really as driven as my mother and the psychiatrist thought.

The transcript's so old it could be a document in a historical society. It shows I took thirteen years to do thirteen semesters of course work. What was I doing the other thirteen semesters? Giving birth, pushing baby carriages in picket lines, studying for comprehensives, teaching part-time, writing my dissertation. Only four times did I manage to take two courses. Nine semesters I took just one course. That looks like a straggle, not a forced march. But it was enough to convict me of the crime of stealing time for myself from my children and my husband.

That's not the way my advisor saw it. At one conference, Al Kellogg thumbed through my folder checking off the requirements I'd met, and said, "Now here's a note from your obstetrician saying that you started coursework the day your first child was born—"

"Not quite."

"Then you took some incompletes and a semester off when the baby was hospitalized, and another semester off when another child was born. *Transcriptus interruptus*," he said, shaking his head. After years of worrying about how my studies were disrupting my child rearing, it made my head spin to hear that childbearing had disrupted my studies. "Then I had to schedule your master's exam as an oral," he went on, leaning back in his swivel chair, "because you were going to give birth yet again in October when the written exam was scheduled. I thought I was going to have to drag in the janitor to fill out a committee that summer."

"I've always thought I passed that exam because I managed to look eleven months pregnant," I told him. "When I couldn't remember all the Shakespearean motifs in *Moby-Dick,* the questioner backed off because he thought the agony on my face meant I was going into labor on the spot."

"You terrified every man there."

"But are they going to kick me out of here for taking so long to finish?"

"You'll need a special extension, but I think I can persuade the committee you haven't been loafing." And he did.

David comes home and drops his briefcase on the stairs. "How was your lunch with Daniel?" I ask.

"Good. He told me how furious he was when Jane was sick so much the first year they were married. She wasn't being the perfect person he thought he'd married."

"Sounds familiar."

"I told him it wasn't your fault you're laid up. And he howled! 'You think that means you're not angry?' he said. 'Don't tell me you believe you're a rational creature!' "

He's got Daniel's intense intonation to a *T.* I hold up my hand and he takes it. We're thawed at the edges but still icy in the center. Maybe no man can be both a body-servant and a lover.

"Let me see if I can cook a simple meal tonight."

I wash two potatoes and rub chicken breasts with oregano and lemon juice and stick them in the microwave while I boil frozen peas. David's delighted. The second quickest way to his heart is through his stomach.

71

The next day my legs take their revenge. I phone Dr. Frederick to ask him to renew my prescription for Percocet. "You have to learn to control the pain by doing less," he tells me, "not with drugs. By trying to rush your recovery, you're setting it back."

"How about some exercises? My muscles have all turned to jelly."

"It's too soon."

"What about physical therapy?"

"Not yet. Give yourself a chance to heal."

Pearl calls. She's lived with rheumatoid arthritis for decades. "I've got some advice for you if you want it," she says. "You do? Okay. Worrying about your illness isn't going to affect the outcome. You have to accept the situation and its timetable. That's not resignation, Joan, it's just realism. Even if you have to live differently, you can still have a rich life."

"I know." But I don't want to know.

"Meanwhile—want to hear some more?"

"Mmm."

"Okay. Meanwhile keep track of your progress, no matter how much it zigs and zags. And ask yourself what's *good* about today. Is the sun out, did you hear some wonderful music, did a friend call, are you any better? Living in the day, you can refuse to be depressed."

I write Pearl's words on the pad of paper still serving as my journal. A wave of shame heats my face. How many times did I call her when she was recovering from heart surgery? Or Carol after her spine operation, or Walter when Jean was dying? I just didn't understand what a strong lifeline a call can be. Even if I had understood, I might have shrunk from pain I couldn't relieve.

• • •

72

After a week of doing nothing, my spine's giving me very little pain. So when my children come to visit, I propose a short walk in the woods next to our house. Brendon rides on Mark's shoulders, pulling yellow leaves off the trees. His wife Norma, who is pregnant, ambles along with me in the rear. Dave bites at Leslie's nose like a snapping turtle. She counterattacks and he escapes up a tree. Brendon loves it and so do I.

"You'd think they were ten and five, instead of thirty and twenty-five," I say to Norma.

"I love your family's playfulness. I hope it's rubbing off on me."

Suddenly my knees wobble and I think I'm going to throw up. Leslie takes my arm and steers me out of the woods to the street. Dave runs home to get a car. Home is less than a block away.

Back on the sofa, I try to listen to my body's signals. After a few weeks, it pays cash. Little by little it lets me walk longer distances, first down the block and back, then to a nearby forest of enormous evergreens. I lean against one tree and watch the treetops merge and separate in the windy blue sky. My dizziness turns to ecstasy.

Why has this sight brought me here for thirty years? I've come carrying babies and trailing toddlers, come alone. To look at rooted trunks and waving branches. To imagine that fixity and freedom, those old antagonists, could actually be complementary. To gather the long, tapered pinecones that fall from these trees, fragrant kindling for winter fires. Now I can't bend over. I pick up cones with a sort of calipers David got me so I wouldn't have to ask him to pick up a piece of paper from the floor or get a box of tea from a high shelf. My picker-upper and my slow moseying make me feel older than my mother. But I see more than at my usual stride. The afternoon sun sets fire to the yellow maple leaves drifting down between the trees. I ache as I do each year when the heart-lifting colors announce that the trees will soon be bare.

But the maples are every bit as alive as the evergreens. They just have different cycles. I am more alive now, horizontal or moseying, mulling by myself or connecting to friends and family over long telephone wires, than when I'm in full leaf.

5

Buried Goddesses

$\mathscr{I}$'ve always wondered what witches do at their covens. On Halloween I'm going to find out. I'm convening the Wise Women who held me safely through surgery in the web of their affection. One is old enough to be my mother, one is younger than my daughter. There's a mathematician and an economist and a psychoanalyst and some poets and professors and a singing gorilla. There are divorced mothers, resident wives, lesbian lovers. Leslie can't get away from Cleveland, but she sends a magic wand full of floating sparkles. "Just wave it," she says, "and—*pffftt!*—you can make anything disappear!"

Nine of us gather on Halloween for potluck. Everyone brings what she likes. A colleague in Women's Studies taught me to "let the Goddess provide" and as always this nonsystem produces a perfect feast. We have tortellini and fish stew and endive salad and homemade bread and wine and cider and fudgy brownies. Since none of us knows how witches should behave, we make up our own rituals. Vicki hands out big black witches' hats and lights the fire. Ilona switches off the lamps. While I lie on the sofa with my feet in Sharon's lap, we take turns waving Leslie's magic wand. First we wave it to make things disappear from our lives and from the planet—nuclear waste and too many meetings are high on everyone's list—and then to bring into being what's missing.

"More joy," says Martha. Our eyes lock. She chairs committees and works in soup kitchens and teaches poetry to women serving life sentences and still can't fill the vacuum in her life where love and pleasure should be. My life is full of love and pleasure. Why have I crammed my life the same way she does?

Eleanor adds a log to the fire. "I want to be the one to solve a hundred-year-old problem in mathematics and put my name on the solution." Firelight dances in her red hair.

"I want more hate," Ann says, waving the wand. Everyone looks up. She nods energetically. "Yes, hate! You have no idea how exhilarating it can be!" Connie found hate enlivening, too. I never have.

"How about an eighth day in the week?" says Vicki. "Or a bubble of extra time you could walk into whenever you need it."

I'm already living in that bubble of time. My own over-scheduled life is last night's bad dream. Vicki hands me the wand.

"I want renewal," I say. I'm thinking of my bones and my marriage. "And I want someone, or something, to thank—the Fates or the Goddess or whoever you think is responsible for things that go right. My surgery. My healing. Our friendship." My voice cracks. "I could almost thank my body for stopping me in my tracks!"

"When the student is ready, the teacher appears," Vicki says. She's spiritual for a gorilla.

"The teacher does come," I say. "In all shapes, over and over again. But who sends her?"

76

"God," Martha says. Eleanor rolls her eyes.

"But if you don't believe in God," I say, "or in the Goddess or fate or lucky stars, why should they bother with you?" I hold up my glass so Ilona can refill it. "And if my healing and our friendship are somehow meant to be, does that mean other people are meant to suffer starvation or war or torture? I don't know what to believe."

"I believe in us," Sharon says firmly. She squeezes my foot.

Hiking boots would give me surer footing on the rocky paths of the forest than my tennis shoes do. At a nearby sporting goods store—a ten-minute drive, my first independent outing—I choose a pair of lightweight gray suede boots, perfectly serious except for fuchsia *V*s flashing along the sides. They promise mobility—as soon as I can bend enough to lace them myself.

On the way back into the house, I pick up the mail. Under the catalogs is the current issue of *Anima,* with my article on goddesses and fairy tales. It's the lead article. That's nice. I take it to the sofa and lie down, nauseated and trembling from my excursion. My new boots excite me more than this essay I labored so long to write. I still don't know why I wrote it.

The ancestors of these sentences I pounded out on my little Olivetti portable typewriter six years ago in our scantily furnished apartment in Florence. The twelve-foot ceilings and marble floors echoed every keystroke. Our first sabbatical abroad! I'd dreamed of living abroad ever since I sat on the floor playing with a bronze horse my father had brought home from Shanghai. I knew he'd been happy when he lived there, and I knew he wasn't happy any more. In Florence I was deliriously happy, though I was uneasy about people at home. My mother was recovering from radiation treatments for the tumor on her vocal cords. Mark was depressed because his environmental studies at the University of Massachusetts were showing him it was too late to save the planet. Dave was all right, managing bike shops in Rhode Island while he tried to figure out how to use his Phi Beta Kappa credentials without having to put on a necktie. Leslie, though, in her first semester at Oberlin, was reeling.

"What am I doing here with all these smart people?" she wrote. I'd read her letters while standing on the crowded bus going to my Italian lessons, or waiting in line at the *supermercato*. I'd sit at my table in the British Institute Library, reading about Demeter's grief at losing her daughter Persephone, and remember how I'd grieved when Leslie decided to spend her last two years of high school with her father.

It might have hurt less if she'd been kidnapped like Persephone. She wasn't moving to the Berkshires just because she hated her suburban high school. She was going after her father. She was getting away from me. It wasn't because we argued. I couldn't get her to argue with me. She'd just pull a shade down behind her eyes and look at me coldly. But as soon as she moved away she lifted the shade and invited me in. Like Persephone returning to Demeter, she came back to me. We wrote long letters and ran up huge phone bills. She called me one night when "the parents" were out.

"I'm thinking about becoming sexually active," she said. Just like that.

"With anyone in particular?"

"Mother! I'm not just trying to get rid of my virginity. It's Johannes—I told you about him. I really like him, but I'm not sure I'm ready. What do you think? Should I go to Planned Parenthood and get a diaphragm, or just carry condoms in case I get swept away by passion some wild night?"

Letting her go, I'd won her back. She went off to Oberlin, I went off to Florence. "Sometimes I think I'm more mature than anyone around me," she wrote me that year, "but other times I'm just a little lost lamb. Here I am at David's college. I'm coordinating the local chapter of Amnesty International, just like you. Last week I rode all night in a bus to Washington to march against the *Contra* war. Am I a grown-up with my own principles or still a Good Little Girl doing what my family thinks is right?"

I'd been studying carvings of Demeter and Persephone, facing one another like mirror images, and reading about mothers and daughters who feel like one person, unable to tell where one leaves off and the other begins, so confused that when the daughter gains weight the mother feels fat. I didn't think I was tangled up that way with Leslie, but maybe she did. "Do you think we haven't separated enough?" I asked her. "Maybe we just finessed separation when you went to live with your father. Maybe we need to do it now."

"You were a tough act to follow," Leslie wrote back. "I guess I had to put some distance between us. But I don't think our closeness now is a problem. I really like it."

So do I. Even now that Leslie is studying to be a doctor—not a mommy waiting for her children to come home—she's still the child I wanted enough to commit *transcriptus interruptus*. Howard couldn't understand it. Why would I interrupt my graduate work to have a baby when I was so obviously harassed by the two little boys we already had? I couldn't explain why I wanted a third child. I was the third child in my own family. Maybe I wanted a family like the one I'd grown up in. The same, only happy.

When Leslie squirmed out of my body, the gynecologist said, "Son of a gun, you got a girl!" He'd given up trying to have a girl after four sons. I fell in love with my daughter on the spot. The boys I'd hurried out of bottles at a year and diapers at two, but I took a deep pleasure in the warm smell of Leslie's damp curls even at four in the morning. I was willing to let her stop being three years old only because I knew she'd find new ways to delight me when she was four. Would I have been so batty about her if she'd been a boy? Or was I so crazy about her because she was female like me, yet nothing like me? Not a "street angel, house devil," like my mother called me. Not a back-talking brat like me to "send back to the Indians," but an adorable, funny little girl I could love to pieces.

That's why I had to have her! It was myself I wanted to give birth to, myself I wanted to mother. I stare at my toes in their gray wool socks. I used my daughter. Made her the child I'd wanted to be. Myself made perfect.

That was a really terrible thing to do to a child.

No wonder Leslie was never bad. No wonder she'd hide in her closet when she needed to cry. Move away from me when she was fifteen. Leave me feeling like a jilted lover. That's how I feel right this minute. Why? Why now, why when Leslie left, why with Connie in the Rollins Archive? No man ever jilted me. I stop wiggling my toes and lie perfectly still. Maybe I'm making Connie stand in for my daughter. Maybe I'm still making Leslie stand in for me. Making them into parts of myself I can't bear to lose but that have the power to reject the rest of me.

My mother is right about introspection. It does make you miserable. I roll off the sofa and struggle to my feet. The copy of *Anima* falls to the floor. "Individuation and Intimacy," I called my article. Hah! Learnedly I pointed out how myths and fairy tales dramatize the timeless struggle between wanting to be a separate person with firm boundaries and longing to break down those boundaries. Succinctly I explained the complicated rhythm of union and detachment that we learn, or don't learn, with our mothers, and then carry over to our children and our mates. And it's taken me six years and major surgery to recognize that any of that was going on between Leslie and me.

If it was boundaries I needed to understand, I certainly went about it the hard way. I wasted four years studying mythology and the history of religion. Irreplaceable time, maybe my last chance to sit in libraries, sit at a typewriter. And I threw it away on *goddesses*. Why? It was their descents into the Underworld that fascinated me—Persephone dragged down there by Hades, the Sumerian goddess Inanna choosing to enter the great Below—but I never understood what the Underworld was or what it meant to go there. I had to fudge it whenever I wrote about it. It was exciting to learn that God was imagined as a woman eons before anyone imagined God as a man. It tickled me to discover that the original Holy Trinity was Maiden, Mother and Crone. But nothing I learned made me want to believe in a divine female presence any more than I wanted to believe in the God of Abraham, Isaac and Jacob.

I head for the kitchen to make a cup of tea. Not quite by accident, I step on the journal. I'm finished with the Goddess.

But she isn't finished with me.

A few days later I dream I'm at a political rally. I climb a steep grandstand. Above me is a very tall, very broad woman in a simple flowing gown. She stops me and accuses me of stealing her jewelry. Me, a thief? I hold up the necklace I'm carrying in my hand—a hollow silver circle on a chain. She admits it's mine, not hers. "These ancient symbols belong to everyone," I say. "Thank God," she says. I'm uneasy. We should be allies, this woman and I, not antagonists. This anger between us feels like my fault.

I know who she is. You can't spend years studying mythology and not recognize a goddess when you meet one. But why would she accuse me of stealing? I've paid tribute to her power in print. I don't need to climb a grandstand to declare my allegiance to womanhood; I do that every day I teach about women and write about women and work for women's right to study their own traditions. So why do I feel in the wrong?

Sharon calls, excited that the mail has brought her copy of *Anima*. "Any idea when you might feel up to reading my chapter?'' she asks. Before my surgery I edited the first chapters of a book she's writing on sexual abuse. Two more chapters are sitting on the coffee table. I don't know if my brain can concentrate yet, but I promise to try. To my surprise I can follow her argument from one paragraph to the next, see how she might clarify or sharpen it. I'll try reading two essays on Woolson that a journal asked me to evaluate. I can explain why one should be rejected and how the other could be strengthened enough to publish. If I can do that, maybe I can go back to work on my own book about Connie's literary relations.

I gather a stack of books, notes, and notecards and arrange them on our king-sized bed like the petals of a flower. Carefully I climb into the center, carefully I lie down. Everything I need is within reach. Except one book I forgot. I can't begin without it. Groaning, I roll over, kneel, and stand on the bed to walk around my notes. Something stabs my groin. My right leg buckles. It dumps me sprawling on my beautiful daisy, shatters its petals, scatters them everywhere. Furious, I kick books and papers onto the floor and flop back onto the bed. I peer down at my throbbing body as if it were separated from the rest of me by an Elizabethan ruff. If I could banish this treacherous body from the royal presence of the ruling brain, I would, I would.

What if I do manage to override my body and write the book whose materials litter the floor around my bed? I'll be back living in my head, that's what. A nice place to visit, but too small, too isolated, too cold to live in. Locked out from the shafts of bliss and floods of tears that have stretched my life since surgery. But if I refuse to live in my head, and I can't live much of a life in my body, where am I going to live?

A few days later the mail brings the first copies of my anthology of Connie's stories. It took years to research and write my article, years to prepare this book, and now they arrive in a single week! I tear open the box. It holds six handsome volumes bound in white with gold lettering. My fingers tremble as they trace the title: *Women Artists, Women Exiles: "Miss Grief" and Other Stories by Constance Fenimore Woolson.* I stroke my own name printed below Connie's, feel the heft of the volume as I flip the smooth pages, admiring a lyrical image, an ironic aside, a tough-minded ending. Wonderful stories. "Connie, you're back in print!" I tell her. "Maybe now you'll get that revival you deserve." I turn back to my long introduction. It looks so different in print than it did in manuscript, bristling with yellow Post-its, bleeding with red ink from my fights with the copy editor.

David buys champagne to celebrate—a selfless gesture since his hypoglycemia splits his skull if he drinks any himself. He pops the cork and fills my glass.

"Here's to your first book all on your own!" he says, raising his glass of Perrier. Fifteen years ago we edited a seven-volume anthology of American literature together.

"Connie wrote all but fifty pages of it. All the good ones."

"That's absurd! You wrote a splendid introduction."

"Oh, it's sound and scholarly."

"And full of ideas."

"But I can't stand the sound of my voice on the page," I hear myself say. "It's so impersonal. It's so respectable."

"So next time write like a wild woman!"

"Would you want to be married to a wild woman?"

"Why not?"

Why not? It would have to be more exciting than this polite minuet we've been dancing since my surgery.

I'm lying on the sofa watching leaves drift down from the maple tree when Carol calls. "Just to say I'm thinking about you." Just like that, the barometer of my day rises. Then it sinks: I called her only once after *her* spine surgery.

"Bless you. How can you think of anything while you're finishing your novel?"

"Oh God. There's a hole in my heroine's motivation. It's killing the plot."

"Maybe that's why you're writing about her, because you don't understand her." Those goddesses have taught me something after all.

"Are there things you still don't understand about Connie?"

"I'll just give you the short list. Did she kill herself? If she did, why did she? Could Henry James have saved her? Could a loving woman friend have saved her?"

"The mystery that interests me," says Carol, who's known me since we were freshmen at Tufts, "is why an exuberant woman like you is so obsessed by a suffering woman like her."

"I wish I knew. If I could write her biography I might find out, but I've gathered every scrap that's survived about her life, and it's not enough."

"Just as well. If you were looking for yourself, you'd be writing *your* life, not hers."

"All biographers do that, really. They just keep quiet about their own stories. Physicists at least admit that where they stand affects the measurements they get. What I'd really like to hear about is that tricky relationship between the observers and what they're observing."

"Why don't you tell that story?" Carol says.

That night I dream that a woman wearing long dark clothes sits before me. I know it's Connie even though she's facing me and all the photos I've seen of her have been in profile. She looks right at me. It's a marvelous face: angular, quizzical, amused despite what it knows of pain. I am fascinated by her boots. They have thick rubber soles and black fabric tops with bold gold Vs on them. They look like my new hiking boots, except that the Vs on mine are fuchsia. I wonder where those Vs are pointing, hers and mine. I tell her I've just brought a volume of her stories back into print, and she's surprised and pleased, but disappointed that I haven't brought her a copy of the book. Have I let her down already? I put my arm around her waist. I want to make some sort of intimate claim. She may not know me, but I've known her for years. We agree to meet on Friday when I don't have any classes. I worry that she won't show up; she accepts so few invitations. The prospect of talking with her, of knowing her after years of thinking and imagining and guessing about her, makes me tremble with excitement.

I can't wait to get her alone, away from the man with a terrible cold who keeps pursuing us. Evading him saps my energy, distracts and worries me. As I drive to my meeting with Connie, I find myself right behind him on an icy road, our bumpers almost touching, knowing we're about to have a terrible collision.

The minute I wake up I know who this man is. He's the literary critic who'll judge any book I write. He's trying to infect me with his values. If I keep following close behind him, I'll never get to my meeting with Connie. I'll wind up in a ditch, or a hospital. My dream is like a cartoon captioned by Emerson: "Imitation is suicide."

The dream hangs over me for days. I call Sharon and tell her about it. "Why are you so fascinated by Connie's boots?" she asks.

"Her boots? I haven't given them a thought. Well, they look something like the hiking boots I just bought. And they remind me of the ugly oxfords my father made me wear. And they make me think of Mr. Ramsay's boots. Have you ever read Virginia Woolf's *To the Lighthouse*?"

"Years ago."

"You remember how Mr. Ramsay won't let Lily concentrate on her painting? He wants her to stop and soothe him the way his wife always did until he wore her out and she died. He pesters her till she finds something about him to praise, even if it's only his magnificent boots."

Lily was a reserved spinster like Connie. I'm bearing down on Connie the same way Mr. Ramsay bore down on Lily, demanding even more than he did. He just wanted her to deal with him. I want Connie to reveal herself to me. She'd have hated that. She'd have pulled down a shade behind her eyes. She'd have been furious at me for prying into her secrets, reading her letters, dredging up the stories she never reprinted because she was ashamed of them. I can smell her hostility.

"Can I call you back?" I ask Sharon. "I want to look up that passage about Mr. Ramsay's boots." I find my battered copy of *To the Lighthouse,* and stumble on Lily's struggle to know Mrs. Ramsay.

> Sitting on the floor with her arms round Mrs. Ramsay's knees . . . she imagined how in the chambers of the mind and heart of the woman who was, physically, touching her, were stood, like the treasures in the tombs of kings, tablets bearing sacred inscriptions, which if one could spell them out, would teach one everything, but they would never be offered openly, never made public.

It was those sacred tablets I was trying to decipher at Rollins. I want to sit on the floor like Lily with my arms wrapped around the knees of the woman who fascinates me. I know I can't. But that's what I want. Woolf knows exactly how that longing feels. "What art was there," she asks, "known to love or cunning, by which one pressed through into those secret chambers? What device for becoming, like waters poured into one jar, inextricably the same, one with the object one adored?" What art, what device? That's what I want to know too. That's what I was trying to figure out in my *Anima* article: how to know someone intimately, not just with your mind, but as if you were one person, the way you'd been with your mother before you were born. With your daughter before *she* was born.

That's what Woolf's talking about. "It was not knowledge but unity that she desired, not inscriptions on tablets, nothing that could be written in any language known to men, but intimacy itself, which is knowledge, she had thought, leaning her head on Mrs. Ramsay's knee."

> Nothing happened. Nothing! Nothing! as she leant her head against Mrs. Ramsay's knee. And yet, she knew knowledge and wisdom were stored up in Mrs. Ramsay's heart. How then, she had asked herself, did one know one thing or another thing about people, sealed as they were? Only like a bee, drawn by some sweetness or sharpness in the air intangible to touch or taste, one haunted the dome-shaped hive . . . the hives which were people.

Pressing through by some art known to love or cunning into the secret chambers of another person. Intimacy which is knowledge. Exactly. Exactly! That's what I was studying in mythology. That's what I want with Connie. Thank God for great literature. Woolf's lines light up my muddle and hypnotize me with their beauty. But they don't tell me how to achieve this intimacy which is knowledge. Certainly not with a dead woman, not when the fabric of the life she's left me is more holes than cloth. I'm angry with Connie. She won't let me write her biography any more than she'll let me wrap my arms around her knees. All I can do is imagine what she would have said to me if I could have leaned my head on her knee. All I can do is ask what there is in the sweetness or sharpness in the air above her head that makes it the hive I have to haunt.

Why did Lily Briscoe yearn and yearn to read the sacred inscriptions in the secret chambers of Mrs. Ramsay's heart? For one thing, Mrs. Ramsay had lived lives that Lily had rejected for herself. That's why I need to know Connie. She never married; I've married twice. She had no children; David and I have six children and three grandchildren. She lived alone, traveled alone, avoided people. Until these months of convalescence I've hardly ever been alone in my life. She was easily tired, easily ill; I've always been impossibly energetic and almost never sick. She was seriously depressed; I've always been ebullient. She almost certainly committed suicide; I've never believed I would. She knows the Underworld like the palm of her hand. She could guide me there, lead me to the buried goddesses whose power is inseparable from their pain. Lead me to my buried selves.

6

The Proud Salmon of the Pond

*Y*ou seem preoccupied," David says while we wait for our frozen waffles to leap out of the toaster. I laugh and tell him the word is exactly right. Ever since my dream of Connie, the geography of my mind has been literally "preoccupied" by a tenant who won't move out, a guest who sits in on every conversation.

David leaves for Rutgers and Connie tags along on my walk to the forest. I see her leaning against a tree, looking up at the treetops weaving in the high autumn wind. My pleasure is sharp and intense. "Why am I so happy?" I ask her. "I should be miserable." I fought for the life I had before my spine broke down: a living marriage. Satisfying work. Travel. Now David and I are polite acquaintances. I can't work, can't travel. But every minute glows.

Connie doesn't answer. She walks away between two rows of pines. Patches of sun move over the tree trunks and the carpet of pine needles. This odd life I'm living must be satisfying desires I didn't know I had. Connie has stopped in a puddle of sunshine, looking away from me. I want to look with my own eyes and speak in my own voice. I want to occupy my own space on the planet. Did Connie put those words in my head?

"I went to the woods because I wished to live deliberately." I know who put those words in my head, and when. I read *Walden* while I was nursing Dave at four in the morning. Funny choice for a new mother, the reflections of a bachelor living alone in a cabin by a pond.

Connie turns and looks back at me. And now you've taken up with a reclusive spinster, she says. In between there were those other solitaries, Hawthorne and Dickinson. Don't you understand that you're one of us?

"I'm not a secret hermit," I tell her. "I'm madly in love with my children. I love talking and teaching and plotting to change the world."

But look what that's cost you, Connie says. The chance to live deliberately.

Why was I reading about the deliberate life instead of gazing deliberately into my baby's eyes? Because Dave's eyes closed as soon as my milk stopped the spasms of his hunger. I marveled that the whorls of his hair and the shape of his fingers were just like his father's, that he was getting bigger drinking milk I never saw, but I couldn't marvel indefinitely. Not during six or seven feedings a day, half an hour each time. I got bored.

And as for living deliberately—well, by the time I got the chance to teach *Walden*, I had three little children. Living deliberately was as impossible as a meal without a spilled glass of milk. "I did not wish to live what was not life," Thoreau says. "Living is so dear." Right. Dear—beloved and costly. But how can you tell when what you're living is life, and when it's not? Did Connie kill herself because she was trapped in what was not life? I turn to ask her but she's disappeared.

David comes home chuckling. "Have you been listening to *All Things Considered?*"

"Well, you could call it that."

"Dan Quayle said the most hilarious thing—"

The phone rings. It's Ilona. "How is your back, my darling? Are you having a lot of pain?"

"Very little. Even my legs are okay if I don't try to do too much."

"You must be going crazy, lying around all day all by yourself."

"I'm ashamed to tell you how much I'm enjoying myself. Mark used to say 'Mommy needs a little piece of quiet!' This must be the first time in my life I've had a piece that's big enough."

David heads up the stairs with his briefcases.

"I don't tell people how much I enjoy my own company," Ilona says. "They think you don't like them. It's not that—"

Half an hour later, David comes downstairs. Ilona and I are still talking and laughing.

"Dinner?" he mouths, eyebrows raised.

I nod and thank Ilona for her call. By the time I roll off the sofa and strap on my brace, he's in the kitchen boiling water for the pasta.

"How's Ilona?"

"Fine. She sends you her love." I can get the salad makings out of the refrigerator by bending my knees, though I still can't bend at the hips.

"How do you know she's fine?" David says coldly. "All you were talking about was yourself."

"Was I?" I keep my anger out of my words but it heats my cheeks. "No, I wasn't. She told me how much she's enjoying her retirement and her solitude."

"Maybe that was after I went upstairs."

He slams the lid on the pot so hard that several spoons fall from their hooks onto the floor. I freeze.

"I'm glad you have such a gratifying social life," he says with icy deliberateness, keeping his back to me, "but do you think you could occasionally postpone some of the pleasure you take in your friends, so you and I might have a few words?" He turns toward me. His face is red. "Did you have to take Ilona's call when I'd just come home? Is thirty minutes of my wife's time too much to ask for?" He's shouting now and I'm backing into the dining room. "I thought since you're not teaching I'd have some time with you. But you're either talking about Connie or you're on the phone. No doubt a dead author is more entertaining than I am these days—"

I'm on the far side of the dining table. He looks ready to throw that spoon in his hand. I don't think my back will let me duck.

"You haven't seemed very interested in talking with me," I say in the tone I'd use to persuade a lion back in its cage.

"Do I have to shout to bring myself to your attention?"

"I thought you were glad I had other people to talk to."

"Nothing's ever your fault, is it?"

"Is it my fault men can't give each other what women do?" My fault his kids live in Minnesota and California? My fault his mother died when he was three?

He sighs, and walks toward me. "Truce?" he says. He's done fighting. He's had his annual explosion. "Here's a peace proposal." He wraps his long fingers around my wrist. "You set the answering machine to pick up on the first ring, and I make a fire, and we take our plates into the living room. We spend the evening talking to each other. That's why we got married, right? So we could talk with each other?"

"Among other things."

"Other things would be nice, too."

"Maybe soon. We see Dr. Frederick the day after tomorrow. I'll flip you to see who asks him." David pulls a quarter out of his pocket. "Heads," I call.

It's heads. We both laugh. It will kill David to raise the question of sex with the doctor, but it will kill us both if we have to abstain much longer.

I phoned ahead to ask Dr. Frederick's office how late he's running, but when David and I arrive in his waiting room, it's full as usual. "Sorry," says the receptionist. "He had an emergency." He always does. I can't sit, so I lean against the wall until an elderly couple vacates a couch where I can lie down. "Can I put my head in your lap?" I ask David. He strokes my hair. His touch brings tears.

So does the x-ray table. When I ask why it can't be padded, Dr. Frederick says most patients have more padding of their own than I do. "We had to use a synthetic fabric to cover your bone graft," he says. "There wasn't enough fat on your hips to transplant."

"I've got plenty on my stomach," I say. "You'd have been more than welcome to that."

He cuts apart the metal staples that have been holding my incision together. It doesn't hurt; it's a relief to get rid of these foreign bodies that have been in me almost a month. Leaving them in so long will give me a nearly invisible scar, he says, but since I can't see it I don't care what it looks like. What I want to see are my x rays. The films shock me. There's a five-inch square of bony matchsticks at the base of my spine. I'd imagined a bone graft as something much more genteel.

"You had an awful lot of arthritic bone," he says. "After I removed it, I made a big graft to stabilize what was left."

"What else did you find?"

"The nerves were inflamed and badly scarred."

I look at David. Two surgeons have warned me that scarred nerves might never heal. Maybe I scarred mine walking around London and Chester and Coventry. What if that reprieve leads to a life sentence of pain? Chilled, I pull on my sweater. Dr. Frederick is talking about the letters he's going to write to my university and my insurance company.

"Will you send a copy to the Boston surgeon Joan consulted?" David asks.

"I'll write him when I see what kind of result we get."

My bones were worse than he expected. My nerves are in shreds. I could be crippled. He's preparing me for that. He didn't tell me how bad things were until I was strong enough to hear it. I shiver all the way home and can't stop shaking. David settles me on the sofa, tucks a soft Irish blanket around me, brings me a cup of tea. Then he kindles a fire with the pinecones I've brought back.

"Do you think you might get warm faster if we took off our clothes?" he asks.

"You forgot to ask the doctor!"

"We can be careful."

"Like two porcupines making love?"

Months of trying to ignore pain has made my body slow to respond to pleasure. It's forgotten the music of arousal and release. Still, touching David's body brings me back to my senses. Afterward we weep in each other's arms "as if we'd been separated by a war," David says.

"Or locked up in adjacent cells."

"Or in a fortress. That's where I've been since the day of your surgery."

"Lonely in there."

"I couldn't find my way out." He buries his face in my neck. "I was terrified of losing you. Until now I just couldn't let myself know that."

Weeping together is better than weeping alone.

I'm an obsessor. I never knew that. All day long all I can think about are my scarred nerves and Connie's death. Writing in my journal just digs deeper holes in the same two patches of dirt. If I could think about Connie's life and my own in some systematic way, maybe she could lead me out of this rut. I've got dozens of files about her in my computer, dozens more in my desk. But I can't sit for more than ten minutes at a time. Not for six months at least, more likely nine. Not until my spine fuses—or refuses to fuse. If I don't find something else to think about I'll lose my mind. I try resting my laptop computer on my stomach. Too heavy for my back. Maybe I could work standing up, the way Connie did. I set the computer on the piano lid. In ten minutes my legs have had enough. What the hell good is this leisure if I can't work?

Connie worked herself sick. There's a fat file in my desk of all the notes I took on her work habits. Today I can drop to my knees in front of the file drawer, pull out a folder and get back on my feet without breaking into a sweat. My legs are stronger since Connie and I have been walking in the forest. I open the folder as I go slowly back toward the sofa. On top is a letter Connie wrote to her former teacher at the Cleveland Academy. She couldn't write sooner, she explains to Miss Guilford, because the work of finishing her third novel had tangled the muscles of her right arm "with the nerves of the same locality and the two hold a witches' dance together that sends me to bed and keeps me there." No wonder! Look at the hours she's been working: "I am called at 4½ a.m.," she tells her nephew Sam. "I take a cup of tea, & go out to walk at 5. Come in at 6, or soon after. Bath; breakfast. . . . Then my stand-up desk, where I remain until 7 p.m., with half an hour's rest at noon." Why so driven?

She's writing in August of 1887 from Bellosguardo. In a few

months she'll have to give up the Villa Brichieri with its stupendous views of Florence. Though the rent is preposterously low, it's more than she can earn, even working twelve-hour days. But her publisher keeps begging for more stories, more novels. I don't understand why she couldn't write them.

I spread the pages of notes across the scratched mahogany of the piano lid. Nothing's in any sort of order. Here's my copy of a letter Connie wrote to Henry James when she was preparing the "fair copy" of her second novel for *Harper's*, working "from five in the morning to six at night" at "the copying—always with me a painful task. I do'nt hold a pen easily, & my hand soon becomes cramped. The arm often aches to the shoulder." I held the original of this letter in the Houghton Library at Harvard. I could feel Connie's hand aching as it wrote the letter, see Henry's finely shaped hands as they held it. Electricity buzzed in those pages. The paper sparked with talent and tension.

They'd met two years earlier in Florence, when Connie first came to Europe carrying a letter of introduction to the man whose early comic novels she'd reviewed for the *Atlantic Monthly*. She was a forty-year-old spinster, slim and swift, her penetrating blue eyes compensating for her muddled hearing, her terrible grief from her mother's death healing in the delight at being in Europe at last, after decades of longing. She had two volumes of stories in print and installments of her first novel coming out in *Harper's*. James was a thirty-seven-year-old bachelor. Connie observed his "beautiful regular profile, brown beard and hair, large light grey eyes from which he banishes all expression, and a very quiet, almost cold, manner." He was just starting his first major work, *The Portrait of a Lady*. Connie charmed him so, with her intelligence and frankness, that he took time from his work to call for her in the mornings, take her around to churches and galleries or just for walks and talks. He gave her quite a rush.

But on one of those sunlit days he drove her to "despair."

The word leaps off the page at me, highlighted in yellow. She was reminding him of one of their first talks, on an "occasion, (which I have no hesitation in describing because of course you have forgotten it; you forget everything) when . . . you said, in answer to a remark of mine, 'Oh I never copy.' And upon a mute gesture from me, you added, 'Do you think, then, that my work has the air of having been copied, & perhaps more than once?' I think I made no direct reply, then. But I will now. The gesture was despair,—despair, that, added to your other perfections, was the gift of writing as you do, at the first draft!"

In the margin I've written myself a note on Connie's willingness to seem pathetic rather than put herself in competition with Henry James, another note on the subtle way she contradicts his "other perfections" with her parenthetical remark that he "forgets everything." But I didn't write a word about my own despair over my own endless drafts. Not one word about my own jealousy of authors who write well at the first draft. I didn't even think about it. I wasn't sitting at the polished table in the Houghton Library to think about myself. I was researching a book on Constance Fenimore Woolson, not trying to haunt Connie's hive, not groping for that intimacy which is knowledge. If I recognized my own struggle in Connie's compulsive revising, I ignored it.

I wish I knew where Connie learned never to be satisfied with what she'd written. I know where I learned it. From the terror of Brookline High School, Mr. Newsome. You had to be interviewed for admission to his creative-writing course, and I remember my horror at seeing close up how his papery skin stretched over his cadaverous cheekbones. Even his shoes—carefully polished but riddled with cracks—looked as if they'd been buried for years. It wasn't just his appearance that terrified. He had a diabolic grading system. There was only one grade—*A*. You kept writing your papers over and over until he thought they deserved an *A*. Until then, you had zeros. The first assignment was to describe a place. Twelve times I described the living room of my house until I was ready to burn all the furniture so I'd have a different scene to describe. By spring we'd all learned to revise before we let Mr. Newsome see our work. Finally I got down to three rewrites, even two. Annie Greep once got a paper accepted on the first try. My jealousy is still warm.

How much worse it must have been for Connie, revising and copying and revising and copying hundred and hundreds of pages by hand, and knowing writers who didn't have to sweat the way she did. Long before Henry James's genius filled her with despair, she'd watched the most famous writer in America, her great-uncle James Fenimore Cooper, turn out book after book before breakfast. She'd even described him doing it. I think her essay about Cooper was her first publication. I wonder if it came back nine times like my first article. I've been standing at the piano too long. Taking the ten steps to my study is like wading through burning coals. I find Connie's essay and carry it back to the sofa, easing myself like an octogenarian onto the pillows.

When I can open my eyes again I find the passage I remembered: "Rising early in the morning, he generally accomplished all his writing before breakfast, which took place at nine." How old would Connie have been when Cooper died? Eleven. She'd spent most of her summers in Cooperstown, probably at her grandparents' house. But she could have hidden in a room off the great hall of her great-uncle's manor house and watched Cooper "walking up and down the hall with his hands behind him, apparently thinking out his next chapters, and now and then nodding his head emphatically at the successful completion of some silent train of thought. . . ." Sounds like an eyewitness report. She'd have wondered if his talent ran in her blood, wondered if she could match him or even outdo him. Did Connie really admire Cooper's books? I can't stand them. I had to stop reading *The Deerslayer* in bed because I kept waking David with loud snorts of laughter at Cooper's wooden characters and impossible situations and unspeakable language. But I can see why Connie wrote the sketch. I know how hard it is to get your first article published. If my middle name had been "Fenimore," I'd have hitched a ride on it too.

But even when the witches in Connie's arm cackled that *she* couldn't write as much in twelve hours as Uncle James could in three, at least she could tell them that her work was as fine as his was crude. What could she do when Henry James told her he never revised? Swallow her despair. But it's disgusting that she apologized to him for her own success. Here's a letter that makes me fume. Connie's first novel is so phenomenally successful that *Harper's* pays her a whopping bonus. Shyly, she mentions that fact to Henry. Then she turns around and tells him that her success "could not alter the fact that the utmost best of my work cannot touch the hem of your first or poorest. My work is coarse beside yours. Of entirely another grade. The two should not be mentioned on the same day."

What is this, Connie, flattery or groveling? It certainly isn't realism. Henry's poorest work could be very poor indeed, and you knew it. You wrote half-a-dozen stories as fine as most of his. Under all that humility you're seething with rage. It boils over in a letter you wrote Henry just six months after you kissed the hem of his garment. I wish I knew what happened in those months to make you so amazingly blunt.

"I do'nt think you appreciated," you wrote, putting your apostrophe in the wrong place as usual, "I do'nt think you appreciated the laudation your books received in America, as they came out one by one. (We little fish did! We little fish became worn to skeletons owing to the constant admonitions we received to regard the beauty, the grace, the incomparable perfections of all sorts and kinds of the proud salmon of the pond; we ended by hating that salmon)."

Where on earth did you find the courage to admit that you hated him for his success? I'm just beginning to understand that hatred. No. I understand it all right. I'm just beginning to admit that I share it. I'm jealous of the proud salmon whose books line the shelves in libraries and bookstores. Of Henry James and Thoreau and Virginia Woolf, of their beautiful sentences and their insight and their fame. I'm even jealous of the jealous little fish. A freckle-faced, loudmouthed kid in pigtails has elbowed her way into my living room and she's yammering about how she's going to be a writer when she grows up. Not a teacher who writes about other writers. A real writer. I'd forgotten she existed. How could I have buried that desire so deep?

A day comes back to me fringed with joy after—what, more than forty years? My eighth-grade teacher is reading my book report on *Uncle Tom's Cabin* out loud to the class. Her bony face is softened with approval. I stare at the graffiti carved on my desk, trying to look embarrassed. In fact I'm ecstatic. If Harriet Beecher Stowe could become a famous writer and help free the slaves, maybe I could too.

I couldn't have given up on that dream in high school or I'd never have braved Mr. Newsome. Never have written the sonnet that won an honorable mention in the *Atlantic Monthly* contest. I saw that sonnet just last year. My mother and I were looking through the big old checkbooks my father used as family scrapbooks. He'd saved a copy of the high school newspaper that reprinted my poem. I just laughed and turned the page, embarrassed. By what? Not the poem. I didn't even read it. By the girl who wrote it, the kid who wanted to be a writer.

Turning that page I was ducking the way I always did when I opened my bedroom door as a child, in case my brother and sister had balanced a roll of toilet paper or a bucket of water on the door to fall on my head. When my sonnet won a prize, I knew they'd call me Shakespeare Shapiro. In our house if you got any "big ideas" about yourself, someone would pull you "off your high horse." I wish now I'd reread that sonnet. All I remember is the title, "Sleeping Child." No, I remember writing it. I was sitting on a train. A little girl fell asleep in the seat across from mine. I watched myself having what I knew were deep thoughts about her oblivion to the lives around her and ahead of her. I know who that sleeping child is. The child I've kept drugged for decades, the kid who wants to be a writer.

What was it about being a writer that made me want it so passionately and then forget I ever wanted it? I stare at the ceiling, tracing the crack whose curve I've memorized. A writer is a person who lives deliberately. Her thoughts are valuable. Her feelings matter. She deserves to be taken seriously, not to have rolls of toilet paper dropped on her head. An honorable mention was nice, my father would have said as he taped my poem in the scrapbook. Now if I really put some effort into my writing, maybe next year I'd win a real award. It was the sort of thing he'd say when I'd bring home a report card with one *B*. No matter how high I jumped, he'd hold the stick higher. That was his idea of encouragement.

But not his only idea. Another day swims up glowing with joy. It's my sixteenth birthday. I come to the dinner table and see only small packages by my plate. I swallow my disappointment and pull my chair out. It's heavy. The white tablecloth slides back and there's the black-ribbed carrying case of a Smith-Corona portable typewriter. I fling myself into my father's arms, then into my mother's, sobbing out my gratitude. My father's arms first, because even if the typewriter was my mother's idea, he'd have been the one to decide about such an extravagant present. His arms first, because he pays only for what he approves of, and he's the only one who earns money.

My throat fills. I look out at bare maple branches stark against the dusk. Did my father give me that typewriter to encourage me as a writer? No. He couldn't have. The year I turned sixteen was the year my father was telling me he wouldn't send me to college. He was a college graduate. He knew writers needed good educations. Forget about applying to Cornell and Brown, he told me, and apply to junior colleges or secretarial school. Wasn't there enough money for college? No, that wasn't the reason. For a while I thought he was kidding. Then I saw he really meant it.

"Why are you doing this to me?" I shouted. "You sent the other kids to college and my grades are better than theirs were!"

"You think you're so smart," he screamed back. "You and your goddamn boyfriends! You're nothing but a baby who pishes in its pants!"

I know those are his exact words. I never forgot them because I never understood them. I was excited about having boy-friends because boys' approval was what mattered. But what did that have to do with being smart or going to college? He sounded jealous, but he couldn't be. I was sure he didn't love me enough to be jealous.

"Then I'll send myself to college," I said, trembling with righteous outrage. "I'll get a scholarship."

"No one will give you a scholarship," he retorted. "Your father earns too much money."

Outrageous! Could the world really be so unfair that I needed his approval to get the education I needed to stop depending on his approval? I ran upstairs and soaked my pillow right through my blue chenille bedspread.

The next day my father gave me a reason for what he'd said. It was a waste of money to send a girl to college who was so interested in boys. If an MRS degree was what I wanted, I'd get there much faster as a private secretary who could get "close to the boss." A married woman didn't need a college degree. It might tempt her into a career that would ruin her marriage.

He was telling me I had to choose between thinking and desire. I could have knowledge and independence or I could have love and sex. Not both. He had to be wrong. I'd show him he was wrong. He was certainly wrong if he thought I'd ever marry a boss, after a lifetime of being bossed by him.

I did take the typing course he wanted me to take. I learned to type seventy words a minute. I let him think I was learning how to transcribe some boss's words when all the time I was learning how to make my own words fit to be seen in public, dreaming that the stories and poems and articles I'd type would free me all at once from being a subservient secretary or a dependent daughter.

I still don't understand why my father would buy me my own typewriter when he was threatening not to let me go to college. He knew bosses provide their secretaries with typewriters. I don't remember why he relented and sent me to Tufts, his own alma mater. I call my mother and ask if she remembers my fight to go to college. She does.

"What made Daddy change his mind? Did you?"

"I didn't always agree with your father," she says, "but no one asked me for my opinion."

She certainly hadn't waited to be asked what she thought of my going to graduate school when my children were small. But my father was dead then.

"I wish you'd let me know when you thought I was right."

"You weren't always right." But why wouldn't you defend me when I was? "He used to destroy you in a terrible fight," she says in her gravelly voice, "and then try to make it up with money. I thought it was awful. I told him, 'Don't you ever try that with me. I'll throw it in your face.' "

"You never told me that!" I can't remember hearing her stand up to my father, not once.

We hang up. I feel soiled. Maybe I should have thrown the typewriter in my father's face. I hate to think that my beloved Smith-Corona typewriter was my father's apology for all the times he lost control of himself. I want it to be his secret encouragement of a daughter he thought had talent.

So what did I write on that compromised machine besides

my assignments for Mr. Newsome? Every paper I wrote in college and graduate school. Stories and poems. My "Original
Declamation" for the J. Murray Kaye Prize Speaking Contest. I
have no idea who J. Murray Kaye was. Why have I remembered
his name? Probably because that contest was the second biggest
event at Brookline High School, ranking just behind the
Thanksgiving football game. I raced home to tell my mother I
was going to be a finalist, they'd liked my funny piece about a
quarrel between a big and little sister.

"I knew you could do it," she said calmly.

She'd never told *me* that. She'd told me the piece I'd submit-
ted was silly. But she took me to Filene's Basement to buy the
formal gown I had to wear for the contest. I think we bought my
prom dresses upstairs, but maybe not. We found a wonderful
dress—slate-blue taffeta, off the shoulder, waltz-length. She
bought me strippy high-heeled sandals too, and had them dyed
to match the gown. And she sat in the auditorium next to my
father and watched me forget my lines, watched me stare into
the darkness until the lines came back into my head and I
managed to finish.

I thought I won because the judges gave me points for going
on as if nothing had happened. Or maybe the eons of silence
were only seconds. I don't remember what my father said when
I came down into the auditorium flushed with victory. But now
I remember what my mother said. Her exact words. She said
the piece I'd written "wasn't worthy of you."

Four words to tell me I could have made her proud of me but
hadn't done it. To tell me I was a superior person while she cut
me off at the knees. David's been telling me for years how cen-
sorious she is. He's right. Lots of people will flatter you, she'd
say, but your real friends will tell you the truth. When she
wrote to me at summer camp, she'd sign her letters "From your
best friend and severest critic." Sharon is my best friend. She is
absolutely honest with me. But severe? Maybe that word isn't

as ugly as I think it is. I roll myself off the sofa and pull the dictionary off the bookshelf. Sever, severance, severe. Unsparing and harsh. Causing intense pain or distress; sharp; violent. It is ugly. Why would my mother want to be severe with me? And why would she tell me her severity proved she was my best friend?

I don't like this. My mother really was my best friend. When I'd break a doll, by making her perform heroic leaps and splits, she'd reattach its head and arms and legs with a couple of big rubber bands and a crochet hook. If the damage was really serious, we'd take the doll downtown on the streetcar to the Dolls' Hospital. The mother I remember took me to Boston Common to ride the swan boats. She took me on her lap and read to me, took me to the Olde Corner Book Store to pick out the books I wanted for my birthday. She invited all my friends to birthday parties, and let me tint the frosting yellow for the daffodils she drew on my birthday cakes. She took me to see the Ballet Russe and *The Student Prince.* When I was sad she'd take me in her arms and make me dance a polka with her around the house, singing "RUM tum tum, RUM tum tum," until I laughed, then tell me that's what her mother used to do with her. When I came home from a date I'd sit on the edge of her bed and tell her all about it. Well, almost all.

She was my best friend. Why was she my severest critic? She was afraid I'd get too big for my britches. Get a big head, get up on my high horse. I hear her say those words, not in the gravelly voice she has now but in the strong, low voice she used to have. Maybe she was jealous of me.

That's crazy. I swat the word away. It's as crazy as thinking my father was jealous of my boyfriends. What makes me think I'm such hot stuff that my mother and father would be jealous of me? They didn't want to be anything like me. They didn't even want *me* to be like me.

I go to the kitchen to make some tea. Sometimes my mother is proud of me, I tell the kettle. Once when David and I visited her in the hospital, we found stacked on her night table the seven volumes of the anthology of American literature we'd just edited. I was astounded. She'd barely acknowledged receiving them. Probably she'd hated seeing my name and David's together on the title page. She was still treating him like a convict on parole.

"Are you really feeling well enough to read?" I'd asked.

"Who reads in a hospital? When I feel low, I brag about you to anyone who'll listen."

If she'd ever bragged about me before, she'd kept it a secret for forty years. When she recovered from her hernia operation and came to visit her grandchildren in New Jersey—which is how she'd say it, so I'd know it wasn't me she was coming to see—I invited her to visit one of my classes. I must have been hoping I could make her brag about me to my face. My students came through. They argued fiercely about the misogyny in Edgar Allan Poe. Afterwards I waited for her to say she wished she'd had such exciting teachers when she was a girl. But she didn't say anything. Finally I asked her what she'd thought of the class.

"You looked perfectly lovely," she said.

I could have killed her. Hadn't she heard a word I'd said? I drop the tea bag in the sink. Did she hate what she'd seen? Maybe she was trying to find something nice to say. She didn't like it when I won a prize for dramatizing my rivalry with my sister. Probably she didn't like to see me encourage my students to argue. She hated conflict. Every fight I had with my father put a knife in her heart. I was so busy fighting him, I didn't feel her hacking away at me. Didn't let myself feel it.

How old do I have to be to stop hungering for her praise?

I want some toast with my tea. And some cheese. The toast sticks in my throat.

So what if my mother refused to encourage me? It's not her

fault I gave up on myself as a writer. What if she'd told me everything I wrote was wonderful? I wouldn't have believed her. I don't know how writers come to believe they have something important to say and the skill to say it. To say, "I'm a writer. Writing is what I do." How did Connie do it? I leave the cold toast on the kitchen counter and stumble back to the sofa.

Here's her teacher's memory of how Connie's classmates at the Cleveland Seminary sat "in rapt attention" while she read her compositions "in her low, cultivated voice." A classmate remembers "the flush of pleasure on Connie's face as her audience breaks into open applause after one of her characteristic essays" is read aloud. I know that flush of pleasure, even though my classmates managed to withhold their applause when Mrs. Thompson read my work to them. Connie was nicer than I was, better liked. And she was just so amazingly good that they couldn't help applauding.

Then she went to finishing school, though colleges were opening for women when she was the right age to go. I wonder if she begged to go to Mount Holyoke. Or if that was too far from Cleveland, how about Oberlin, just twenty miles from home? Probably her parents thought Holyoke was too evangelical and Oberlin too radical. Maybe all Connie cared about was getting to New York for the opera and theater and museums that were the breath of life to her. Her parents must have worried that even Madame Chegaray's elite academy for young ladies would turn their brilliant daughter into a bluestocking and a spinster. Her sister Clara has a vivid memory of how the "literary talent in her led her to do things that those *not* thus gifted, did not do." Like ignoring her mother's warning not to carry her inkstand up and down the hotel stairs. They were at a resort near Boston, celebrating Connie's graduation from Madame Chegaray's. Connie came "down the steep hotel stairs" carrying on top of her "limp portfolio . . . her ink bottle with no cork in it!" Predictably—deliberately? Why else did she leave the cork out of the ink bottle?—Connie "stumbled and went down and the whole bottle of black ink poured over her lovely dress!"

You can't miss the gloating in Clara's voice. And you can't mistake Connie's intent. At the very age when I was burying my desire to be a writer, she was flaunting hers. She carried her ink bottle around the hotel like a warning to prospective suitors, fell down the stairs and ruined her belle's dress so she wouldn't fall into her mother's life. She'd be a writer.

Now I remember when I stopped writing fiction and poetry. Thirty years ago. I'd just finished John Holmes's course in creative writing at Tufts. And now I remember why. I'd discovered I didn't know a thing about life. Having to be right in all my fights with my father had concealed that truth from me until then. But I was stumped trying to figure out how to live a fuller life than being somebody's wife or somebody's mother or some pathetic spinster. No one would want to read about experiences like those. And what other adventures were there for a woman who wasn't Marie Curie or Amelia Earhart?

My friend Carol was in John Holmes's course with me, as well as every other English and philosophy course I took. I call her now. She's finished her morning's writing but hasn't gone to her office yet.

"Do you remember what John Holmes said to you about your writing?" I ask her.

"Do I remember?" She pauses for dramatic effect. "I saved every paper I wrote for him. He wrote 'God bless you' on a sketch I wrote of my father just after he died. And he told me I'd be a writer. But I didn't believe him."

"He was right about you. He was right about me too. He said I had a lot of energy and word-sense and would keep on writing. But he didn't say I had talent. Did he help you?"

"By being there, by living a writer's life, he did," she says. "Remember Robert Frost was his friend?"

"Sure. John brought him to Tufts and I literally sat at his feet."

Carol got married in our junior year, a few months before I did. She had three babies even closer together than mine. She divorced her husband a year after I divorced Howard. She remarried a year after I did. I gaze at the crooked path of women discovering their own desires.

"I think it was John's faint praise," I say, "that told me writing was not the way to distinguish myself."

"It made sense for you to keep on doing what you'd gotten recognition for doing," Carol says. "You were Phi Beta Kappa."

"So were you."

"No, I wasn't."

"I may have looked pretty good at Tufts, but I knew I wouldn't have looked like much at Radcliffe."

"Do you know I was accepted at Radcliffe and didn't go? They offered me three hundred dollars less than Tufts did. But the real reason I didn't go was because I was afraid they'd find me out."

"You too?" My laughter has an edge of hysteria. "I thought I was lucky to graduate from Tufts before they figured out how I'd fooled them."

"And before Professor Burch could see our pregnant bellies!" We laugh. He had called me into his office to say he could get me a graduate fellowship in philosophy at the University of Chicago. He was stung when I turned him down. The truth was that while I loved to talk philosophy, I hated reading it. But it was easier to tell Professor Burch I couldn't go to Chicago because I was getting married.

He'd lifted his huge bushy black eyebrows and said, "What? You're going to be a little hausfrau who stays home and cooks fudge?"

When was that? 1956? What a rare man looked out from under those eyebrows!

"No," I'd said with all the dignity I could summon. "I'm going to do graduate work in literature here in Boston until my husband finishes dental school."

When Howard did finish, I hid behind oak trees at his graduation so Professor Burch wouldn't see me. I certainly looked as if I'd cooked and eaten a lot of fudge; I was seven months pregnant. I really think it was Professor Burch's taunt as much as my own restlessness that sent me off to graduate school when Dave was six weeks old.

Carol says, "Will you ever forget how he told me not to be a little hausfrau who stays home and cooks fudge?"

"Carol, it was me he told that!"

"Really? I've told that story to my own students for so many years, I could have sworn it happened to me!"

So I became a college professor to prove that two men were wrong, the professor who believed I wouldn't use my mind and the father who believed I shouldn't. I buried my longing to be a writer and became a scholar and a teacher so I could go on sitting at the feet of the Robert Frosts, hanging around the cafés where the great writers met, bringing them espresso and absinthe and wiping off their tables, forgetting that I'd ever wanted to sit down at the table myself. If I couldn't have it, I didn't want it.

My stomach turns over as I wonder what other passions I have refused to admit.

7

Sisters of Charity

$\mathcal{I}$ strap on my brace and go out to get the mail. I should
have worn a jacket. The wind is cold and the air smells
of wet leaves. They drift across the driveway—leathery oak
leaves, maple leaves like faded sunsets. I hate raking. This year
I can't do it! Cheerfully, I pull a wad of envelopes out of our
mailbox and lower the red flag. Doctors' bills. Appeals for
funds from organizations with names like alphabet soup—
CISPES and NARAL and WILPF and AIUSA and ACLU. This
year all I can do is write checks. Not load trucks with medical
supplies for Nicaragua, not march in Washington for women's
right to choose abortion, not raise money. Knowing that unties
a knot I hadn't felt constricting my chest.

Is this me, feeling that relief, that pleasure? These causes are
as much a part of me as the color of my eyes. I'm hardly burned
out. I've been off duty for seven months. I walk back up the
driveway, shuffling through sycamore leaves the size of dinner

plates. If I can't be active, I should be sorry. If I'm not sorry, does that mean I'm joining the Me Generation? I never asked myself why I was fighting discrimination or unjust wars. It needed doing. I needed to help do it. Fine. But what if my fight to free a prisoner of conscience freezing in a Pakistani jail deafened me to the voices of people I've imprisoned and deserted, like the little girl I just met who wanted to be a writer?

I dump the mail on the kitchen table. On the bottom is a big manila envelope from Suzanne Gardinier. It's not the latest stanzas of her epic poem, *The New World*. It's a hand-lettered "Healing Poem for Joan":

> *Last night I dreamed you and I were walking*
> *on new grass, in the raw spring, at the edge*
> *of a pond we circled once; you were holding*
> *new sun in your hair and on your shoulder.*
> *You were telling me a story: then a catch*
> *stopped your voice a second, then another,*
> *like thorns stopping shirtsleeves on an uncleared path.*
> *Tears wet your cheeks. When we faced each other*
> *I took your hands, as you had taken mine*
> *once, to give back something I had lost.*
> *Leaf buds had hardly opened; the early sun*
> *had just intent enough to warm the ground*
> *for us to lie and rest on, and the sound*
> *of words I thought might help your pain was just*
> *clear enough to hear, but not to understand.*
> *I sat beside all your fierce courage stretched*
> *on the lawn, held all your openness*
> *in my eyes, and, instead of speaking,*
> *in a wordless voice I hardly knew, sang.*

I lean against the kitchen table with cheeks as wet as Suzanne imagined them. She's right about how "raw" my new life feels, how the "new sun" in my sky barely warms the ground. But why does she think it takes "fierce courage" to lie on a sofa and wait for your bones to heal? I don't understand how my pain can give *her* something I couldn't give when I was active.

It must have been sixteen years ago, the first time she came into my broom-closet of an office. I'd thought some graduate student had slipped into my introductory course. "Please come see me," I wrote on her first paper. "Let's talk about what you're planning to do with this talent." The author turned out to be a sixteen-year-old freshman with thick carroty hair. She begged me to tell her how to learn enough about the world to be a writer. Just then I was up to my ears coordinating the Pakistani case. I invited her to help. Strange, I'd been thinking about that just before I saw Suzanne's envelope. She's told me Amnesty International opened the world for her. Now she's confidently finishing an epic poem that manages to love the world whose brutality enrages her. And telling me there's something about my trouble that helps her find a new voice. I'm deeply moved, and baffled.

I pull on heavy wool socks under my hiking boots, David's faded blue down jacket over my sweatpants, a stocking cap over my unwashed hair, and walk briskly down the rocky trail into the forest. It was right here that pain first announced there was something very wrong with me. That was last March. Late in September I was just coming out of anesthesia. In more ways than one. In October Dave had to rescue me with the car after I'd walked in these woods for ten minutes. But now that all the leaves are down but a few stubborn clumps clinging to the oak trees, now I can hike for an hour! Down the hill, over the bridge, along the stream, up through the forest of evergreens. No stabbing in the groin, no burning in the legs. I double my pace as I climb the last hill. How brilliantly I'm healing, just six weeks after surgery! I really could organize the spring delegation to Nicaragua.

Sharon calls. "Do you think you could sit long enough to go to the theater? Olympia Dukakis is performing the myth of Inanna at her Whole Theater in Montclair."

"Dukakis and Inanna in New Jersey? That I have to see!" Sharon's read my article on the Sumerian goddess Inanna—the feistiest female in mythology, and one of the most ancient. "I wouldn't even be breaking parole. Dr. Frederick said that when I could walk an hour, I could sit for fifteen minutes."

"So if you lie in the back seat while I drive, and sit in the last row so you can stand up when you need to—"

"Let's do it. I haven't been out in public for almost two months. You'll have to tell me how to behave."

A whole group of actresses is making Inanna's descent to the Underworld. Standing in the back of the small theater, I'm puzzled. Then I nod. It's not just the woman hero who makes this journey. Connie's leap out the window must have been the last step of *her* descent through countless dark nights of the soul. If I can understand Inanna's descent, maybe I can understand Connie's. Maybe I can even understand why I need so badly to understand it.

The Inannas are stripped of their jewels, their shining robes, their scepters—all the symbols of civilized power. Waiting for them in the Underworld is their suffering sister Erishkegal—Dukakis herself. I watch her grieve and storm and rage, rip her clothes, tear her hair, and see women suffering from Inanna's day to mine. I see a daughter sacrificed for a good wind. I see a mother's face when her husband orders her newborn daughter suffocated in the ashes. I see foot binding and clitoridectomy, hareems and purdah, the burning of millions of witches, rape. Earthquakes and plague, wars and hunger.

Maybe that's what it means to descend into the Underworld: to take on yourself the whole mountain of human pain that I glimpsed in Coventry Cathedral. Not just the tiny piece you choose to work on so you don't feel helpless. All of it. Unbearable. Unendurable. But Inanna has to bear it. Erishkegal beats her and hangs her on a peg like a piece of meat. Finally some women come to groan with Erishkegal. Soothed, she agrees to let Inanna go if someone else will take her place in the Underworld. Inanna returns to the community. Now she understands suffering. She's ready to assume her throne.

In the lobby, Sharon looks shaken and I feel drained.

"Is the descent about being immersed in pain," I ask her, "in death, even, without knowing if you'll ever be rescued or reborn?"

She nods. "It's about hopelessness and helplessness and chaos," she says. Then she tosses her long purple scarf over her shoulder. "I'm starving. I want an ice cream sundae!"

We walk around the block and find a café. "You know what I'm really hungry for?" Sharon says as we sit in a dark wooden booth. "For a community of women. I watch those women comforting Erishkegal, and I'm so angry that my mother died young. I'm so angry that I spent all those years ignoring other women and talking with men as if they could tell me what I needed to know. That's why our closeness matters so much. I even get jealous when you talk about your other friends!"

I smile and take her hand. The waiter brings Sharon's hot-fudge sundae, my coffee ice cream with butterscotch sauce. He gives us a funny look. Probably he thinks we're lesbians. Let him. I have to break the news to Sharon that David and I have decided to leave for California on the first of January. He's on sabbatical, and Dr. Frederick says there's nothing for me to do now but walk a lot and wait for my bones to fuse. Walking will be easier in balmy California than in icy New Jersey, and doctors there can follow my progress.

"You're leaving?" Sharon's green eyes widen. "Abandoning me?"

"I wish you'd come too. I even dreamed we were traveling together."

"You and me?"

"We were driving for miles, looking for a special pond. When we finally found it we dove in and swam underwater, side by side. We stayed underwater so long I thought I must have grown gills. When I woke up I was tremendously happy. I think it was because you and I were traveling together, horizontally and vertically."

"Together and separately," Sharon says, "in the same car and in the same pond, but doing our own diving. Like a descent into the Underworld."

"Like Inanna's? But hers was terrible. This was wonderful. Maybe because you were there with me."

"The way I couldn't be when you had surgery. Don't you think that was a kind of descent? You were dead to the world a long time, and then you couldn't move for days, like Inanna on the hook."

"But it wasn't terrible." She gives me a dubious look. "It wasn't, Sharon! Not like your falling through that trap door into depression."

"That's about not feeling mothered."

"I've never been so mothered in my life. I still haven't made the descent. Maybe I need to."

"What would it do for you, to make that descent?"

"I don't know." I lick my spoon and put it down. "I think there's power down there, stored up from years of confinement underground. Power that's all tied up with pain."

"Have you ever wondered why you spend so much time writing about other women's suffering?" Sharon scrapes the last of the fudge sauce out of her dish. "Isn't that what your articles on women in Egypt, and in Brazil, and in Central America, are all about? Pain?" She's right. "As I read them, I found myself thinking it was a surprising preoccupation for such a happy person."

She's right about that too. I could give her reasons why I might have done that research and written those articles. Liberal guilt. Self-righteousness. But those labels wouldn't explain why suffering magnetizes me. Especially women's suffering. I don't understand it.

"You know, Connie did the same thing," I say, "burrowing into other women's pain. It's funny, I published an article on the stories where she does it, but I never saw any connection with what I did in Egypt and Brazil."

We get up to leave the café. Something stabs my groin and my right leg buckles. Sharon grabs my elbow. "You all right?"

"Fine. Just sat too long."

A week later I bundle up and head for the woods. By the time I reach the wooden bridge there's a persistent ache behind my knees. It gets hot and spreads up my thighs, down my calves. Burning, the way it did on the walls at Chester. The way it did yesterday and the day before. What's going on? At home I strip off my sweaty long underwear and take a hot shower. My legs still buzz and burn. I take a couple of aspirin, spend a couple of hours on the sofa. My legs aren't impressed. I call Doctor Frederick. To my surprise, he interrupts his office hours to take my call.

"Why should I be getting worse?"

"It could only be adhesions," he says. "I told you the nerves to your legs were badly scarred. Shreds of the nerves must have gotten stuck to your bones. Walking stretches them and sends your leg muscles into spasm."

"But I hiked for an hour last week with no pain."

"Last week the scar tissue hadn't attached itself."

My heart drops into my stomach. "So what do we do about it?"

"Do you have any Valium left from last spring?"

"I flushed it down the toilet."

"I'll phone in another prescription. The Valium will relax the muscle spasms."

"But it puts me to sleep. How about physical therapy?"

"It's still much too soon. Try half a Valium and let me know in a few days how you're doing."

I hang up and find tears pooled at the base of my neck. My operation could be a complete success, my bones could fuse like a rock, and I could *still* be incapacitated. The cushion under my head is damp. I don't like these tears. They're not the flushing-out kind, just self-pitying. The hell with that. I wipe my face on my shirtsleeve and get two little volumes of Connie's early stories from my bookshelves. Before the Valium comes and puts me to sleep, I'm going to reread those stories about investigating other women's pain.

I lean against my desk and open the faded brown cover of the first book. Words, my drug of choice. I've never read this way, hunting for myself. Highly unprofessional. Grounds for banishment from scholarly ranks. But that's not why something's fluttering under my ribs. What am I afraid of? That Connie won't mirror my own life? That she will?

I turn the brittle pages. Clever titles, Connie, like arrows pointing the reader away from the real subjects of the stories— their narrators. Your stand-ins. You can drop those disguises. I know it's your own "habit of studying persons very closely" you've given to that sweet old auntie in "Jeannette." I'll bet you liked to be "swept along in the train" of other people's passion and heartbreak as much as she did. You put on a thicker disguise in "Wilhelmena," but I know it's you, glueing yourself to that poor girl waiting for her sweetheart to come home from the Civil War. It's you feeling how Wilhelmena's "slender form throbbed," how "pulses were beating under my hands wherever I touched her." And when the soldier comes back and abandons her, as you know he will, it's you who draws the girl's head down on your shoulder because it's "better the soldier should not hear" the weeping whose "anguish thrilled my own heart."

Now that's really sickening. This narrator writing the script, directing the play, performing all the parts, thrilling to other people's pain—don't tell me she isn't you. You know you're committing Hawthorne's Unpardonable Sin. You said Hawthorne was one of your gods.

He's one of mine. I wrote my dissertation on his artistic dilemmas. This was one of them, this fear that he would become "a cold observer, looking on mankind as the subject of his experiment, and, at length, converting man and woman to be his puppets, and pulling the wires that moved them. . . ." Puppets is right. That's what your narrators make of other people. I know you did it too.

Didn't you say that your favorite of all Hawthorne's works is *The Blithedale Romance*? I thought that was a bizarre preference. Now I get it. Every important character in the book commits the Unpardonable Sin. The narrator even stirs up tragedies to give himself the pleasure of writing verses about them. It relieved your guilt, didn't it, recognizing your own predicament in Hawthorne's? I bet you never thought anyone would put those pieces together.

I see Connie standing in the center of the room. Her back is to me. The skirt of her black dress touches the pale-green rug. I could touch her, make her vanish, but I don't. I take a few steps back. Really, she's pathetic. All that vicarious living, all that feeling other people's pulses because she couldn't, or wouldn't, act on her own desires. Revolting.

She turns around. Pain creases her mouth but her blue eyes are steady. Those stories are confessions, she says. Penance.

What kind of confession do you call that, hiding behind your narrators? I ask her. Is it penance to publish a story that rewards you with a check and builds your reputation as a writer? You sinned again in the very act of punishing yourself!

Connie squares her strong shoulders. And what about you? she asks. You wrote about other people's suffering.

I don't have to pry into other people's love stories, I tell her. I've got my own love life. I don't have to live vicariously. I've always been actively engaged with life. Maybe too actively.

Then why did you spend more than a year holed up with Hawthorne? Connie asks. And why have you been haunting me for more than three years, and no end in sight?

She thinks I've been haunting *her*?

Not that I'm trying to get rid of you, she goes on, but why do you think you've spent so much time with the likes of us? And in between, with the suffering goddesses and the suffering women of what you call the Third World?

I don't know why. That's what I'm trying to find out. Just the other day I copied into my journal something Nadine Gordimer wrote about writers' peering into other people's lives. "Powers of observation heightened beyond the normal"—like Hawthorne's, like yours, Connie, maybe like mine—imply "excessive preoccupation and identification with the lives of others, and at the same time a monstrous detachment." A perfect description of what you're doing in "Jeannette" and "Wilhelmena"—identifying with the suffering you exploit. It *is* monstrous. But I don't see how a writer can escape it. I walk to the window and press my forehead against the cold glass.

You're leaving out love, Connie says. To observe deeply is to love. You can't help it. And the art you make from that love is not detached. Every verb you choose is part of it.

I turn back from the frozen gray grass and find myself alone in the room.

· · ·

On burning legs I wander back to the sofa and stuff pillows under my knees. I still don't know why I'm caught in the undertow of other women's pain. Asking why is getting me nowhere. When was the first time I looked at suffering as a serious investigator? Where was I?

Egypt. 1973. And I wasn't looking for pain. I just stumbled into it. Habu had brought us to Cairo to lecture at his university. The shabby concrete building was braced with sandbags, the classroom windows camouflaged with dark-blue paint. Sometimes we could hear shooting from the Sinai, fifty miles away. I gave the first talk because David couldn't get out of bed. Crossing Tahrir Square on overpasses packed solid with thousands of Egyptians had flattened him with culture shock. I thought I'd give Habu's students a mild culture shock by pointing out that women writers work in a different climate than men. When I finished speaking the young women sat silent in their elegant Western clothes. Habu had a question for me.

"Aren't you exaggerating the differences between the sexes?" he asked, and smiled engagingly. "Surely you'd agree that men and women are both human beings? That they experience life in essentially the same way?"

I was trying to think of a polite way to ask him if he thought Egyptian women's lives were unaffected by the veil or by their fathers' and husbands' right to beat them and lock them in the house when several women rose to their feet. "No! She's right!" they said. "Women's lives are nothing like men's!"

"Look what happens when I introduce a feminist to my students," Habu said, taken aback but laughing. "Right away we have a revolution!"

That evening David had recovered enough to go out for dinner. Habu wanted us to meet a group of distinguished intellectuals, all men. Sitting in a little seafood restaurant on the Nile, he told them about the "palace revolt" I'd fostered among his students.

"Really, women in Egypt have very little to complain about

at present," a journalist said. "Excision is hardly practiced any more."

"What's that?" I asked innocently.

"Female circumcision," he said. "Clitoridectomy. My older sister contracted a serious infection after hers was done when she was ten—old women come in to do it, and their knives are not clean—so my father decided not to circumcise my younger sister, not even in a hospital, though all our relatives warned him no man would marry her."

My stomach twisted. I put down my fork and looked at David. He was studying the shrimp on his plate. The other men kept eating. After all, this was old news to them.

"These days, a sophisticated Egyptian man will marry an uncircumcised woman," said a diplomat.

"Not peasants, though. In the countryside they still display the blood-stained sheet to prove the bride was a virgin," said the journalist with obvious disapproval.

"Ah, well, in the countryside!" said a philosopher. "There a father still kills his daughter if her husband claims she was not a virgin on their wedding night."

It was my turn to be sickened by culture shock. A few days later, one of Habu's students asked to meet me for lunch. She wanted to show me a portfolio of her drawings. In one, a naked woman looked sadly at a shard of jagged glass. It seemed to have been the instrument that had separated her head from her body and her legs from her torso. In horror and outrage, I wrote an article about the various mutilations of Egyptian women and my own struggles to understand them. Nine journals rejected it. The tenth gave it a prize of five hundred dollars. That's how it all got started—my investigating, my writing.

So you built your credentials as a writer on other women's pain, just as I did. It's Connie's voice.

But that wasn't my motive. Their suffering hurt me. I couldn't stop it, but I had to bear witness to it. That's different from exploiting it.

Oh, you've changed your mind, then? she asks. When I bore witness to a real woman's pain, you said I was using her.

You said you were using her! It's that admission that makes "In the Cotton Country" such a powerful story.

There she doesn't hide behind her narrator. She's the "solitary pedestrian" from the North who walks through cotton plantations ruined by the Civil War, following a flock of crows through devastated fields that mirror her own inner landscape. The crows lead her to "one solemn, lonely old house. Now if there had been two," she writes, "I should not have gone on. . . . Two houses are sociable and commonplace; but one all alone on a desolate waste like that inspired me with—let us call it interest, and I went forward."

What is it she's *not* calling it? Some uncontrollable need to see who could survive a life even more desolate than hers? She knocks on the door. A gray-haired white woman appears. "I could not very well say, 'Who are you, and how came you here?' and yet that was exactly what I wanted to know. The woman's face baffled me, and I do not like to be baffled." Of course not. She's a writer. "The next afternoon I wandered that way again, and the next, and the next. I used to wait impatiently for the hour when I could enter into her great silence. How still she was! If she had wept, if she had raved, if she had worked with nervous energy, or been resolutely, doggedly idle, if she had seemed reckless, or callous, or even pious; but no, she was none of these."

Why don't you finish that sentence, Connie? If the Southern woman had wept, had raved, then what? Then you'd have understood her and walked away. You can't walk away because you don't "like to be baffled." There's a piece of yourself locked up somewhere in the other woman's pain and you can't back

123

off until you make the other woman tell you how the war destroyed everything but her pride and her contempt for the blacks who'd picked her cotton.

I could say about you what you say about her: "The eyes haunted me; they haunt me now, the dry, still eyes of immovable, hopeless grief." I'm just as stubborn as you are. I won't go away until you tell me your whole bitter story. I don't believe for a minute you fell out of that window in Venice. I need to understand what made your life such a torment that you killed yourself when you were just my age. You baffle me, and I don't like to be baffled.

I thought you'd never see it, Connie says. Of course this story is about *us.* I'm the desolate woman and you're the solitary pedestrian who won't leave me alone until you've dragged my story out of me. I hope you don't imagine that makes you a "Sister of Charity bearing balm and wine and oil for those who suffer." Look how that poor woman pushed me away. "No, you cannot help me," she said.

> No one can help me. I can not adjust myself to the new order of things; I can not fit myself in new soil; the fibers are broken. Leave me alone. . . . It will not be until such as I have gone from earth that the new blood can come to her. Let us alone; we will watch the old life out with her, and when her new dawning comes we shall have joined our dead, and all of us, our errors, our sins, and our sufferings will be forgotten.

You made sure their sufferings would not be forgotten, I tell her. That woman was a nightmare image of your own life—stuck somewhere in the past, immobilized by pain she refused to relinquish. If you could give her despair a voice, evoke compassion for a woman whose racism appalled you, maybe you could forgive yourself for some unspeakable crime you feel you've committed. You could get unstuck and move on. Sounds therapeutic. But it just piles on more guilt, doesn't it? Maybe your compassion for this woman saves you from the Unpardonable Sin, but you're still using her to "open an intercourse with the world." That's why Hawthorne said he wrote—to connect himself with people without taking the risks of relationship. Isn't that why you wrote, too?

What about you? she says.

What about me? I'm no recluse. And I'm hardly stuck in the past. I'm still trying to remember "what it was to be me."

That doesn't mean you're not stuck, she says. You're searching out your own buried pain in mine. Isn't that the very same thing you were doing with all those women in Egypt and Brazil, all those years ago?

Is it?

Two years after our trip to Egypt David and I went to Brazil. Since he'd lived there for a year as a Fulbright professor, Amnesty International hoped the people he knew could help him find out if an Amnesty mission might help the victims of torture piling up in Brazil's prisons. I wanted to find out why so many women supported the military regime that tortured dissidents and made them disappear. I honestly don't think I was looking for stories about pain. I just wanted to talk to women about their lives. Would a different interviewer have met different women, asked different questions, gotten different answers? Probably.

Between the cracks on the ceiling I see green mountains plummeting to the sea. David and I are on a beach in Rio de Janeiro. We're trying to keep our minds on the girl from Ipanema in her tiny string bikini, but all we can talk about is the tortured bodies we've been hearing about for three weeks. Our informants have taught us how to talk in code on bugged telephones. When we want to know if someone has been arrested, we ask if he's in the hospital. When we want to know if she's been tortured, we ask about her surgery. In São Paolo we look over our shoulders as we photocopy documents. At first, the stunning beauty of the mountains and beaches makes this undercover work seem preposterous. Soon, the reality of what we're hearing makes Brazil's beauty seem preposterous.

We learn that the government is trying to eradicate "subversives," who are defined as anyone who objects to anything the government does. If you point out that the real "economic miracle" in Brazil is not the country's growth but the fact that all the poor people haven't yet starved to death, you're a subversive. If you teach poor people to read, you're a subversive. If you rent a room in your house to someone who knows someone suspected of being a leftist, you're a subversive. If you defend someone accused of being a subversive, you're a subversive. No charges will be brought against you. You won't be arrested. You'll disappear. You'll be tortured. You may or may not reappear. We are staggered by the number of people who take these risks and double them by talking to us.

Our days we spend interviewing, our nights weeping. When I touch David's skin I feel the marks of torture on other bodies. One night we give a joint talk at the American Cultural Center in Rio. Afterwards, a striking woman with olive skin and wavy black hair introduces herself to me.

"I was so glad to hear you read that poem by Adrienne Rich," she says, "about her solidarity with a Soviet political prisoner. It's a favorite of mine too."

So she understands why I read this poem—as a covert invitation to members of our audience to tell us what they know about prisoners of conscience here. We agree to meet at her home the next afternoon for tea. As we sit on her leather sofa, I discover that her life mirrors mine with astonishing exactness. Maria Luiza is a professor of American literature, a feminist, with children the same ages as mine. We eat grapes and chat about our universities and the uneven progress of the women's movement in our countries.

"I trust you as another feminist," she says finally. And she closes the doors and tells me about the day the soldiers came into the room where we are sitting to arrest her daughter for passing out leaflets at her university criticizing the government. She even lets me tape-record her story:

> I was in the bathtub when they came. By the time I got a robe on, the soldiers were aiming machine guns at the younger children. My thirteen-year-old son tried to comfort his sister: "Don't be afraid, it's only a gun." "It's loaded," warned the soldier. "Of course it's loaded," said Paolo. "What good would it be if it weren't loaded?" As soon as they left the house with my daughter, I threw on clothes and tore out of the house to get her sister, who had already gone off to school. "You're going into hiding," I told her. "Don't ask any questions. If they arrest me, I won't tell them where you are. I'm a coward, but I'm a mother first."
>
> When my arrested daughter was finally released from prison she told me that five men had stripped her naked and beaten her. One man they called "the nurse" put electrodes on her hands and in her vagina to give her electric shocks. They confined her in an "icebox," a freezing room so small she could only crouch in it. But they couldn't make her give them a false confession until they told her the girl screaming in the next room was her sister. If she had only known that I had already hidden her sister! Eight days after her "confession" they released her. No formal charges were ever filed against her. She is still suffering from the injuries to her kidneys and back muscles, and her uterus was so badly burned, it will probably never hold a baby.
>
> I could do so little—for her or for the others. All I ever did was hide them, help some get away, try to heal them when

127

they were hurt. The kids knew what was going on, although I never told them any details. The less you know the less they can torture out of you. But they all knew why these strangers were in our house. And they never talked. Never!

As I listened I knew that if I had been born where Maria Luiza was born, I would have been telling her story. It would have been my son standing up to soldiers, my daughter screaming in a torture chamber—acting on the values I'd taught them. I don't think my identification with her anguish was "excessive." My tax dollars were paying the men who tortured her daughter.

David and I went home and started to write furiously. He wrote an Op-Ed piece for *The New York Times*, a poem, an article, finally a screenplay about the kidnapping and torture of an American missionary working in Brazil. A true story. We heard Fred Morris tell it at Drew, soon after he was released and expelled from Brazil. When we were still hoping the film might be produced, David proposed they split any money the film might make. Fred agreed: "After all, I did do the research."

What gave us the right to report on other people's devastating "research" a hemisphere away? But how could we not tell stories that people had risked their lives to tell us? I told those stories in churches and high schools and universities. People would come up afterward to tell me how brave I was. *I* was! If I learned anything in Brazil, I learned that nothing that had ever happened to me was really painful. Nothing I had ever done was really brave.

David could write about torture but he couldn't talk about it. He'd break down. I could talk about torture but I couldn't write about it unless there was another person in the room with me. I thought I was afraid to be alone with the torturers. Now I think there was something else in the room. Excitement. Oh God. My mind skids away from the truth. I pull it back. Yes. It *was* thrilling to soak myself in danger and grief without being hurt myself. This wasn't the harmless thrill you get watching a scary movie. I was reliving the pain of real people, people I'd taken walks with, drunk tea with. So that's why I was afraid to be alone. I was afraid of what I might find out about my own capacity to enjoy other people's suffering. I am afraid now.

Connie's doing her job. I could fire her, but then I'd be stuck in this awful place by myself.

All right, Connie, I admit it. I benefited from other people's pain as much as you did. When I wrote and spoke about torture and murder in Brazil and Egypt, and later Nicaragua, I was showing how suffering people had trusted me. How moral I was, how sensitive, how brave. Touching real danger gave me glamour. Exposing injustice and pleading for change gave me stature. But all that righteous indignation about genital mutilation and the torture of dissidents—I don't know how much of it was just an evasion of my own vicarious excitement at other people's pain and danger, an evasion of pain I've brought to others. An evasion of my own pain.

I'm still interrogating sufferers. I'm doing it right this minute when I try to make you tell me how it feels to live in hell and why you're there. I can't pretend I'm exploiting your pain in order to relieve it. No one can relieve it now. I'm not sure anyone could have relieved it when you were alive. I'm using you to find the truth about myself. Using your passions to find my own. What a ghoulish enterprise!

The soul keeps trying to tell the truth, Connie says in tones so gentle they sting my eyes. It tells it through the pain of others if only that is bearable. We draw near to others' suffering when we ourselves are in pain and cannot speak it.

Then it's time to speak it. If I used those women to experience my fair share of the world's suffering while I hid from my own, I don't want to use you that way. I want you to keep me on the track I glimpsed after surgery, the trail that leads to the deep mountain lake inside me, or to the minefield, if that's where we're going. Anywhere but back to my old ignorance.

129

8

Maternal Mirrors

I take a Valium and the minute I stop walking I'm asleep. I take half a Valium and I can't walk. Dr. Frederick says I'll feel better when my bones fuse, and I'm careful not to ask him how fusing is going to unglue the shreds of nerves tugging on my bones. He says there's no reason why we can't leave for California on New Year's Day. "As long as you don't carry anything heavy or sit too long at a stretch, it won't hurt you to fly," he says. "You want to visit your mother in Boston? Go ahead. It'll be a good trial run."

My niece Ellen meets me at Logan Airport. She looks more like me than any of my own children do—same straight eyebrows, same square face. "I left the baby at my parents' house," she says. "They can't get enough of him, and I—"

"Sometimes you can. I remember how that feels." I recline the seat of her car and slip off my shoes so I can put my feet on the dashboard.

"Is your back giving you a lot of pain?"

"A little, from sitting on the plane. If I could just live lying down, I wouldn't have any pain at all."

"But who wants to live lying down?"

"It's been anything but boring," I tell her. "I've been keeping a journal for the first time in my life."

"I haven't written a page in my journal since Steven was born," Ellen says, buckling her seatbelt. "I'm probably scared to see what I feel written down in black and white."

I hand her money for the tunnel. "It's a good thing we only have to be 'good-enough' mothers, not perfect ones."

"But what's good enough? I'm not crying quite so much now that I'm back at work—"

"Postpartum blues?"

"Steven's eight months old! When does it stop? And what's he learning when he sees himself reflected in such a sad face?"

The tunnel closes around us. "I've been thinking about that a lot," I tell her, "the idea that children get their sense of themselves from the mirror of their mothers' faces."

That theory attracts me because it would explain so much about Connie's life—her terrible depressions, even her suicide. The first mirror she looked in was the face of a mother out of her mind with grief. There's Connie, a little white bundle in her mother's arms. Then there's Connie, a big white bundle on a cold Venice pavement. She was two days old when one of her sisters came down with scarlet fever. Three weeks later the disease had killed two-year-old Julia and three-year-old Gertrude and five-year-old Annie. Emma and Georgie, who were seven and nine, got well. Connie never got sick. Her mother's milk must have protected her from the disease. But I don't think anything could have protected her from Hannah's despair, not in infancy, not later.

I can't stop telling myself this terrible story. I see Hannah looking at Connie and seeing the three little girls who died when Connie was born. That must be why Connie's own face never looked right to her. She hated to look in mirrors, hated to be photographed. When she couldn't escape the camera she offered it as little as possible of her face. These half-portraits she's left me—just one eye and half a mouth, an outline of high forehead, straight nose, firm chin—show exactly how much self she was able to construct out of the shattered mirror of her mother's face.

"You know," I tell Ellen, "this emphasis on the mother's gaze makes perfect sense to me as long as I'm thinking like a daughter. But the minute I think like a mother, it seems crazy. It's outrageous to blame mothers for their children's sense of themselves. You could never count all the people and all the things that shape a child."

I never take credit for Dave's courage or Mark's generosity or Leslie's resourcefulness, because if I did I'd also have to accept the blame for Leslie's guardedness and Mark's overeating and Dave's bravado. If I argue that depressed or grieving mothers like Hannah depress their children just by turning sad faces toward them, if I concede that mothers' subjectivity—their pain and fear and anger—damages their children, then I have to conclude that only a woman with no inner life of her own could be a good-enough mother. And I won't concede that.

"I don't think it's bad for babies to know that their mothers are real people with complicated feelings," I tell Ellen. "Real people can't be smiling mirrors all the time."

But what if a baby's birth brings the deaths of three other children, what if the house is abruptly emptied of the singing and laughing and wailing of three little girls? Scraps of letters and journals tell the terrible story. Hannah "nearly lost her reason." Jarvis lifted her and their surviving children into their carriage and drove from Claremont, New Hampshire to Cooperstown, New York. They moved from one to another of the big houses belonging to Hannah's relatives. Hannah was no better. Finally Jarvis parked the big girls with an aunt, lifted his wife and baby Connie into his carriage, and drove across the whole state of Pennsylvania and half of Ohio on ungraded roads, full of mudholes in wet weather and iron-hard ruts in dry. Close friends in Cleveland persuaded them to stay for the winter. By the following March, they'd decided to stay indefinitely. Jarvis started a new business from scratch, they rented a house of their own and sent for poor abandoned Georgie and Emma. The family was finally reunited around Connie's first birthday. That would have been the first anniversary of the other children's deaths. The ghosts of the children Hannah could never talk about would always hover in the flames of the candles on Connie's birthday cakes. She'd blow furiously at them, trying to make them go away. But every year they'd be back.

I can't stop thinking about the first year of Connie's life. Did Hannah cling to her baby, weeping over her for what she had lost, pouring all her longing and despair into her? Maybe she was overwhelmed with guilt, wondering if God had punished her for wishing her daughters had been sons. Maybe she turned her face away from her baby. How could Connie learn to be alone without withdrawing, to be close without suffocating? That rhythm of intimacy and individuation comes hard to me, and Connie couldn't dance to it at all. Impossible to learn to bond and separate from a mother whose own identity was in shreds.

My mother's face is peering anxiously from her kitchen window as Ellen pulls up to her apartment. What did I learn, looking at that face? My stomach knots while we wait on the stairs listening to my mother opening three sets of locks.

"Welcome to Fort Knox," she says. "And pardon my voice. I still sound like Gravel Gertie."

"I think it's sexy." When I put my arms around her I feel every rib.

"My great-grandson doesn't," she says. "He cries when I sing to him."

"Thanks for the ride, Ellen." I kiss her good-bye. "Call me.

One of those evenings when the baby won't stop crying." It's easier to comfort a niece than a daughter because her griefs aren't even conceivably my fault.

"Where's your suitcase?" my mother asks, locking the door behind Ellen.

"Everything's in this bag." I never stay more than one night in Boston.

"I'm afraid coming to see me is too much for your back."

"My back feels fine." She doesn't have to know about my legs. "The doctor said it was all right to come."

"I hope you're not taking advantage. Here, hang up your coat. Can I give you something to eat? A cup of tea?"

"Tea would be great. I'll make it. Will you have some?"

"I'll have hot water and milk." She shuffles along the pale-green carpeting as if she doesn't trust the ground under her feet. She seems much frailer than when I saw her in June. But I've never gone six months without seeing her before, except when I was living abroad. "You look terrific," she says. "Have you lost some weight?"

"Mmm." I've lost so much weight my trousers hang loosely even over the bulk of my brace, but I always feel fat when my mother looks at me. I feel her eyes on me as I reach down two cups and saucers in her flowered china. Every bite I ate off those plates made me fatter than my mother. No man's gaze could make me as conscious of my bodily mass and density as hers does. As hers still does. I still let her define my body, and surgery has taught me how my body defines my self. So how can I deny the power of the maternal mirror?

The kettle whistles. I fill the cups and bring them to the mahogany dining table. Here's the same scratch I used to trace over and over with my finger while my father and I were wrangling and my mother was choking on her food and going to the bathroom to throw up her dinner. Is it possible she was bulemic? Maybe that's how she could eat so much and still keep her size-eight figure, and her status as the only thin person in the house. Maybe she needed us to be fat.

"I don't know how you've stood all these months of inactivity," she's saying.

"I like having time to myself."

"You may like it, but I don't. Since I fell on the ice, I've had to give up all my volunteer work, even sorting books at Brandeis. It was boring, but at least I was good for something. Now that I can't do anything, I hate myself."

She shocks me. More than that. She warns me. If I'm what I do and nothing else, and if I can't keep on doing the things that give me value, then I can turn into a wretched old woman who hates herself. "What a terrible way to feel!"

"It is terrible. I hope you never live to find yourself with no necessary purpose in the world."

"You're necessary to me." I take her arm in its red polyester sleeve. It's just bones.

"You don't need me."

"Of course I do!"

"What for?"

"To be there! To be my mother and love me and argue with me."

"I say the most awful things to you!"

"I want you to tell me what's on your mind."

"Are you sure?" She laughs. "Then I'll tell you. I've gone past my stop. Did you know my grandfather lived to a hundred and two, sitting on his *tuchas* and letting his children support him? Promise me you'll take me out in the back yard and shoot me before I get that old."

"I promise. The minute you pass a hundred and one."

"Oh, please don't wait that long. I keep singing the line from 'Old Man River'—I'm tired of livin' but scared of dyin'."

"Can you tell me what you're afraid of?"

"Well, no one knows what's on the other side," she says, putting down her cup. "I might meet your father."

"He's the one who should worry about that, not you."

I see her sitting at this same scratched table with her head bowed, biting her lip while my father's unfocused rage washes over her in waves. My old, passionate need to rescue her from him washes over me now.

She shakes her head. "I should have done things differently."

"Mother, I'm sure you were more sinned against than sinning."

She shakes her head again. Then abruptly she turns on me. "Joan, you're very bright, but you've got me baring my soul!"

I sit back in my chair stunned. "I wasn't trying to be bright," I finally manage to say. "I thought you wanted to talk."

"Well, I don't any more," she says, and gets up from the table. The cups and saucers rattle in her hands.

"Here, let me do that."

"All right, but don't put the sterling in the dishwasher," she says. "I'm going to the toilet."

I stand at the sink, flushed with shame and anger. Don't pry, don't badger me, don't argue. None of your back talk. Her familiar words bounce off the kitchen walls. Now I get paid to pry and badger and argue, I think wryly. I teach my students to talk back to the authors they read, to disagree with me and with each other. Students say they like it. My mother doesn't. I didn't like it much when my own children did it, either. It used up too much of me. It felt like having my life sucked up with my milk. Maybe that's how my mother felt. And what I didn't suck out of her, she vomited up. No wonder there's so little left of her.

I wipe my face on a paper towel. Babies have a right to their mothers' milk, I think as I squirt detergent onto a sponge, but what right do I have to my mother's secrets? I don't blame her for throwing my questions back in my face. Carefully I wash the curly handles of the spoons. I used to sit at that mahogany table tracing this intricate design on my spoon while my father complained that the brisket was too tough or too tender, demanded to know why my mother hadn't straightened out that butcher who was taking advantage of her. Is it possible my mother really did do something awful to my father, some crime that makes her hate herself now? Or did she always hate herself?

"Are you all right, Mother?" I call.

"Yes, I spend half my life in here."

I open the drawer of the cherrywood chest that always stood in the dining room on Winthrop Road, and stack the spoons in their padded compartment. I loved to put away this shining silverware after one of my mother's bridge parties. I'd come home from kindergarten to find the living room full of ladies who smelled sweet and powdery when they kissed me and pinched my fat cheeks. Suddenly I see myself sitting at a low kindergarten table, cutting—not very neatly—blue triangles out of construction paper. Charlie Baron says we need more blue circles. I look at the sheet of blue paper in my hands and wonder with an intensity so fierce it blazes up at me after nearly fifty years whether blue looks the same out of Charlie's eyes as it does out of mine. I look in the other children's eyes. There's no way to know what they see when they say "blue." They're all positive that blue is just blue, but I know they can't prove it. Since blue might not look blue to other people, I tell them excitedly, then everything we see might look different to other people. Everything we say might mean something different to them. The debate gets noisy, and Miss Kilburn comes to our table to scold me for distracting the children from their work.

So there's a piece of myself that hasn't changed since kindergarten: my passionate need to know how the world looks through other people's eyes. Was I still trying to find out if blue looked blue to other people when I asked nosy questions in Brazil and Egypt and Nicaragua? When I asked my mother about her sins?

I settle myself on the tightly upholstered sofa where I read my first books. My mother shuffles into the room.

"I weigh ninety pounds dripping wet," she says. "Isn't that awful?"

"Why aren't you eating?"

She sighs. "With these dentures I can't chew anything. Since the radiation treatments I can hardly taste anything. The last thing I enjoyed eating was that minestrone you made me."

"I'll make it tomorrow."

"There won't be time. Tomorrow we have to go through all the things you've sent me. I want you to take home everything that's yours. I won't have room for anything in the nursing home."

"*What* nursing home?"

Painfully she settles herself in a high-backed blue chair. "I dread it. They all stink of urine. You can't even have your own room. But I can't go on living alone. Look at this dress. It's the only thing I own that I can still put on by myself. It must be filthy, but I can't see well enough to know if it is or not. That's why old people wear dirty clothes, you know. I can't get in and out of the tub by myself, so I can't bathe until Adele comes to clean. Probably I stink, but I can't smell well enough to tell. Mostly I take sponge baths." She laughs. "You know, I wash down as far as possible, and then up as far as possible, and then I wash possible."

"You need help, but it doesn't have to be in a nursing home. What about that congregate care place we looked at last spring?"

She sighs. "You know where I'd really like to go?" She gestures upward with her thumb.

I put my arm around her. "Can I help you get ready for bed?"

I put drops in her eyes and unzip her dress. "I can't do buttons," she says, "my fingers feel like I'm wearing mittens." I unhook her bra—"Did you ever see a belly like this over such skinny legs except on a child with rickets?" she asks—and drop her nightgown over her head.

"I won't ask you to take my teeth to the bathroom and clean them," she says, "but if you're brave I'll let you see how I look without them. My mouth looks exactly like a hen's ass."

"Where did you ever see a hen's ass?" I ask, laughing.

"We kept chickens in Somerville. And a donkey that came and brayed at the window because he liked the dishwater my mother threw on him. It was the country then. Go to bed, *mein kind*. I can see how tired you are."

I kiss her and close the door of her den behind me. My mother doesn't eat because she hates her life, but she can't die because she's afraid of meeting my father. My brace seems to confine me in her terrible trap. Velcro snarls as I pull it off. I shove the window open to the December night and take into my lungs as much cold air as they can hold. My mother's not afraid that God will punish her. Her own mother taught her that God wouldn't punish her for eating *chomotz* during Passover. It might make her sick, but God wouldn't care. It's my father my mother's afraid of. She's thinking about the dead the way a child would think. I sit on the bed and kick off my shoes. I don't remember being afraid of the dead when I was a child, but I spent a lot of time looking at a picture of my dead cousin Jeannie. I'd go to my Aunt Helen's house to practice the piano after school, because she liked having a little girl in the house again. I'd look up from Czerny at Jeannie's picture and imagine how my parents would grieve if I died. They'd say what everyone said about Jeannie—that I was the best of all the children, the smartest, the sweetest. I knew I couldn't compete with Richard because he was a boy or with Ruth because she was good. Dying young would make me special.

Some memories are fuzzy, things I saw dissolving into things

I'd heard. But this one is sharp-edged. It brings back the words of a song I sang for company. I'd stand beside the piano in my shiny Mary Janes while my father played, and sing "They always always pick on me." That's how it started. It ended like this:

> I know what I'll do, by and by,
> I'll eat some worms, and then—I'll—die!
> And when I'm gone, you wait and see,
> How they'll *all be sorry* that they picked on me.

How old could I have been when they taught me that song? Four, five, maybe six? I always knew the song was a joke. Eating worms would be disgusting but it wouldn't kill you. It was stupid to feel so sorry for yourself that you couldn't see it wouldn't do you one bit of good to have people feel sorry for you after you were dead. I pretended to laugh right along with everyone else, but I was angry. Everyone *did* pick on me.

The other kids performed too. I remember Ruth singing

> Come to me, my melancholy baby,
> Cuddle up and don't be blue;
> All your fears are foolish fancies, maybes,
> You know dear that I'm in love with you.

Richard's song, I remember, was a love song too:

> I'm in love with you, Honey;
> Say you love me too, Honey;
> No one else will do, Honey;
> Seems funny but it's true.

Amazing to find myself letter-perfect on these songs after fifty years. Was I the only one who had to sing about killing myself?

It was supposed to be funny. Or teach me something I evidently needed to learn about self-pity. Vaccinate me against thoughts of suicide. Maybe it did.

Connie must have stood in front of her sisters' pictures imagining how her parents would mourn for her if she died. Both of us imagined we had to be dead to be loved. Connie never outgrew that fantasy about death. I did. But I've replaced it with another one: that a dead woman cares about me. Maybe she doesn't love me the way I love her, maybe she gets huffy when I guess her secrets and exasperated when I guess wrong. But she's there. I feel her pull me this way, tug me that way as if she really were an active force in the world.

So what makes me so sure my mother's wrong, as usual, when she says my father is waiting for her on the other side of the grave? The room feels cold. I close the window and climb into bed.

In the morning my mother comes out of her bedroom in a striped nylon bathrobe she wore twenty years ago.

"Oh, you're not dressed?" she says. "I was going to ask you to get my newspaper. The goddamn newsboy left it halfway down the path. No matter how many times I call and tell them that I can't manage the door and the steps—"

"I'll get it."

"Not in your pajamas!"

I slip on my coat—not because I think I need it but because I know my mother thinks I do—and unlock the front door of her apartment.

"Here, take the key," she says.

"Why, are you going to lock me out?"

"Wise guy. The outside door will close on you, and then I'll have to come down and unlock it for you."

"I can hold it open," I say, hating the fuss I'm making as

much as the fuss she's making. At the foot of the stairs I hear Canada geese honking and look out the glass door to see mallard ducks swimming on the river that early morning clouds have tinted pink. The snow is pink too, except along a line of black hemlocks where it's almost blue. Holding the door open, I find the thick Sunday papers are out of reach. My mother is watching from the top of the stairs, keys dangling from her fingers. With my foot I hold the heavy door open. Stretching hurts. I drag the papers toward me. It hasn't gotten any easier to admit that my mother is right.

"My poor baby brother," my mother says when we sit down to bran muffins. "He's completely blind now." Her voice is barely audible.

"I thought he still had peripheral vision."

"He's losing it. And I'm going to be blind too."

"Is that what your doctor tells you?"

"No. But I know. I see double. I see two of you right now."

"Where are your glasses?"

"I hate them, those thick lenses with the prisms in them."

"But do you see double when you have them on?"

"No," she admits reluctantly. "But I can't read with them. All the letters blur."

"I thought you had another pair of glasses for reading."

"Yes. What a goddamn nuisance."

"Mother, I've worn bifocals since I was forty! I can't read a word without them. What do you expect at eighty-six?"

"I don't know, miracles maybe. I certainly didn't expect to *be* eighty-six. Believe me, Joan, long life is no gift."

"I do believe you," I say. "But as long as you can't turn your back on it, you might as well look at it."

" 'Keep your eye upon the doughnut, and not upon the hole,' " she says. "Remember that sign in the coffee shop on Boylston Street?"

"The one with a conveyor belt in the window, so you could watch the doughnuts being made?"

"That's right."

"I loved to watch the doughnuts flip over when they were brown on one side. They smelled wonderful."

"They never tasted as good as they smelled," my mother says, and laughs. "I guess I'm the sad sack who keeps her eye on the hole."

She goes into the bathroom to rinse the bran muffin out of her dentures while I rinse the cups and plates before putting them in the dishwasher because my mother insists the crumbs stick to the plates if you don't rinse them. If I admit that my legs are throbbing or that my mother's sight is failing, or even that crumbs will stick and doors will lock, then I'll have to live in her world of holes without doughnuts. It's a terrible world. I'll do anything I have to do to keep out of it.

I have to admit that as a description of the world, my optimism is no more accurate than my mother's pessimism. But I'm damned if I'll let her add my pain to hers. She's a pain collector. That's more than a world view, it's a power play. When my father had a stroke and someone said, "Poor Dave!" my mother said, "What do you mean 'poor Dave'? 'Poor Frances!'" The caretaker, the worrier, was the one who really suffered. I felt guilty when I broke my ankle. If I told her how my legs are burning now, she'd turn that to a reason for me to worry about *her*. Poor Frances has power.

It's hardly news that some women parlay their suffering into power they can't get any other way. I saw Brazilian mothers use their husbands' adulteries to bind their children to them. I saw Egyptian mothers use their confinement the same way. I know how few channels most women have for their energy. So why has it taken me until this very minute to admit that my mother uses suffering this way? Because I hate it. I hate her when she does it. And I don't want to hate my mother.

She shuffles into the living room and stands looking out at the river.

"Did you notice how pink the water was this morning?" she

asks. I put my arm around her. I love my mother. "I'll miss this view when I move," she says, dazzling me with the skill with which she's just converted another doughnut into a hole.

"Can I help you get dressed?" I follow her to her bedroom. As she opens the top drawer of her mahogany dresser with handles made of gilded acorns, I smell the French perfume that used to rise from her slips when I'd run my fingers from the lace to the satin and back to the lace, white, black, and pink. I'd forgotten her glamour. Now she takes out a dingy polyester slip. From the closet she pulls out the same faded red polyester dress she was wearing yesterday. The closet is full of well-tailored skirts and pants, bright silk blouses with matching handknit cardigans, a few suits and dresses, an aqua velour bathrobe I gave her with the tags still hanging from the sleeve. "I've lost so much weight my skirts and pants fall off me," she says.

"Do you want me to see if I can take them in?"

"No, they're too hard to put on anyway. Oh, here's a beautiful dress I can't wear any more. Try it on."

It is a beautiful dress, jade silk piped with navy, simply styled, fully lined. The label says size six.

"It's lovely, Mother, but I wear size ten. Sometimes eight, but never six."

"Is it only a six? It's cut big. Try it on."

"But I'm four inches taller than you are."

"I left a deep hem when I shortened it, and you're so thin now—"

Seduced, I take off my pants and sweater and brace and try on the dress. The waist is two inches too short, and when I fasten the buttons I can barely move my arms.

"It's a lovely color on you," my mother says, "but I guess I didn't have you in mind when I bought it."

How could I fall into her trap like that? I glare at her reflection next to mine.

"I look in the mirror and wonder who let that old woman in here," she says. "And then I hear my mother's voice saying 'A hand is going to come out of the mirror and smack you across the face!' I used to sneak a peek at myself and duck."

"Why'd she say that?" My words come grudgingly.

"Oh, I used to strike tragic poses in front of the mirror. I was a dancer, and I thought I was a great *artiste.* My mother knew how to take me down off my high horse." Her tone is approving.

So that's where she learned it. I tug at the tight sleeves to get my arms free. "But you *were* an artist. You danced with Ray Bolger."

"He was the artist. He'd stay at the studio rehearsing after everyone else went home. I was never that serious. Once our dancing school sent us out to do an exhibition together—did I ever tell you this story?" She laughs. "We did a ballroom number together and then he did a solo with a flying split and ruptured himself! We were supposed to do a tap duet next, but since we couldn't finish our performance they didn't pay us the three dollars they owed us. We had just enough money between us to limp home on the streetcars."

I strap on my brace. She was free once too. "But you were good! Why'd you give up dancing? Did Daddy make you stop?"

"No, by the time I met him I was just teaching dancing. I must have been seventeen, maybe eighteen, when I was offered a job replacing another dancer in a road company. Papa asked, 'What happened to the other girl?' and I had to tell him she died of TB, so of course he said I couldn't go. I went mooning around the house like Sarah Bernhardt. So Papa took me to New York and we went to theaters and nightclubs."

"To cheer you up?" I'm jealous. My father never took me anywhere, just the two of us.

"No, to show me what an awful life dancers had. Of course I

thought it looked wonderful. I wanted it more than ever. But I got over it. Come, let's go through your papers and letters so you can take what you want. I won't have room to store these things in a nursing home." Her voice is a raspy wisp. I'll argue with her later.

On the card table where she usually does crossword puzzles and pays bills is a thick file folder and a pile of journals. On top is my anthology of Woolson's stories. So she did receive it. She never said anything.

"Have you read any of these stories?" I ask, picking it up. "Some of them are really wonderful."

"I've just read some of your introduction." She sits down in a hard bridge chair. "I couldn't read much of it. The print is very small."

"I'm afraid I couldn't control the way the book was printed," I say through clenched teeth, "only what went into it." Isn't she proud of me? Isn't she glad I didn't have to give up my career the way she did?

"I don't understand why Woolson took care of her mother all those years," my mother says, "when you say her mother never appreciated her."

I sit down across the table from her and look her square in the eye. She looks back with perfect innocence. "There's a letter she wrote after her mother died," I tell her, "about rowing her mother up and down Otsego Lake in Cooperstown, and stopping at a big rock to build a fire and make coffee for her, and then she says something like 'my dear mother, what a loving heart she had!' *She* had! I think Connie was hoping that if she was very very good, some day her mother might love her back."

"And she lived with her mother until the old lady died?"

"Yes."

"That must have been a liberation for her."

"It devastated her." I'm not waiting for you to die, Mother. "I think it was because she finally knew she'd never, *ever* get what she wanted from her mother."

My mother doesn't react to the italics I haven't been able to keep out of my voice. The bridge chair digs into my back and I move to the bed, where I lean against the big green bolsters I upholstered for her. I run my fingers along the edges of the cushions. I cut and sewed this welting, yards and yards of it, because I couldn't buy any the right color. Some daughters row, I tell myself, other daughters sew.

"Giving all those years to her mother," my mother says, "that was a big sacrifice. By the time the old lady died, Woolson was too old to get married."

"I don't think she wanted to get married."

"Why not?"

"I think she was afraid of it. She'd seen her two older sisters die in the early years of their marriages."

This is another story I can't stop telling myself. Connie's big sister Georgie won herself the nickname of "Romping Granite" from Great-Uncle Fenimore. She must have chased bullies down the street when they teased her bookish little sister. She must have been the one who taught Connie how to row on Lake Erie. When she was nineteen and Connie was ten, Georgie got married and moved to a house just five minutes away. Connie could run back and forth every day, help Georgie find a rhyme for the witty verses she wrote to ask her mother for an egg, play with Georgie's baby, puff herself up with the dignity of an aunt. This is the best part of the story.

Then everything goes wrong. Connie's other big sister wants to get married. Emma's the one who gives Connie music lessons and sings "I Know That My Redeemer Liveth" in the church choir with a spirituality so intense that it stirs everyone who hears her. The young minister is so stirred he wants to marry her, but though he's handsome and rich, he has a mysterious illness. Emma's parents send her back to boarding school to get over him, but she pines away so alarmingly that they finally let her get married. Jarvis agonizes over it to a friend:

> It is a hard thing for a Parent, in my opinion, to *refuse to consent* to a connection which carries with it the best affection, and the happiness, perhaps, of the whole life in this, at best, troublous world. The responsibility for such a refusal, I have never been willing to take upon myself where no serious or unconquerable obstacle existed.

I love Jarvis for this letter, but I shudder when I read it because I know what his compassion and humility are going to cost him. He lets Emma marry T. Jarvis Carter, whose name must have been part of his allure. Those Woolson girls all adored their dashing father. Six months later the young minister dies and Emma comes home to her parents. She moves into the front bedroom and Connie watches her fade away. Three months later she's dead of the "quick consumption" that killed her husband, and of her own heartbreak. Emma is nineteen. Connie is twelve.

Grief and guilt make Jarvis and Hannah so sick that they decide to close the house and take the three young children away on a long trip, but Georgie gets pregnant with her second child and they stay in Cleveland to see her safely through. But she doesn't make it through. Three days after giving birth to a little girl, fifteen months after Emma's death, Georgie asks to see her little sisters and then she dies of childbed fever.

I hate this part of the story.

Now Connie's five older sisters are dead and she's the oldest child. She works and works to be best at everything, at biology and rowing, singing and French, history and composition. Her younger sister Clara says when she's old, "There was no possible use for *me* to attempt anything in any line because Connie, from her earliest girlhood, had been at the head in *every* line." Connie has to work all the time to deserve to be alive. Then she begins to menstruate and learns what it means: that her own body can bear children who'll die young and break her heart or who'll kill her being born. She's seen what love and marriage and childbirth do to women. They'll never happen to her. She'll be an independent woman. She'll have a career. That will save her from the grief on her mother's face.

That's what I thought, too.

9

Brass Horse, High Horse

*D*eeper than the puckers around my mother's mouth and neck are the creases between her eyes and across her forehead. I've never seen her without those frown lines, not even when she laughs. I used to sit on her lap and try to press the creases flat with my fingers, but they'd bounce right back. At bedtime she'd press an adhesive butterfly between her eyes, but the grooves were still there in the morning. I remember her with hands on hips, scowling. My father I see with one hand inside his belt and his face twisted with discomfort.

"Did Daddy have ulcers when you married him?" I ask.

"No, just a bad gall bladder. And psoriasis. Remember those white cotton gloves he wore?"

Yes. Within weeks after my father died, my own hands cracked open like his and bled whenever I bent my fingers to tie a shoe or write a word. To peel a potato or rinse a diaper I had to wear rubber gloves, and at night I wore plastic gloves sealed with tape at my wrists because they were supposed to work better than the cotton gloves my father wore. I thought my hands were punishing me for not being able to mourn for my father. At his funeral I'd looked at the waxy face in the coffin and felt only shock that the person who had been my father was obviously not there. What was sad was not that his life was over—abruptly, at sixty, from a massive brain hemorrhage—but that it had been such torment. I'd hated him. Now I pitied him. I told myself he must have loved me to scrutinize my life with such care. To go every day to work he detested so I could have new saddle shoes and roast beef for dinner. To stay in the hot city working so I could stay at a house near the beach. But it didn't feel like love.

"The Depression gave Daddy his ulcers," my mother is saying. "When Ruth was born he said, 'If someone would offer me forty dollars a week for the rest of my life, I'd sign my life away.' Those ulcers ruined my marriage. The ulcers and that darling doctor who told me, 'That man must not be aggravated.' Good trick! Life aggravated your father."

"I certainly aggravated him."

"That you did. Richard respected him, and I think feared him, and Ruth adored him and would do anything in the world for him, but you—you always gave as good as you got!"

That's how Richard remembers it too. "I can see it so clearly," he told me recently, "the basic family scene. Maybe you were six, so I'd have been thirteen, and you'd asked Dad for permission to do something, and of course the answer was no, and you'd stomp off to your room, and halfway up the stairs you'd turn around and say, with all the sarcasm you could muster, '*Thank* you!' and run up the rest of the stairs and slam your door. Ruth and I were very impressed."

"Impressed?"

"Because we could never stand up to Dad."

"But Mother hated it—"

"Because she couldn't do it either."

Now my mother is uncrossing and recrossing her legs. They're still elegant at eighty-six, still a dancer's legs. "Of course your father loved to fight," she says. "He'd take any side of an argument, just to get the exercise. But I was a lousy fighter. I couldn't think of a smart comeback till the next day. It would have been much better if I'd argued with him."

"*Really?*" I look at her in astonishment.

"Your father—he wanted things out in the open. I couldn't do it. Or I wouldn't. I think—I think he resented it."

"You were following the doctor's orders."

"But it would have been much better if I'd communicated with my husband."

So I got it all wrong. It wasn't my back talk that aggravated my father and kept his ulcer from healing. It was my mother's silence. If she'd stood up to him, I might not have had to. Maybe he needed his ulcers. They helped balance the power my mother won through her silent suffering. No. That's wrong. His ulcers made him rage and his rage made my mother suffer and her suffering made her powerful and gave him more reason to rage.

This story is as terrible in its way as the Woolson family tragedies.

I pull an afghan off the bolster and wrap it around my shoulders.

"Of course there's more than one way to communicate," my mother is saying. "I could squelch Richard and Ruth with a threatening look, but you?" She laughs. "You'd look away!"

I remember doing that. I knew what I'd see if I caught my mother's eye. Not just disapproval or anger. Suffering. I pull the afghan tight around me. I was smart to look away. It's dangerous to see yourself in your mother's grief.

"You were hell on wheels," my mother goes on. "But I told your father, 'This one has a spark that's special.' I didn't want him to break your spirit." She laughs. "Now I think nothing could have broken it!"

"It could have been broken." I take her hand.

"You made my life hell," my mother says. I know how I did that. I talked back. I wouldn't keep quiet when my father told me to become a secretary or when he said welfare just made people lazy or black people deserved what they got. I'd disagree, my father would explode, my mother would go to the toilet and throw up her dinner. She'd never say *he* made her life hell, just me. He was a good husband. He didn't drink or gamble or run around with other women. He was not a distant, absent father. He was right there, right on top of us every minute.

Richard calls. My mother says, "Joan's spine? It's not too bad." She hands me the phone and shuffles out of the room.

"Am I remembering right?" I ask him, running my eyes along the shelves of knickknacks and framed photos. "Did Dad really scrutinize every move we made?"

"His eye was on the sparrow," Richard says, laughing, "and God help the sparrow if it turned left when it should have turned right!"

"Am I paranoid, or did Dad really pick on me more than he did on you or Ruth?"

"Of course he did. You were the one who was most like him."

Here it comes: I'm my father's spit 'n' image, contentious like him, self-righteous, aggressive—

"You had the pioneer qualities that made him go to China when he was twenty-one," Richard says. I'm stunned. I stare at the brass horse my father brought home from Shanghai. It could have been something *good* in me that infuriated my father. Something he'd lost before I was born, something he missed and couldn't get back.

"I see you as the Robert Kennedy of our family," Richard is saying.

"The what?" Flattery is a rope pulled across the road to send you sprawling. I learned that growing up on Winthrop Road.

"Remember what he said? 'Some people look at things as they are and ask why, but I look at things as they might be and ask why not.' You weren't arguing with Dad about why we had to have dinner at six o'clock. You were trying to expand the horizons of your universe."

He's not teasing me. The big brother I idolized actually thought I was something special. I never knew that. I get up to hang up the phone and my right leg buckles. I fought my father to expand my horizons and now my own body is shrinking them.

I hear the toilet flush and my mother comes back into the room. "We're not making much progress with these papers, are we?"

On her bridge table is a stack of journals with familiar covers—my articles on Egypt and Brazil and Central America, my articles on goddesses and on Connie. I sent them all to my mother and she saved them all. If she was proud of me for writing them, she never said. Preserving the spark in me didn't mean fanning the flame. But why should it make her proud to see me analyze and argue, to watch me wield the words my father used as weapons against her? Why should she admire me for writing about other women's suffering when I looked away from hers?

I wrote those pages for her. I wrote them to make amends for making her life hell. I should have known mothers don't accept reparations like that. I can't bear to touch the journals.

"I'll start the minestrone," I say. On the kitchen shelf I find cans of kidney beans and tomatoes and a package of macaroni. Here's the big dented soup pot my mother used for cooking bean and barley soup. I heat olive oil, peel and chop garlic and onions, crush oregano and basil in my hands. Soup is a form of restitution my mother accepts.

She shuffles into the kitchen. "Need any help?"

"Want to wash the parsley?"

"As long as I don't have to chop anything. I can't tell my fingers from the carrots. Tell me, what do you hear from Leslie?"

"She's helping deliver babies. Can you imagine your granddaughter doing that?"

"I thought she was going to be a mother who stayed home with her own babies. Do you remember the day she came home from kindergarten and told you that's what she was going to be when she grew up?"

What I don't remember is giving my mother that ammunition to use against me. I stir the carrots into the onions with a blackened wooden spoon. "She says she doesn't see any children in her future except other people's."

"Does she have a boyfriend?"

"No."

"Probably she doesn't have time."

"I don't think she's very interested in men right now."

From time to time I invite my mother to let me know that she knows that Leslie is a lesbian. Each time she lets me know that she doesn't want to know. Recently she told me how disgusted she was by a Gay Pride march she'd seen on the television news. "I don't care what people do in private," she said, "but why do they have to flaunt it?" Her politics are generally progressive, so I explained that the march was a human-rights demonstration by people who get beaten up and discriminated against. I pointed out that heterosexuality is flaunted on every billboard and TV screen, that most people have no choice about their sexual orientation, that having to hide it says it's something shameful. "I'm sorry," she said, "but I think it *is* shameful. They might as well go to the toilet in public." When I reported this conversation to Leslie, she said, "The last time I saw Gram she told me gays should go back in the closet, or back under the rock they crawled out from."

155

My mother doesn't want to hear that her darling Leslie who can do no wrong is one of *them*. We decided not to tell her. Leslie was still bruised from coming out to her father. Why was her sexuality so easy for me to accept? When she told me, first I was surprised. She'd had plenty of boyfriends. Then I was sorry, thinking of the extra hurdles in front of her. But then I was glad. What a wonderful choice of lovers she was going to have! I know dozens of marvelous women, but I think a good man is very hard to find.

I never could see what was so awful about being a lesbian. Maybe it's because I taught Women's Studies and studied lesbians' lives, or because I'd loved Suzanne for years before she discovered she loved women differently than the way she loved men. This new fact about her didn't change anything, not even the way I felt when we hugged. Hugging men who aren't related to me always feels complicated by sexual possibilities, but hugging other women feels natural and good. I suppose that's because every woman loved another woman's body at the beginning of her life. The way I must have loved my mother's.

The carrots are tender now. I open the cans of beans and tomatoes and dump them in the pot along with the cubed zucchini and some water. "Would you set the timer for fifteen minutes?" I ask my mother.

"Just fifteen minutes? I used to cook soup for hours."

"That's Jewish soup. Italians cook their vegetables *al dente*."

"*Al dente* is nice if you have your own teeth."

"If it's too hard to chew, I'll cook it longer. Let's sit down while it simmers." My legs hurt. I'd take a Valium but I need all my wits about me.

"I never dreamed I'd live so long I'd have to put up with indignities like false teeth," my mother says. She walks carefully into the living room, holding on to the backs of the chairs. The river is deep gray now, spotted with geese. One flies up off the water. Then two more. Then a flock of them. Wherever they're going, I want to go too. I lie down on the sofa.

"Didn't they rename you for your grandmother so you'd have a long life like hers?"

"It was a superstitious custom, but it worked. Too well!" She eases into her reclining chair. "I was sixteen and they thought I was dying."

"What was wrong with you?" What's wrong with me, that I know exactly why Georgie and Emma and Annie and Gertrude and Julia died, but not why Frances almost died?

"A bowel obstruction, six weeks after an appendectomy."

"Do you remember your grandmother?" I never knew mine.

"Oh, sure. She was a charitable soul. Her fancy German family disowned her when she married Grandpa, who was just a Russian shingle maker. But during the First World War the relatives who'd stayed in Germany were starving and she sent them money. Her life was no bargain, either. She had twenty-one pregnancies."

"*Twenty-one?*"

"She raised only seven children to maturity."

I fold my hands over my stomach. All those months of morning sickness and back aches, all those racking childbirths with nothing to ease the pain, not even a living child at the end of it, only exhaustion, grief, and breasts engorged with milk. Here I've been obsessing over Hannah Woolson losing three little daughters and two grown daughters without even knowing that my own great-grandmother suffered everything she did, and more.

"Grandma was the one educated person in my *yichis*," my mother is saying. "She could read and write both in German and in Yiddish. I don't know if her booklearning helped her feed seven children on what Grandpa earned."

"Was he still a shingle maker after they came to America?"

"No, he was a junk man," my mother says. "He used to drive a horse and wagon through the West End and shout 'Any rags, any bones, any bottles today?' The junk yard was in their back yard, and I loved to go there and play in huge bins of old books and magazines."

I wonder if any of them were in German or Yiddish. I wonder if my great-grandmother read books in the middle of the night while she nursed her babies, the way I did. I wonder if books opened a window on her life, and if the wider view just made her miserable, the way Shanghai did my father.

My mother laughs. "Maybe it was in the junk yard that I got attached to old papers. I've saved a lot of your letters. Everything's in this folder. Take what you want, and throw out the rest."

I want everything. I need to know what it was to be me. The timer buzzes, and I carry the fat brown folder with me to the kitchen. I stir some macaroni into the soup and set the timer for another ten minutes. Inside the folder I find blue airmail letters typed on the clunky Olivetti portable I used in Florence, and smeary letters typed on my electronic typewriter in Oxford. Under them I find a penciled postcard postmarked January of 1943:

Dear Mother, It seems to me that when you are here it is a lot better. I like Aunt Louise and Uncle Eliot, but I like you more. I'm glad for your sake that you went away but I still miss you.

Love

Joan

X X X X X X X X X X X X X X X X X X X X X X X X X X X X X

O O O O O O O O O O O O O O O O O O O O O O O O O O O

I was six when I sent my mother all those hugs and kisses. Old enough to know she needed a vacation from me. Here's a slip of notebook paper on which my father has penciled in "Date?- 1944-?" I'd have been eight.

158

Mom, I am not eating any supper thank you
hatingly yours
Joan
P.S. Please do not come in and kiss me tonight.

I adored my mother, I hated her. Nothing's changed.

The timer buzzes. "Soup's ready," I call to my mother. "Come taste it and see if the vegetables are soft enough for you to chew."

I lift out a cube of carrot on a spoon and blow on it, the way she used to cool my food for me. She laughs, remembering too, and opens her mouth wide for the spoon.

"Delicious," she says. "You're a good cook. You never learned it from me."

She was a good cook too, but I didn't learn to cook from her. I wasn't interested in learning how to live her life. After lunch I say, "What about a nap?"

"I hate to waste the time while you're here."

"I'll rest too." I help her out of her dress and onto her bed.

"Do you remember how I used to lie down with you to get you to nap?" she asks. "Then I'd fall asleep and you'd sneak away!"

She remembers so much I've forgotten. Yes, I remember lying beside her, watching the pain drain from her face. I knew I'd put it there. That's why I only looked at it when she was sleeping. Otherwise I'd have to pay for making my mother's life hell with a lifetime of suffering like hers. Connie paid that price. Not me.

I close the bedroom door and go back to the den. In this low cabinet my mother keeps the family scrapbooks. My father used to sit at the dining-room table with these checkbooks and his scissors and tape, a short, stout man with thin gray hair and bifocals that hid his eyes.

I drop to my knees and haul out the scrapbooks. Sitting on

159

my heels hurts. Awkwardly, I flop onto the floor and sit against the wall with my legs sticking straight out in front of me. I pull one of the heavy scrapbooks onto my lap. Here's a newspaper photo of my mother wearing a white blouse and a severe man-tailored suit. She's receiving a check for the Hadassah work-shops she ran, sewing clothes for Jews who'd survived Hitler and gone to Israel—Palestine, it was then. She's smiling, but be-tween her eyes the frown lines are deep. Here she's receiving an award for her outstanding service to the Red Cross. For years she worked at the Veterans' Hospital, writing letters for men who'd lost their hands, chatting with men who'd lost their legs, holding hands with men who'd lost their minds. "How can you stand to look at them?" my father asked her. "I just look in their eyes," she said.

My mother sought out other people's pain, too.

She's told me how she'd resented her own mother's charities. "I never know who I'll find in my bed with me in the morning!" she'd complain. "You take in every stray dog and cat."

"Here," Rose would say to her, "take this five dollars and a dozen eggs to Bessie Fisher, you'll have a *mitzvah*."

"Sure," said Frances, "with ten *mitzvahs* I can buy a cup of coffee."

"But you'll go," said Rose.

And Frances went.

When I worked in the Civil Rights movement, and then the antiwar movement, she approved. "Jews have an obligation to cry out against injustice," she said. Except at home, I'd thought, meanly.

Here's a clipping about me. I'm eighteen, round-faced, sitting on a hospital bed, smiling down at a man who's smiling up at me. I remember begging the reporter not to write the story. "Why not," he said, "you're a heroine! The guy would have drowned if you hadn't saved him."

We'd been sailing together. He'd gone for a swim and gotten

a cramp in the cold water. He was upwind and I couldn't sail back to him fast enough. I had to swim for him, haul him unconscious back to our overturned sailboat. Another sailboat picked us up, the police took us to the hospital, the reporter saw the police report.

"But my father will kill me when he finds out!"

I was afraid he'd haul me out of my college dormitory and make me live at home where he could keep his eye on me. What a damned fool thing to do, he'd say, risking your life like that. But he saved the clipping. Maybe he was proud of me. My mother wasn't. When the Humane Society sent me a medal the size of a saucer she laughed. When she met the man I'd rescued she told him, "Joan would have done the same for any stray dog or cat." He wasn't worth it, she told me later.

The minestrone isn't sitting well in my stomach.

Here's a yellowed clipping from the *American Legion Magazine:* MY TWO DOLLAR ULCER CURE. And on the next page, clippings from the *Boston Globe:* NEW OPERATION FOR ULCERS LETS ULCER CURE ITSELF, NEW DRUG RELIEVES ULCER PAIN RAPIDLY, SMOKING AND DEATH RATES IN MEN. These are my father's clippings. No awards for service like my mother's or heroics like mine. "NERVOUSNESS" REALLY FAILURE TO GROW UP. Why did my father save this? It describes a person who's "unhappy, discontented, often a poor eater, a poor sleeper, never feeling vital, usually vaguely uneasy about things in general, often feeling physically low with vague aches and pains." Sounds familiar. An "ambitious, tense person in a hurry to get what he wants or in a rage because he didn't get what he wants or complaining that he can't get what he wants." My God! That's exactly how I saw my father! He saw himself the same way. He saved this brutal self-portrait. He must have wanted to change. But the article only says that the "nervous" person is using childish techniques to control the world, and should grow up. That's all. Just do it. It was 1954. Only crazy people went to psychiatrists then.

My father wasn't crazy. He was just miserable. He'd been miserable ever since he came home from Shanghai.

I put down the checkbook and pick up a real scrapbook with a leather cover and heavy black pages. My father's photos of his two years in China. He's twenty-one years old, younger than my youngest child. A civil engineer fresh out of college, building flour mills in Shanghai. No wonder he's grinning. Next to him is a coolie with a rickshaw. Coolies could run all day because they smoked opium, he told us. It was cheaper than food. Coolies were lucky if they were pulling people. Some coolies had to empty outhouses and haul the excrement in "honey carts" to farmers who spread it on their fields. You could die from biting into a peach or brushing your teeth with water that hadn't been boiled. Maybe that's how he got so fussy about his food.

Did he actually take this picture of a man with a pigtail being executed in the street? He took this one, of a woman with her feet bound into tiny triangles. Women could barely hobble, he told me. They had to lean on someone while they tottered around. If I'd been born in China, I asked him, would you have bound my feet? You weren't even a gleam in my eye when I was in China, he'd say. But I knew if he'd tried, I'd have run away while I still had big feet.

Shanghai was a dangerous place, a cruel place. People were so poor, he told us, that they'd maim their own children—gouge out their eyes, lame them—to make them better beggars. It was blackmail, my father said, a con game. If you gave money to one beggar, you'd have a mob of them all around you, pushing and shoving. I couldn't understand how he could have been so happy there. He'd walk down narrow streets choked with beggars, walk past fortune-tellers and barbers and old men taking their pet birds out for the air and babies peeing through split pants. He'd buy silk kimonos beautifully embroidered by little boys. Buy brass horses and gongs and bowls, cigarette cases enameled with dragons. Servants would cook his food and smooth satin sheets on his bed. In the morning he'd walk out the door and step over the bodies of people who'd died overnight of starvation. Living in Shanghai would have made me a socialist, a communist maybe. It made my father a Republican who thought the New Deal had ruined America.

But Shanghai was thrilling, exotic, addicting. After Shanghai, life was gray. He warned us not to travel. We'd come home and be discontented with our lives. He'd had to come home long before he wanted to. His brother told him he'd better come home if he ever wanted to see his parents alive again. That would have been, what, 1922? My grandfather died just before I was born, so he was alive until 1936. My grandmother lived another year. So Uncle George called my father home fourteen years before he needed to. My father was a good son. He came home and got married and had me and lived unhappily ever after.

Naturally, I didn't follow his advice. I lived in Florence, planned my next sabbatical in Rome. I was packing for that trip when I found out that the lump in my mother's throat was malignant. I called her doctor. No reason not to go, he said. She should tolerate the radiation well. It would be at least a year before they'd know if there was a recurrence. I called my sister.

"Go," Ruth said. "There's nothing you can accomplish staying home."

"But it's not fair that so much of Mother's care falls on you."

"It's not your fault you live two hundred miles away. You do your share by keeping her debriefed on the phone. Go. Have a wonderful time."

Uncle George wanted to clip my father's wings. Ruth wanted me to have a wonderful time. So I went to Rome. I walked in Connie's footsteps and brought primroses to her grave and wrote articles about her and planned my anthology and fell in love with her. I'll call Ruth and thank her for that. I wish I could call my father. I want to ask him about China and tell him about Egypt. We could talk about how it feels to walk streets where you can't read a sign. To learn about clitoridectomy and foot-binding. My father and I could have had a real conversation.

No. We couldn't. I know exactly what would happen. He'd embark on one of his monologues. I'd try to say something. He'd cut me off. I'd tune him out. I wouldn't learn any more about him and China than I know now. He wouldn't learn any more about me.

I wish things could have been different. But I see now that when my parents looked at me, they saw parts of themselves they'd had to bury: my mother's back talk, her artistic ambitions; my father's pioneering streak, his questing spirit. They couldn't bear to see what they'd lost when the Roaring Twenties of their twenties turned into the depressing Depression of their thirties. If my parents had been happier, I could have been happier, too.

But I've refused to be wretched like my father or to suffer like my mother. I've refused to descend into the gloomy Underworld where they lived. I looked away, walked away. The only way I know it must have hurt to be me is by how shocked I am to discover that Richard thought I was a visionary, shocked that my mother wanted to protect a spark she saw in me, shocked that my father was proud I'd saved someone's life. I remember being angry but I must have been sad, too, like the kid in the song who's going to eat worms.

I struggle to my feet. My spine aches. That's all right, it's not fused yet. I walk toward the door. My legs stop me in front of the brass horse. That's scarred nerves tugging on my bones. That's not all right. Pain has caught up with me. Maybe chronic pain, for the rest of my life, like my father's. I'm going to have to learn about pain.

Maybe I should turn my ear to the Great Below. That's what Inanna said when she was ready to descend into the Underworld. She went voluntarily, like Orpheus going to hell for Euridice, or Beowulf diving into the dark lake to kill Grendel's mother. But hers was a woman's descent. She can show me how to do it. I dump the green bolsters with their neat green welting onto the floor and stretch out on the bed. I pull my mother's afghan over me and close my eyes.

Soon I'm walking down a steep ramp like the entrance to a pyramid. Huge gray stones wall me in and roof me over. Finally I see a dim light. Standing in front of smoky torches at the bottom of the ramp is my sister Erishkegal. She steps forward. She's huge, like the goddess on the grandstand in my dream. Through the wild black hair that nearly covers her face I see her eyes. They're cruel.

Strip yourself, she says.

I hand her my necklace with its hollow silver circle. She throws it on the stones at our feet.

Drop your titles, she says.

Doctor of Philosophy and Professor of English shatter as she knocks them to the hard ground.

Give up the strength and speed and sensuality of your body.

My knees buckle. I fall on the sharp splinters of my titles.

She's not satisfied. Give up the love of your children, she says. Give up the love of your husband.

But then who will rescue me? I try to rise from my bleeding knees but Erishkegal shoves me down. How can a woman like myself, my own sister, do this to me? I ask her, Who are you really?

I am the Mater Dolorosa, she says. I suffer not just because the world is forever crucifying my son and raping my daughter and murdering their father, but because it is my nature to suffer. Ohhh, my womb! Ohhh, my heart! Ohhh, my head, my back, my legs!

I didn't cause your pain, I tell her. I can't fix it. What do you want of me?

She doesn't want me to stop her pain. She wants me to feel it with her. She wants me to say, Ohhh, your insides! Ohhh, your outsides! Oh, how you suffer! I can't make myself say it. If I could rescue her, if she even wanted to be rescued, I could love her, but she clings to her pain. It gives her power. I hate her self-pity as much as her cruelty. I hate all women who make other women suffer—the mother who binds her daughter's feet, the mother who holds her daughter down while another woman cuts off her clitoris, the mothers all over the world who do the same thing without knives or strips of cloth, producing the diminished females men will accept.

What do you really want of me, I ask Erishkegal.

Your life, she says. She wants to live my life.

You can't have it, I tell her. I won't give it up.

Then I'll destroy it, she says. She drags me toward a hook on the wall. She wants to hang me there like a piece of meat. She'll make me live her life of knowing nothing but her own suffering. That's what hell is.

Someone knocks her down. Someone seizes my hand, pulls me to my feet, drags me back up the stone ramp. I hear Erishkegal howling down below but she can't follow us. Daylight filters into the tunnel. I find myself standing in the desert, blinded by the sun.

You can't rescue Erishkegal, says Connie's voice. Or the mutilated women of the world. You can't rescue me, or your mother. All you can rescue is the truth.

I open my eyes. A shaft of sunlight surrounds the bronze horse with fire.

10

*Spirits from the
Vasty Deep*

I strap on my goggles and ease into a vacant lane in the YMCA pool. This is my first swim since surgery. Dr. Frederick said it wouldn't hurt, and I'm hoping it will help my muscle spasms. I push off from the wall and my hair lifts from my scalp, my body stretches out in the water, light and free. A quick bite of air, a cloud of bubbles. With the first kick the backs of my legs knot up.

Easy, easy, I coach myself. This is not a race. Try the breast-stroke. If I had to swim for shore from a shipwreck, that's how I'd swim. The first kick stabs my groin and shoots my knees up to my chest. The sharks would get me. Sidestroke's no better. Walking to the ladder is worse than swimming.

It takes me three tries to unlock my locker. In the shower I keep dropping the soap and shampoo. At home, I leave a message for Dr. Frederick and take half a Valium. For my legs. For my panic. Beside the sofa is a pile of folders I've been sorting to decide what to take to California. Now I take my brain in my hands like a drill and aim it away from the throbbing in my legs, force it to bear down on the words on the page.

The top folder is labeled "Woolson-Cooper Family History." The top sheet is headed "New York State Historical Association, Cooperstown." The words are a little smeared, like all the notes I've typed in archives on my electronic typewriter. My machine was paralyzed after a night in the trunk of my car at five below, I remember. I had to drive back to the village for new batteries. That was when I could still climb over snowbanks. Just a year ago.

I stuff another pillow under my knees and point my drill back at Cooperstown. The morning sun glittered on the snow while Beverly Woolson drove me around town, pointing out the big, solid houses where Connie's grandparents, aunts, and cousins lived. Later Jim Woolson handed me a beautifully engraved calling card inscribed "Miss Constance Fenimore Woolson." My fingers buzzed as I held it. I hated to give it back. It was much more exciting than the yards of computer printouts that showed how Jim was descended from Connie's great-great-grandfather. My fingers tingled again when Henry Cooper handed me a book inscribed by Connie's grandmother. He's descended from James Fenimore Cooper. While our snowy boots dripped in the hall of his fine old house, Henry lit a fire and told me he thought Connie's articles about New York would have made fine "Talk of the Town" columns for *The New Yorker*, where he worked.

"Woolson was a much better writer of fiction than Cooper's daughter Susan," Henry said, pouring red wine in my glass. "But Susan's nonfiction was pretty good. And there was another Susan—Cooper's granddaughter, who would have been Connie's age—who had psychic powers. She'd load a mahogany dining table with books and seat the heaviest man in Cooperstown on top of the books, and then she'd move the loaded table across the room using just her two index fingers."

"I wonder if Connie ever saw her do it." I spread Brie on a piece of warm French bread.

"She might have. Susan performed for anyone who asked her. Then a spirit told her these powers came from the devil, and she renounced them."

"Didn't her father go to seances?"

"That's right. And his sister was a famous ghost."

"Ann Pomeroy, Connie's grandmother? I don't know that story."

"She came to the door of her house holding a candle, and gave a stranger accurate directions to the rectory. When the rector showed the stranger photos of old residents, he picked out Ann's picture right away. She'd been dead for years."

I laughed. "Maybe Connie inherited her grandmother's talent for giving directions. I could swear she led me to some letters about her brother's drug addiction that weren't even catalogued. Maybe she wants me to know her family secrets. But I can't get her to tell me why."

A year later I still can't. Her imprint in my life just gets deeper. Amazing that a woman who's been lying in a Roman cemetery for nearly a century has managed to etch herself in my mind deeper than the fossil of some prehistoric fish or fern. She must have ghostly powers of her own.

I can't think how else she could have made a mark on me so much deeper than any made by my own dead relatives. I've trekked to Cooperstown to explore Connie's relation to her mother's uncle but I don't know anything about my own mother's uncles. Of course, none of them could have been a world-famous author like James Fenimore Cooper. They could barely spell.

Dr. Frederick calls. He's finally persuaded my insurance company they'd rather pay for a Spinal Stimulator now than have to pay for a second operation later. My machine has just arrived from Texas. "Once your bones fuse, you'll feel much better."

"But my back isn't what hurts. How about physical therapy for my legs?"

"It would do you more harm than good. Start wearing your Spinal Stim and be patient," he tells his least patient patient. "These things take months."

I know fusions take months. I can wait months. But adhesions last forever if there's no way of breaking them, and if there were a way to do that, I'm sure Dr. Frederick would have told me. I pull dead leaves off the plants, wipe off the kitchen table, take a book from my study. I can't read. Valium relaxes my eye muscles long before it does a thing for my legs. Or for the panic roiling my gut. Here's a tape of old family movies Ruth left at my mother's for me. I stick it in the VCR and adjust my reclining chair so I'm nearly horizontal.

Peering down over my chin I see my father. He's wearing knickers. His dark hair is slicked back from a center part. My mother has a cloche pulled down around her face, wavy hair sculpted on her cheeks. They're on a boat called *The Thousand Islander*. They must be on their honeymoon on the St. Lawrence River! Good Lord. They're young enough to be my children. She is elegantly slim, he is short and sturdy but not yet the fat man I remember. He steals the captain's hat off his head. Mother laughs. She's nobody's mother yet, but within two months she'll be pregnant.

Then there's Richard, a round-faced baby in a high chair. Then he's a beautiful toddler being cuddled by Grandma Fanny. She has the delicate features of a Russian princess. I never knew her. There's Grandpa Saul helping Ruth down some stairs. What year did they come to America? Where did they live in the Old Country, and how did Grandpa support the children who were born there? I don't know. I've never tried to find out.

Here are my mother's parents. Rose is playing "London Bridge" at Richard's birthday party, wearing a beautiful linen dress. Who's that fat baby Sam is bathing in a dishpan? Ruth? A thrill goes through me as I see the handsome grandfather I adored look up and smile at the camera. He was crazy about children and horses and good food. When he first came to America, Sam sold matches on street corners, and when Rose came she worked in a raincoat factory, but I don't know what years they came.

But I know exactly when Connie's great-grandfather William settled Cooperstown and named it for himself. 1790. I know his wife had been so unnerved at the prospect of moving her seven children from their comfortable home in New Jersey to a settlement where bears roamed the forests and panthers and wolves howled on the ice of Lake Otsego that she sat herself down in her chair and refused to budge. I know that when persuasion failed, her husband picked her up chair and all and put her in the wagon and that's how she rode to Cooperstown. Henry Cooper let me sit in that chair. I've stood in the family graveyard at Christ Church and looked at the row of tiny gravestones half covered with snow where five of Hannah's brothers and sisters were buried after they'd lived only a week, a month, five, ten, and fifteen months.

But I've never visited my own grandparents' graves. I don't know how old their brothers and sisters were when they died. I don't know when they came to America, or from where, or exactly why. For the first time that strikes me as extremely odd.

Of course it wouldn't have been easy to reconstruct my own family history even if I'd wanted to. These old home movies are all the archives my family has. None of my relatives wrote memoirs, or even letters, so far as I know. If they did, no one saved them, no archive catalogued them and preserved them in acid-free boxes.

But there is one document in my family archives. Not fact but fiction. A few years ago I tried to imagine one of the grandmothers I'd never known. Grandma Rose's sayings had come down to me through my mother: You children will fight over the last scrap of bread, not before. You told a lie? From lying comes stealing, from stealing comes murder, from murder comes the electric chair. If you stare at yourself in the mirror, a hand will come out and slap your face. The threats of a mother with five rambunctious children and a husband traveling forty-eight weeks a year. I made up a story about her, out of the stories my mother told me. It was in that folder of papers she gave back to me last week.

Rose is sitting on the front porch of the big house in Somerville, picking brown leaves off a wilted geranium in its clay pot. She's pregnant but she doesn't show yet. Her bust gets big faster than her belly.

"Philip, stop teasing the baby!"

Eliot is penned up behind a wooden gate so he won't walk off the porch. Philip zooms around the porch. Racing down the stairs he collides with a heavy black woman slogging up the hill in front of the house.

"Apologize to Mrs. Wright, Philip. Awful heat we're having." Rose is always friendly to the neighbors. She brings *lokshun koogle* to Mrs. Antonelli and takes home spaghetti and meatballs. Mrs. O'Malley brings her corned beef and cabbage and she gives her *putterkuchen*. Mrs. Wright stops but doesn't answer. She stares at the little girl at her feet. At four, Frances has the skinny, sharp face of an old woman. The huge blue ribbon in her sparse hair doesn't help. She sits, fully dressed, on a chamber pot on the sidewalk.

"The baby walks and she doesn't? Why don't you make the big one walk?"

Rose tells her Frances can't walk. Something's wrong with her legs. Doctors can't fix it. She doesn't tell her what her own mother says when she watches Frances scrape around on the chamber pot: "That one's a born cripple."

"Take the child to the country." Mrs. Wright sounds as if

172

she were reading the Ten Commandments. "Go where there's a lake and bury her in the sand up to her shoulders. Not at the ocean. Near fresh water. You do it every day until she walks."

Rose nods noncommittally and stands up. Mrs. Wright moves slowly up the hill. "Philip, you watch Eliot and Frances. And no *mishigas*. I'm going to take a bath and change before your father comes home."

Sam comes home. The children squeal and fish in his pockets. Jelly beans today. Last week he brought baby chicks! Rose tells him what that old battle-ax told her.

"So try it," he says. "Take the pony cart tomorrow and go to Billerica. In this heat, the kids'll like that."

It's ten hot, bumpy miles in the pony cart, but better than riding the streetcars and buses, with all those people and those smells, and worrying whether Philip is going to tell some woman he doesn't have any mother and will she take care of him? She'd murder that child if he weren't so handsome, and so smart.

Now Philip helps her dig a big hole in the sand. Rose lifts Frances into the hole—a heavy child for one all skin and bones—and piles the wet sand around her. When the sand reaches her neck she starts to cry. Then she screams. Long, hysterical screams, tearing screams with no sob between them. Philip runs down the beach so he won't have to hear. Rose sits and nurses Eliot while the screams bounce around in her skull. She'll have to wean him soon. A neighbor had told her to put tobacco leaves on her breasts to wean Philip. Maybe that spoiled her milk and ruined Frances's bones. Maybe Mrs. Wright's advice is just as bad.

At dusk she digs Frances out. She brushes her off and carries her and Eliot, one under each arm, to the pony cart. Philip she finds at the far end of the lake. He's been telling an old man that his father's in jail and there's no food in the house. She makes him give back the nickel the man gave him. Her jaw is set, her eyes narrow. She drives home.

But she goes back the next day. And the next. Every day for three weeks while the screaming gets shriller. Frances still scrapes through the house on her chamber pot, the scratches on the floors a map of her travels.

Sunday, Sam is home from one of the forty-eight trips he takes to Chicago every year trading horses. Rose says she won't go to the lake, but he says he'll come too. He listens to Frances scream for three minutes and digs her out.

"Come on, baby. Stand up. That's right. Let me brush the sand off. It's all right. Just stand there. Steady. That's it. Now, walk to me, baby. Just a few steps. Come on, sweetheart, walk to Papa."

And she does.

Tears stream down Rose's cheeks, as they always stream down mine when my mother tells this story. Maybe Mrs. Wright was right. Maybe the wet sand unknotted some tangled muscles. Or maybe Frances hadn't wanted to walk, wanted to be the baby longer, but after three weeks in the sand, decided she'd rather walk than scream. Anyway, she walked—of course to Sam, the magician, with his diamond stickpin or the pawn ticket in his pocket still the same charmer, with that smile and that look that stops even Philip without a word. Rose struggles heavily to her feet. It's only the sixth month, but this time she's showing already.

My mother has written corrections in the margins. So she did read it. It was Eliot, not Philip, who was the colossal liar. It was Grandma Sarah, not Grandma Rachel, who called her "crooked legs" and said she was a born cripple. She doesn't remember geraniums on the porch in Somerville. I wasn't trying to write history. I was trying to summon an ancestor I'd never known. Like a medium at a seance summoning the spirits of the dead, like Owen Glendower calling spirits from the vasty deep, I wanted to raise a ghost and transcribe her words. I was practicing for Connie.

Rose would have been a generation older than Connie. Their lives overlapped. But if they'd met, what would they have said to each other—the girl who crossed the ocean in steerage and slept on an ironing board in her cousin's crowded apartment, the girl who came to Cooperstown in her father's carriage and stayed in the best houses in town?

I see Connie's ancestors and mine assembled in front of a stately home as if they were posed for a daguerreotype. The photographer has their heads in vises so they won't move during the long exposure of the plates. They all look as if they have rigor mortis. Some of Connie's relations are wearing velvet and lace and white feathers. Others wear suits of armor and stand with their beavers up. One looks like Natty Bumppo, wearing fringed deerskin and leaning easily on his rifle.

My relatives stand off to the side and the rear. The men hold their caps in their hands; the women wear aprons, and look ready to dash back through the servants' entrance to the kitchen of the great house in the background the second the photographer's flash releases them. If Connie's ancestors belong in *The Last of the Mohegans,* mine belong in *Fiddler on the Roof.*

Her relatives founded new settlements among Mohawk Indians and wolves in central New York State. Mine crowded into Boston tenements full of Irish and Italian and other Russian immigrants. It's as plain as my father's nose on my face that Connie's relatives would have turned up their noses at nobodies like my grandparents. Connie might even have turned up her nose at me.

Would she? I never thought about it when I was climbing over snowbanks in Cooperstown. She was still "Woolson" and I was a scholar. Her family history mattered, mine was irrelevant. Her class views had nothing to do with me. I took notes on them. They're here somewhere.

Here's a review she wrote for the *Atlantic Monthly. That Lass*

o'*Lowrie's* is an absurd book, she says, for suggesting a gentleman can happily "marry an inferior." Everyone knows that "no
after training can ever eradicate entirely the habits of the common working girl"—a girl like my grandmothers—"or supply
the requisite little refinements which . . . are the most powerful
adjuncts of the lady." Adjuncts presumably indispensable to
the gentleman's marital bliss.

Snob! When she wrote that review she was working ten-hour
days writing stories that would pay the bills for her mother and
herself in cheap southern boardinghouses. But of course she
was never a "common working girl." No matter how poor she
got, she was always a lady. She could still feel like somebody by
looking down at someone else. Someone like me.

Connie's mother liked to give herself airs, calling herself
Lady Elinor Eglantine St. Clair when she was a child, and
"Lady Han" in her teenage journals. I know what Grandma
Rose would have said to her: "Who do you think you are? I
know your mother and your father." That's what she said to
my mother when she got up on her high horse.

But even if Hannah was hoity-toity, Connie sought out people as humble as my grandparents—coal miners in Ohio, fur
trappers along Lake Superior, berry pickers on Lake Erie's islands. She recognized herself in the hungry souls stuck in desolate places, and she wrote about them even though "Mrs.
Van-Something" would tell her, "I never care to read about the
lower classes." Connie knew more about working-class people
than I do. I never sought them out. When I typed for a paper
company the summer I was nineteen, I never went down to the
warehouse to meet the people who lugged around huge rolls of
brown kraft and sisal. Just last year I spent two long days in a
jurors' lounge with auto mechanics and construction workers
and custodians. While we waited for our numbers to be called, I
found a quiet corner and read Toni Morrison's novel *Beloved*.
Soaking up a literary account of slaves while I ignored their living descendants! Who's the snob?

"Coffee's ready," David calls. I wander into the kitchen. Would Connie see me as the granddaughter of men who bought and sold old rags and bottles, I wonder, or would she see me as a university professor? Would she look up to me for my superior education, or look down on me as a Jew?

"Do you think of yourself as married to a Jew?" I ask David as I pour milk into our coffee mugs.

"Only when your mother tries to teach me Yiddish expressions," he says, leaning against the stove. He makes a point of mispronouncing *lokshun koogle.*

"Were there Jews in Mansfield, Ohio?"

"Some. I remember my father making some anti-Jewish remarks."

We've never talked about this before. I look at David. I've never seen him as gentile because I don't see myself as Jewish. I don't think about Jewishness from one year to the next. David's the one who's studied the Nazis' persecution of the Jews. But now I'm seeing myself with Connie's eyes. To her I'd have been a Jew. She wrote some things about Jews, but I don't remember what. I can't look them up now. It's time to go pick up my Spinal Stimulator.

It's at the office of a spine specialist who's participating in the study of its effectiveness.

"Why don't you wait in the car," I tell David. "I'll only be a minute."

I expect the nurse to hand me an electronic garter belt, but the box she's unpacking is big enough to hold a television set. First she pulls out a soft brace and straps it around me. It covers everything between my breasts and groin. Then she digs out a pair of heavy rubber coils the size of turkey platters. These she attaches to the front and the back of the the brace with wide Velcro straps. Each coil contains an electric generator, she explains. The coil on my stomach she connects to the one on my back with a short cord. The long cord sticking out the side attaches to a box that will pulse current through me once a second for eight hours every day.

I'm in shock. "It weighs a ton!" I croak.

"Oh, it's much too heavy for you to walk around in," she says quickly, helping me lie down on the examining table. "You wear it to bed."

"People *sleep* in this?" It's like lying on rocks.

"Well, some people can't. They wear it during the day."

Eight-hour days. In this. "For how long?"

"At least three months. If it doesn't work in nine months, it's not going to." She looks at the x rays I've brought from my last visit to Dr. Frederick. "No sign of fusion yet. Do you know if your surgeon took live bone from deep in your hip? The spine specialists are finding that fuses better."

I have no idea. What an idiot I was to let a general orthopedic surgeon operate on me! The nurse unstraps the coils from my body and puts them back in the box.

"Don't try to carry this yourself," she warns me. Apparently she doesn't see the absurdity of telling me to wear something too heavy for me to lift. She lugs the box out to the car.

"What's wrong?" David asks as he drives off. The tears I've blinked back for the last half-hour are spilling down my cheeks.

"Wait till you see it! It's a portable electric chair!"

"But it really does the trick?"

"So they say." But I know my bones. I won't be hurling this machine off a cliff after three months. I'll be lucky if it works in nine. It's almost nine months since Dr. Frederick sent me to bed last April. I could have had two babies in the time this is taking out of my life.

At bedtime I put on the harness and ask David to help me hate it.

"I think it's kind of cute. Can I get my arms all the way around you? It *is* kind of like hugging an electrified armadillo," he admits.

I lie down on my back. The rigid rubber plates dig into my spine, no matter how I jiggle. Lying facedown is forbidden. It's impossible to lie on my side with all these coils and cords snaking out of me. After three sleepless hours I rip off the harness with a screech of Velcro. David stirs, curls himself around me and goes back to sleep, but I lie there stiff and raging. The monitor clicks off the seconds, the minutes, the hours.

In the morning David goes off to give a final exam. I strap the brace over my pajamas, attach the coils to the brace and to each other, and carry the box to the sofa. The electric outlet is near the floor. Bending's impossible. So's squatting. Groaning, I disconnect the coils, rip them off the brace, plug in the box, strap the coils back on, reconnect them to each other and to the box, and collapse among the sofa cushions. I should have brought a box of Kleenex but I'm not getting up again for anything less than a fire alarm. I wipe my eyes on my pajama sleeve and switch on the machine. How many seconds are there in nine months of eight-hour days? I watch the digital display click off the seconds like a prisoner marking off the days on the cell wall. I *am* a prisoner. I'm disabled. I can't pretend I'm not.

Sniffing, I take the "Social Views" folder off the brass table. I've got to be ruthless with every page that doesn't deserve to go to California. We're leaving next week. I've sorted everything here but these papers clipped together and headed "Jews." I hesitate. There could be bad news here. This is not the morning for bad news. But my other folders are in the bottom drawer of my file. To get them I'd have to take off the Stim and put it on again. So it's going to be Connie on the Jews.

I fan out the pages like a gambler squeezing apart the cards on which he's bet the ranch. Here's one of Connie's forgettable early stories. Schoolteachers are spending the summer picking raspberries for some German Jews with accents as thick as the jam they manufacture. The Jews hold back half a day's wages when their workers are too upset to go back to work after one of them is arrested for murder, but they treat their workers so well that the schoolteachers end the summer "well and strong, with more tan and flesh than we had ever had in our lives." And the really sinister money-grubbers in the story—the man who killed for money and the detectives who come to collect the reward for finding him—are *not* Jews. Clipped to the story is a note that tells me Connie treats Jews the same way in the only other story where she mentions them. I wouldn't call those stories anti-Semitic. In Connie's time, stereotypic treatment of Jews was nearly as routine as the generic use of "man." If I let myself be offended every time a writer made women invisible or Jews mercenary, I could never have made a career of literature.

What else? Copies of the articles Connie wrote for *The Daily Cleveland Herald* in 1871, the pieces Henry Cooper admired. I'd forgotten that one of them was about the Jews of New York City. Apparently Jews were news because Temple Emanu-El was new, and because there were enough wealthy Jews in New York to build what she calls the most magnificent church in America. All places of worship were churches to her, and she raves about this one. Even the worshippers are superior: "a visitor . . . finds but little difference between the temple and many places where Christians worship, excepting, perhaps, the superior courtesy with which he is treated at the temple: a good seat being instantly offered and prayer books politely given by the nearest neighbors." So these Jews are just like anyone else, only nicer.

And more beautiful. Sometimes Connie sees a woman's face "so perfect in its Oriental loveliness that the mind reverts to the ideal pictures of the women of the Bible." A different stereotype, the Beautiful Jewess, the Exotic Other. The "Jewesses of New York" dress in "sweeping velvets and satins, glittering with gems, golden chains and bracelets" that "would overload an American woman"—Jews are clearly not Americans to her—but that seem "not inappropriate to the majestic forms and dark beauty of these daughters of Israel."

She must be looking at the wives and daughters of the Guggenheims and the Bloomingdales, the German Jews who were already making fortunes in America while Russian Jews like my great-grandparents were still trying to escape the czar. I can't tell if this opulent Jewish sexuality made her feel like a dowdy spinster in her plain black dress, or like a lady who detests vulgar displays of wealth.

I detest them. Especially by Jews. Why? It can't be just conspicuous consumption that offends me, because I also hate seeing a stiff wig covering the bald head of a plainly dressed Orthodox Jewish woman because her own hair would distract men from their study of Torah. Why am I more outraged by that sexism than by the sexism that veils Moslem women's heads? Why do I find traditional African or Indian dress attractive, but squirm when I see Orthodox Jewish men in long black coats over their hollow chests and black fedoras above their wispy beards? It can only be because I'm afraid people will think I'm like them. And I want everyone to know I'm a nice assimilated educated mannerly American whose parents just happened to be Jewish. A person they'd like.

I don't like that person. I don't want to know her. I squirm to shift the hard coil to a different place on my spine and turn back to Connie. Here she's saying that the Jewish nation has "so preserved its characteristic outline that you can tell it in an instant no matter where you find it." Uh-oh. Characteristic outline? Like a hooked nose? Does she think she could have detected that "characteristic outline" in my features? All my ancestors were Jews, but I've been mistaken for Irish in Ireland and for Christian in Egypt and for Protestant in New Jersey.

In the back yard, brown oak leaves still hang from their branches though all the other trees are bare. I see those trees the way I first saw them, when a realtor showed me this house in 1958. She wanted to know what church Howard and I attended, so she could tell me where the closest one was. Supposedly.

"We don't go to church," I told her.

"Do you attend a synagogue?"

"No," I said. The truth but not the whole truth. But I'd be damned if I'd let her put me in the position of trying to "pass" as Christian. "We're nonobservant Jews," I said.

Soon after we moved in to this house, right down the street from her own, she gave a party for us. One of our new neighbors had a few drinks and leaned across the piano to ask if I knew that Mary had canvassed every house on the street to see if anyone would mind if "a nice young Jewish couple" moved in.

"If she hadn't asked, nobody would have known the difference," he said. "Your name could be Christian, and you don't look at all Jewish."

"So I've been told."

He expected me to say "Thank you." I was incensed. But I have to admit I like it when supermarket checkers tell me I look like Shirley MacLaine. I would not like being told I look like Golda Meir—not just because she's homely but because she's homely in a distinctively Jewish way. In 1958—maybe even today—realtors were telling people with unambiguously Jewish names and faces the same thing they told blacks: that they "wouldn't be happy" in certain neighborhoods.

"I told the realtor I reserved the right to be unhappy where I pleased," a Jewish woman told me. "I wanted an old Colonial house, but I wound up in a split-level on the south side of town with all the other Jews."

She opened my eyes. Jews and blacks were supposed to ghettoize themselves because their presence in a neighborhood would arouse viciousness in their neighbors, and if rocks were hurled through their windows or crosses burned on their lawns it would be their own fault. I'd heard people say that rape was women's fault because they arouse the uncontrollable lusts of men. Why not lock up the rapists and the racists, I thought, instead of confining the women, the blacks, and the Jews? That must have been the first time I saw the link between racism, sexism, and anti-Semitism.

I shuffle together the papers I've been reading. There's just one more sheet labeled "Jews." "You must have had a fine time with your Israelitish princess at Bergen Point," Connie writes from Cooperstown to the eminent critic who befriended her and helped her sell her first stories. "If you admired the little Israelite, probably you admire Daniel Deronda; the man I mean; not the book. But how, how can you?"

I feel as if I've stuck my finger in an electric socket. How, how could I have sat in the Butler Library at Columbia and read and copied and then managed to forget that ugly crack? I must have heard the unmistakable tone of voice in which she says "Israelitish princess." That's what she really thought of the elegant women at Temple Emanu-El. That's how she would have talked about me behind my back. Abruptly, I feel intensely Jewish. And furious. *This* is the woman I've asked to be my guide? *This* is the woman whose reputation I've worked so hard to restore? The ungrateful bitch! After all I've done for her, look how she's betrayed me, the rotten anti-Semite!

That's the end of our love affair. My parents warned me not to fall in love with a *goy* who'd get me pregnant and abandon me. That's exactly what Connie's done. I'm full of my mission to recover the selves I've abandoned, and I can't do it without her. If I abort it, the year of disability—the years of disability—stretching out ahead of me is no golden opportunity. It's just pointless loss.

Two hours and twenty minutes, says the monitor. Five hours and forty minutes to go. I stare at the familiar crack running across the ceiling. Why do I feel like a Jew only when I'm confronted with blatant anti-Semitism? The rest of the time—and that's most of the time—if you asked me who I am I'd say a woman. A feminist, a Democrat, a professor. At a big party I might say I'm David's wife, and at the PTA I used to say I'm Dave's mother, or Mark's or Leslie's. Those identities are not without their own complications, but they feel like my own. I've chosen them, or at least, like my gender, affirmed them. I've neither chosen nor affirmed Jewishness.

I really don't know why. But look how often I've chosen to avoid Jews! I battled my mother to let me go to a camp where I'd be one of three Jews among two hundred campers, and I went back there for five summers. I bought a house near a forest and a decrepit farmhouse in the Berkshires where no Jews had ever lived. I married David, a non-Jew. But I loved the camp because I could ride horses there every day, and I loved this house for its fireplaces and paneled doors, and I loved the Berkshires for its mountains and lakes, and David because he speaks the language of my soul. Why should I be deprived of these good things because they were to be found among gentiles? I wasn't trying to avoid Jews. At least not consciously.

But it's strange that I should know so much more about the worship of ancient goddesses and of Jesus Christ than I do about Judaism. I've gone three times to Egypt and never crossed the border to Israel. Why? Why are there no Jewish organizations on the list of charities I support? If I'm so outraged by injustice, how come I can overlook what's done to Soviet Jews? Why am I haunted by the ghost of an Episcopalian woman rather than by the ghosts of the millions of Jews murdered by the Nazis?

Because you don't want to feel like a survivor, says Connie's voice in my head. She knows plenty about survivors' guilt. You don't want to be a person who needs to be rescued, she goes on. You want to rescue everybody else. A man from drowning. Brazilians in torture chambers, Nicaraguans in bombed-out hospitals. Your mother. Me.

She's right. I can't stand to feel like a victim. I haven't felt like one since I escaped from my father. Not until today. But I'm a victim only of my own body. Jews have been the victims of everybody: of the pharaohs, Herod, the Inquisitors, the czars, Hitler. I refuse to identify with these victims, but I also refuse to identify with Jews who refuse to be victims but victimize others, like the Palestinians. The Jewishness of people who are neither victims nor victimizers I ignore. Looking away from this long history of pain that belongs to me has left me sitting in spiritual limbo. I can't worship the Goddess any more than I can become a Unitarian. To convert would be to abandon a faith my ancestors died to preserve. To convert would join me to the anti-Semites who tried to force Jews to convert.

Can I get up now?

You think I'm an anti-Semite, Connie's saying. Why do you suppose it took you so long to notice that? You denied it, the same way you've denied your own snobbery, your own Jewishness, your own anti-Semitism.

Me an anti-Semite? It's a full minute before the angry flush leaves my cheeks. All right, Connie. I've stereotyped and avoided Jews at least as much as you have. I admit it. As I do I feel something momentous has happened. Some festering sore I never knew I had is open to drain, some injury like Romeo's lovesickness, a scar that never felt a wound. But mine seems to be a spiritual wound, like the Fisher King's in the Grail legend. An injury that has to heal before the kingdom of my life can be restored.

Look at me, a Jew with her head full of Christian voices! I have no idea how to tell a true voice from a false one. But Connie's voice, her presence, feels at least as real as the electricity pulsing invisibly through my body from one coil to the other.

11

*Not All of Them Will
Love You*

"What smells so good?" Dave lifts his head from the steaming pot. Tomato sauce dots his dark beard. Just in time I stop myself from wiping it off.

"Anchovies, capers, black olives—it's called *salsa puttanesca*, because a prostitute can cook and eat it between customers." He doesn't laugh. "Dress the salad, will you?"

"If you trust me to 'make every leaf glisten' with olive oil before I add the vinegar."

"I trust you." He always teases me about the way I make salad dressing. Why that acid edge in his voice tonight? I dump a mountain of cooked spaghetti into the sauce. David walks in, looking fit in his velour warm-up suit. I've chosen his tennis night to invite Dave for dinner.

"Oh hi, Dave." He shakes Dave's hand. "How's the publishing business?"

"I spent the week negotiating with printers."

We sit at the dining table in the seats we've always occupied. "I thought you were editing books," David says, passing Dave the pasta.

"They keep promoting me out of what I like to do." He piles his plate. "That's why I'm going to Central America next week. I'm thinking of going back there to work."

David steered Dave to his first job in Costa Rica. Our friend Fred Morris needed a managing editor for the human-rights newsletter he founded when the Brazilian military was done torturing him. "It'll be a great experience for your son," David said then, "working for someone just as brilliant and opinionated as he is."

"Going back to work in journalism?" I ask now.

"I'm through asking people to tell me how miserable they are so I can write a story about it," Dave says. Is that a dig at the writing David and I have done about Brazil and Nicaragua? "I've been thinking about working with a priest I met in one of the poorest cantons in El Salvador," he goes on, "but I heard today that my visa application was rejected."

A fist I didn't know was squeezing my stomach starts to relax. I've been reading about the stepped-up bombing of rebel-held areas in El Salvador. But Dave doesn't need a visa for Guatemala or Honduras or Nicaragua. They're not such healthy places either. "Is that the priest from the village where you got caught in crossfire and spent the afternoon in a ditch?" I ask.

"Near there," Dave says shortly.

I forgot the wine. Getting it from the kitchen, I hear David say to Dave, "I'm sure you're disappointed, but it must be gratifying to think the Salvadoran authorities read what you wrote about them." It's tremendously gratifying to me. I'm so proud it's embarrassing. I tear the seal off a bottle of Chianti. "Have you asked yourself why you want to work in Central America," David's asking, "rather than some other place on the globe?"

"Like Newark?" says Dave.

"Or Argentina, or Israel."

"I didn't feel at home in Israel."

"Because you couldn't speak the language?"

"I could learn Hebrew. The Israeli struggle just doesn't feel like my struggle. I don't know why."

The corkscrew goes in crooked. I bring the bottle to the dining room and hand it to David. "Maybe you don't identify with Israelis," I say, "because you didn't grow up identifying with American Jews."

"I never got a chance to identify with any Jews," Dave says curtly. "I wasn't even bar mitzvahed. I really resent it, now that I'm learning what I've missed."

Is that why he's so prickly? He's been going to work an hour early twice a week to study with the Orthodox scholar who edits Judaica books for his company. He'd seem closer to me working with a Catholic liberation theologian in El Salvador than studying with an Orthodox Jew from Brooklyn.

David fishes the mutilated cork out of the bottle and pours me a glass of wine. "Your father and I would have felt like hypocrites sending you to Hebrew school when we didn't believe in God," I say. The defensive tone in my voice irritates even me.

David gets up from the table. "You'll have to excuse me, I need to stretch before tennis. Leave the dishes. I'll do them when I come home." The only time I'm glad to see David leave a room is when Dave is in it.

"I'll do them," Dave says. "Go lie down, Mom."

"In a minute. Want to finish the pasta?"

"I'll put it out of its misery," he says, dumping what's left of it onto his plate. "So tell me, without Judaism how do you answer the fundamental questions about life?"

"Which ones?"

"Well, what's the purpose of my life, if any? By what rules, if any, do I conduct myself? From what moral source, if any, do I derive those rules? To whom or what am I responsible?"

"Oh, *those* questions." Serves me right. I'm the one who urged him to study philosophy. "I just make up my life as I go along."

"But you told me your work on Woolson is making you confront your Jewishness. So you have to answer those questions." He shakes his head at my offer of wine.

"No I don't! Why do I?"

"And you need to know what she believed."

"I know what she said she believed. She was a good Episcopalian who was sure that God knew best and that an afterlife would explain human suffering and set everything right. Of course if I'm right that she killed herself, I have some explaining to do. Or she does."

"How do you explain your agnosticism?"

"I don't even try. Haven't since college."

"That was pretty young to make up your mind for good. Did something happen to you?"

"Something did, actually." I haven't thought of this in years. "In the middle of Kol Nidre services, a young cantor I really liked and respected dropped dead in front of my eyes. He was a Holocaust survivor." I'm seeing the women weeping into their fur collars, the men ashen, the rabbi trembling as he uttered the benediction. I'm spilling wine on the table. "The shock forced me to ask what kind of God would send a man through hell just to kill him off."

"I know how that feels. But sometimes I'll see a tree and be so stunned by its beauty and its intricate connections with everything else on the planet that I practically fall off my bike. Then I rehabilitate God." He smiles. "I'm sure He's grateful. Or She is."

"Any God I can imagine needs a lot of rehabilitating," I tell him. "I'd rather live in a meaningless universe than one governed by a God who'd permit the Holocaust."

Dave tilts his chair back, and I stop myself from telling him he's going to break its legs. "One of the people I am agrees with you. But right next to that card-carrying agnostic is a hard-core mystic."

"What does he think?"

"The mystic? He doesn't think at all. He just experiences something—it's hard to talk about. There's a flash and colors turn liquid and I find myself purring along like a race car over the salt flats. All doubts gone, all questions answered. I'm flowing along with the spiritual force of the universe. Then the moment's over. It makes the rest of life taste like plain noodles after *pasta puttanesca.*" He smiles at me.

"Do you think it's a vision of God?"

"A Unity, I call it."

"Is it something you worship?"

"It doesn't need worship."

"Doesn't sound much like Jehovah."

"I don't think it matters what you call it or how you reach it. I like Jewish tradition for its spiritual power and wisdom."

"You think it's wisdom when rabbis say it would be better to burn the Torah than teach it to women?"

"Women are supposed to have their own ways of cementing their relationship with God."

"Does it cement a woman's relationship with God to have to worship behind a screen so she won't distract men from *their* relationship with God? It makes me furious to see Jews, of all people, putting women in a ghetto!"

"The idea is to keep children's crying where it won't cause distractions."

"Distractions to whom? To the men who are assumed to have a serious relationship with God that women aren't capable of having?"

Why am I so fired up about a relationship I don't want with a deity I don't believe in?

"You don't like any tradition because you grew up resenting all authority," Dave says.

"True. So did you. That's one reason you're going to Central America next week."

"True. And *that's* why you're arguing with me about Orthodoxy, because you don't want to admit you're worried!"

"Your mother didn't raise a stupid child." I stand up and rub my back.

"Come on, Mom, lie down and let me do the dishes."

I plod upstairs to get my Spinal Stim. Dave has my father's love of argument—and mine—but not the terrible insecurity that made my father wield his brains like a battle-ax. I'd have given anything to be able to talk with my father like this. I'm arranging myself and my machine on the sofa when Dave comes into the living room drying his hands on his pants.

"What a fiendish contraption!" he says. "I never imagined it was that big!" He leans over me, investigating the coils and monitor box. David comes running down the stairs with his tennis racquet. He bends over the back of the sofa and gives me a long kiss. "Good night, sweetheart. Have a great trip, Dave." Howard was jealous of my closeness with Dave, too. The door to the garage bangs shut.

The phone rings. It's Ruth. "You're okay?" she asks. "I thought you'd want to know that Mother went to the hospital this afternoon with fibrillations. They're adjusting her medications. I don't think it's terribly serious."

"Does she have a phone?"

"Yes, here's the number."

I dial. My mother answers. "What are you doing in there?" I ask.

She laughs. "Seeing what's for excitements." That's what her mother-in-law used to say when someone would ask her why she wanted to go shopping.

"What are fibrillations, anyway?"

"Irregular heartbeats. I've had them before."

"How are you feeling?"

"Better. Everyone is wonderful to me here."

"Is that a really-truly story," I ask, "or a make-up story because there's a nurse standing right there?"

"Yes!" she says. "How did you guess?"

"Get as much rest as you can. I'll call you tomorrow. I love you."

"I love you too," she says, and hangs up. What we feel for each other is, among other things, undeniably love.

"I should go to Boston," I tell Dave.

"I'll go."

"You're leaving for Central America!"

"You're leaving for California. I'll drive up Friday night after work."

"She'll love that." My mother has always called Dave her E.S.B.—Extra Special Boy. He was born just a month after my father died, and everyone was so happy my baby was a boy I could name after my father. For days I hesitated. I didn't want my father's name echoing in my house. Finally I told myself that David is a beautiful name, that this child's life could redeem my father's. It's doing that.

The next afternoon I'm on the sofa in my Stim when Vicki comes by. She's wearing the red-and-white striped stockings and high-topped purple sneakers that go with her chicken suit. Not a gorilla today.

"I've got a going-away present for you," she says. In the box is a sort of asymmetrical cat's cradle of leather strings tied to a hoop of twisted vine, with a long feather hanging from the center. "It's a Dream-Catcher. I got it from John Dancing Crow, also known as the Shaman of Dreams."

"Where'd you find *him*?"

"In New York, at a workshop. We sat on the floor and drummed. It was supposed to represent the heartbeat."

"What a wonderful gift!" I reach up to give her a hug. "I'll hang it over my bed in California. Though why I'm going three thousand miles away from my friends is more than I can understand."

"There's a reason you're going," Vicki says. "You'll find out what it is."

Sunday night I'm lying in the Stim when Dave calls. "Gram's doing fine. I had to work hard to beat her at gin rummy."

"Thanks for going. I'm glad you're back. Whenever you drive the Mass Pike I think of your car accident." David picks up his book and goes upstairs.

"Me too," Dave says. "It still seems miraculous I wasn't killed." He'd been sleeping with his head away from the door that got crushed. "I keep seeing myself lying on the highway with cars whizzing by me. It felt like some great warm hand had put me down so gently I didn't lose anything but some skin."

"Sometimes I wish God did exist, so I could ask him to keep my children safe."

"They say there are no atheists in fox holes."

"Did you pray when you were lying in that ditch in El Salvador?"

"No." He's silent a long time. Did he hang up? "I've been wanting to tell you—but I couldn't—" His voice is shaking. "I lied about that. There *was* a battle. I got there the day after it happened. People showed me the ditch where they'd lain and listened to their friends dying, and I imagined what it would have been like if I'd been there. But I wasn't."

"It would have been you if you'd been there a day earlier. The danger must have seemed so real." I realize I've never really believed this story.

"You taught me the difference between a 'really-truly' story and a 'think-up' story when I was three. But lots of times I don't tell you the truth. I doctor it to make myself look smarter or more important to you." His words are tight with pain.

If he were here I'd take him in my arms. It's a good thing he's not.

"It sounds like you're doing the first and hardest thing right now, by telling the truth about it."

"It's easiest being by myself," he's saying, "like when I cycle across the country, but sometimes I'm unbearably lonely. I've never been able to sustain a serious romantic relationship because I just can't believe anyone could love the person I really am."

If he feels unlovable it can only be my fault. How can it be my fault? I love him so much I can barely speak. "You think that's why you lie?"

"It must be. Low self-esteem, the classic goddamn fucking reason for everything that's wrong with everyone, right?"

So Dave doesn't suffer from my father's insecurity? Whichever way I twist the Stim digs into my spine. "Right," I say. "I'm just learning how hard it is to tell the truth. If we weren't leaving next week, I might look for a therapist, if only to keep me digging. What about you?"

"Yeah. As soon as I can get up my nerve."

If he goes into therapy, I'll need all my nerve. He's going to find out how angry he is with me. "Thank you for trusting me with this."

"I really don't have anyone else," he says.

That has to be my fault.

That night I dream I'm looking in a mirror. I'm shocked to see that my eyebrows are gray. So is my bushy mustache. The mirror also reflects a woman making a bed where we've slept together. She wants to marry me, but I don't love her. Would it be worth it, I wonder? Or is my loneliness bearable?

194

Not All of Them Will Love You

. . .

I've dreamed I'm a man! I turn on my Itty-Bitty Book Light to write down the dream in my journal. I've never envied men their sexual equipment, dangling in front of them all exposed, only the privileges penises bring. But the man in my dream isn't enviable. He's choosing between loneliness and a loveless marriage. I must be dreaming about lives I haven't lived: being a man, being single. I write several pages about roads not taken when my handwriting turns ragged. I know who that mustached face in the mirror belongs to. Dave.

It was so obvious, like widely spaced letters on a map, that I couldn't see it. I didn't want to see it. I don't want to feel his misery. I never have. I force my hand to keep writing. I pretend my children's lives are wonderful. I pretend their difficulties are minor or temporary. It's a lie. I lie to myself the way Dave lies to me. My children have to be wonderful so I can be their wonderful mother. Dave lies to make himself the wonderful person I need him to be. My lies protect me from his pain the same way they protect me from my own. That pain, his and mine, is here, right now. It's sitting on my chest, squeezing the breath out of me. It's taking up so much room it's a wonder it hasn't shoved David out of bed.

I switch off my light. Long after my body stops shivering I'm still awake. If I'm not sleeping I should be clocking hours in my Stim, but I can't make myself get up and put it on.

The morning sky is that dead gray that means snow, but no snow falls. I take my journal to the sofa. A line catches my eye, a quotation from Adrienne Rich that I copied out months ago: "not all of them will love you, whichever way you choose." The line socks me right through the Stim. I should paint it on the ceiling. If I could give up that preposterous fantasy that I can make everyone love me, my children wouldn't have to prove how wonderful I am.

Back Talk

. . .

David loathes Christmas but he feels like an orphan if nothing marks the day, so we've planned dinner with Jane and Daniel. I stuff some zucchini with creamed spinach and talk David through making a crabmeat dip. While he drives us to Princeton I lie in the back seat, running my Stim off its battery. I leave it in the car. Even convicts get time off on Christmas.

Jane opens the door with its handsome wreath. A black-and-white springer spaniel leaps on us. "To-by!" Daniel says fiercely. A fire is burning in the fireplace, "but we saved the other lights until you got here," Jane says. Tall and slim in her long dress, she turns on the tiny blue and white lights on the Christmas tree. Daniel lights the menorah. The flames flicker in his glasses. He and I sing the Chanukah blessing that I still know as well as the alphabet. Jane and David look on. Acutely, I feel that David's and mine is a mixed marriage.

Over the salmon and hollandaise sauce, Jane asks, "What are you going to be writing on your sabbatical, David?"

"A novel," David says. "My hero's going to track down the history of my natural family. I told you I found out last year that my real grandparents came from Germany. It was on my mother's death certificate. Joan dug it up when she was working in an archive in Ohio. I can't stop wondering about them. You know I've been reading compulsively about Nazi Germany for years."

"Was there Jewish blood in your family?" Daniel asks. He's stopped work on his book on Victorian poetry to write his life as a Jew.

"I don't know," David says.

"Maybe writing this novel, you'll find out why Germany haunts you," I say, taking his hand under the table.

He squeezes it. "*You*'re the haunted one in our family."

He's right. And the ghosts of my buried selves are getting

bolder. What if the ones who've emerged so far are just tiger cubs, and their mother is crouching in the underbrush waiting to spring? Connie could unleash that tigress on me. She did it to Henry James. She loosed on him the reeking breath and the savage teeth of the truth about himself. The ferocious images are his, not mine. They're from "The Beast in the Jungle," his great story about what Connie taught him. In the silver bowl filled with holly I see reflected not Jane's red tablecloth but Connie's yellow armchair. Henry James is sitting in it. He's reading through Connie's papers. He's hurried to her Venice apartment, certain her death was a suicide, anxious to take possession of anything she might have left behind that could expose or incriminate him.

Reading through her notebooks, he finds the germ of the plot of "The Beast in the Jungle": "To imagine a man spending his life looking and waiting for his 'splendid moment,' " Connie had written, "but the moment never comes." He finds his protagonist there too: "Imagine a man endowed with an absolutely unswerving will," Connie had written. "Extremely intelligent, he *comprehends* passion, affection, unselfishness and self-sacrifice, etc., perfectly, though he is himself cold and a pure egoist. He has a charming face, a charming voice, and he can, when he pleases, counterfeit all these feelings so exactly that he gets all the benefits that are to be obtained by them." James stiffens with shock as he recognizes himself in the terrible clear mirror of Connie's gaze. He turns red with anger. Then with shame. Blankly he stares out Connie's window while the ripples quiver on the Grand Canal like the candlelight shimmering on my crystal wineglass.

Connie's words are louder in my ears than the voices of the people sitting around the table with me. Henry James hears her words over the shouts of the gondoliers. He tries to drown them out by remembering words Connie meant for him to see. The "deepest charm of your writings to me," she had written

197

him three years into their friendship, is that "they voice for me—as nothing else ever has—my own feelings; those that are so deep—so a part of me, that I cannot express them, and do not try to . . . your writings . . . are my true country, my real home. And nothing else ever fully is—try as I may to think so."

James had squirmed away from those words. Effusions of a solitary spinster, he'd told himself. But sitting in Connie's yellow armchair, feeling her body's imprint under him and around him, he finally understands. She could see the worst of him, describe him with terrifying precision, and still love him. If he'd been able to accept the treasure she offered him—the love that needs no illusions—he might have saved her life. And she would have saved him from his life as a counterfeit.

Connie was a lonely virgin but she knew how to love in a way that I do not. If I had given my son what she offered Henry, Dave might not be suffering now with his terrible loneliness. I don't trust myself to lift my wineglass.

David is laughing at something Daniel has said. They won't miss me. I go back to Henry. It was ten years after Connie's death before he could transform his sickening shame and horror into art. He created a hero "to whom nothing on earth was to have happened" because "no passion had ever touched him." He stands the man at the grave of the woman who loved him, just as Henry had stood again and again at Connie's grave at the Protestant Cemetery in Rome. That's where the beast springs. "The escape would have been to love her; then, *then* he would have lived." I know the words by heart. "*She* had lived—who could say now with what passion?—since she had loved him for himself; whereas he had never thought of her (ah, how it hugely glared at him!) but in the chill of his egotism and the light of her use."

Is that how I loved Dave? My heart pounds so loud I look up to see if the others can hear it. I saw Dave in the light of his use to me. I made him redeem my father's life and my own un-redeemed fury with my father. Made him the child I could talk to about literature and philosophy and politics the way I could never talk with his father, or with mine. Maybe Dave smoked pot and flunked math to refuse to let me use him that way. The same way Leslie pulled down a shade behind her eyes and went to live with her father to keep me from turning her into the good girl I'd never been able to be. An ache races up one arm, across my chest and down the other arm. I grip the edge of the table as if it were trying to run away.

Chocolate mousse and huge dark strawberries pull me back to the present.

"I'll build up the fire," Daniel says as I hobble into the living room. "You look chilled, like you've seen a ghost." He's smart, Daniel. "I've always been interested in the idea of summoning spirits. I read a lot about spiritualism when I was researching my book on Yeats. You must have studied it when you were writing about Hawthorne."

"I never liked the way he used it. Mostly I ignored it." I slip off my shoes and lie down on the soft white sofa.

"Paranormal phenomena fascinate me." Daniel drops a log on the fire and sparks spurt up.

"A real plunge into irrationality would take courage I don't have."

"I don't think of courage any more as a trait one has," Daniel says, "but as something one builds up to. It took me three full journals of gnashings and thrashings to find the courage to admit I wanted to write autobiography."

"Can I read it?"

"I really didn't write it for anyone but myself, and Jane. It's a howl of anger at my parents for denying me my Jewishness. For sending me to fancy Christian schools where I played Jesus in the Christmas pageant but never even telling me about the

Holocaust. Do you know I'm preparing for my adult confirmation as a Jew? It's only thirty-five years late. I want you and David to be there."

The universe is ganging up on me and I'm sick of it.

Early the next afternoon Sharon arrives. She pulls off her purple down coat that looks just like mine.

"Good grief!" she says. "The Stim is all *that*? No wonder you can't sleep in it."

"If I start to tell you how much I hate it, we won't have time for anything else."

"Today we will! Today you don't have to stop talking to make sure there's enough time for me to talk. This afternoon is our Christmas present to each other."

"I have another present for you." I hold up two short silver necklaces. "While I'm away, I'd like to think of you wearing one of them while I wear the other."

One is a thick twisted chain holding an *ankh*. The Egyptian women in Habu's classes gave me this ancient symbol of rebirth. I haven't worn it much. It looks too much like a cross. The other pendant is two moon crescents framing the goddess's double axe. This one I bought for myself at a Women's Studies conference.

"You don't care which one I take?" Sharon asks, holding one necklace in each hand. "Are you sure? Then I want the moon and the axe. I've seen you wear it so many times that it feels like a piece of you to keep with me. And I like its power!"

The pendant shimmers against her aqua sweatshirt. As soon as I see it I realize she's chosen the one *I* want to keep. "I really want you to have it," I tell her. "But there's a greedy little girl in me who wants to take it back!"

Sharon laughs. "She'll just love the kid in me who wants all your time for myself."

"How do we get rid of these kids?"

"We don't. We teach ourselves to love them."

"I'm amazed I was brave enough to let you see that greedy child in me."

"You know you can't impress me. It's not your accomplishments I see when I look at you. I love you even though I'm mad as hell that you're leaving me for eight months!"

My eyes fill. David's love surrounds me with powerful arms that keep evil at bay, but I wouldn't dare dispel his illusions about me. My children love me, but I'm afraid they'll stop as soon as they figure out what I've done to them. But Sharon just loves me.

"Why weren't you my mother? It would have saved so much trouble!"

"Don't idealize me," she says. "You notice I'm not offering to give the necklace back! Let's clear this infernal machinery away. I have something for you."

I move the Stim's heavy electrical box to the floor and Sharon unpacks a bell, book, and candles from a canvas satchel. "Women's symbols for centuries before the Church took them over," she says, arranging them artfully on the brass coffee table. "And these are the Motherpeace cards. I want to do a Tarot reading for you."

I've never seen a Tarot deck before, and never hoped to see one. Still, I'd go along with something much sillier if Sharon asked me to. She lights the candles. I smell lavender. Then she sits crosslegged at the low table and hands me a stack of round cards, too big to hold in one hand. "First shuffle them slowly and thoughtfully. That's right. Then cut them very deliberately. Now turn over the top card. It signifies the general influence covering you right now." It's an infant bursting from a fiery egg, its creative energy pulsing to the edges of the card. "The Ace of Wands! What more could you ask for? It's the perfect card to launch a journey of self-discovery."

"I hate that word," I say, "that and 'self-exploration.' 'If I am for myself alone, what am I?' "

"Have you forgotten the first part of that aphorism? 'If I am not for myself, who will be for me?' Hillel's wisdom is in the balance."

"If there's one thing I'm learning about myself, it's that I'm off balance. What's the next card about?"

"The root. It's about your foundation, the set of your unconscious mind."

I lean on my elbow and turn over the Six of Disks. A woman is stroking the exact spot on a man's back where my bone graft is. "It's about healing, isn't it? I couldn't be more conscious about that."

"What might be unconscious is knowing you're the one who does the healing as well as the one who needs to be healed," Sharon says. "Did you notice the woman is stroking the man's head as well as his back?"

I hadn't. "No doubt my head needs healing as much as my spine."

"The next card is about that—about your consciousness."

It's the Daughter of Wands, a woman wildly leaping, a unicorn running, birds flying across a rocky landscape. "All that freedom," I say. "Doesn't look much like me these days."

"Look at those arid rocks. She's finding power in a desert. Maybe your desert is your lack of trust in your body."

"With excellent reason. What's the next one about?"

"The near future."

I turn over a picture of a figure hanging upside down from the branch of a tree. A great snake twined around the tree forms a noose that holds the victim's foot.

"I've never gotten that card," Sharon says. She flips through the book that explains the symbols. "In most decks it's called the Hanged Man, but here it's Artemis the Hanged One in her sacred grove. She's surrendering herself voluntarily to death and resurrection, it says, the way Inanna did when she descended to the Underworld. That goddess really is after you, isn't she?"

"The way she's hanging there reminds me of the 'parrot's perch,' " I say in a shaky voice. "That's one way they tortured people in Brazil."

Sharon turns the page. "You see that golden halo around the figure?" I hadn't noticed. "It says that's the ecstasy that comes with relinquishing control and listening to the Goddess Within. I guess it's not just torture. Hanging like that must give you a new point of view."

"I already have a new point of view—the horizontal one." I lie back on the sofa cushions. My shirt is plastered to my back.

"When you get this card in a reading, it's a call to turn deliberately to your higher self."

"What's that?"

"Something like that goddess in your dream, maybe. The one way up on the grandstand who said you'd stolen something from her."

"Stolen something from my higher self? That doesn't make any sense. Let's finish this so you can do your cards."

"Hopes and fears is next."

I turn over the Ten of Swords. Women are leaping off a cliff ahead of the invaders. I think of Masada, where Jews threw themselves to their deaths rather than be captured. Of Connie's suicide multiplied by ten. "I can see the fears, all right. But where are the hopes?"

"The book says it's about sacrificing the self to preserve it from a greater peril. I'd say it's about slaying the giant Should who tells you what you ought to be. Killing him feels like jumping off a cliff."

"It sure does. Especially when you see what your false ideals have done to your children." I've asked her to recommend a therapist for Dave.

"The worst thing we do is fail our children," Sharon says, "and it doesn't help that we can't help doing it. But you must have given Dave something extraordinary for him to trust you with his naked soul. That's something for you both to build on." I sigh. The Stim won't let me take a deeper breath. "Your last card's about the outcome."

I turn over the Six of Swords, women flying together amidst roses and knives. "You and me," I say. "Passion and truth. I have to admit that some of these cards are right on target. Do you actually believe in what they say?"

"You could say I pay respectful attention."

"I'm not looking for something to believe in," I tell her, flopping back on the pillows. "Not Judaism or Goddess-worship or any other system of faith I've ever heard of. But for years I've been telling myself that one of these days when I had nothing more pressing to do, I'd see if I could develop the spiritual side of myself. I've developed my mind so I could teach and write, and my body so I could swim and play tennis. But the spiritual part of myself is still a baby! It's not just young. It's stunted. You know, Sharon, of all the desires I've ignored and all the pain I've denied, I think the biggest secret I've kept from myself is my hunger for a spiritual life."

Two days later the mail brings an envelope from Dave. It's not a letter, just a photocopy of a page from a book he's editing about a Silesian Jew in the seventeenth century. A priest turns him down when he tries to convert to Christianity because his refusal to take myth literally shows his Jewishness is ineradicable. In the margin Dave has written, "Thought this might interest you. David." What interests me most is my son's signature. He does call himself "David" on the phone now. He gave up his name when I remarried and we had to distinguish between the two Davids. No, he didn't give it up. I took his name away from him. I couldn't possibly have called my husband "Dave" because my father was called "Dave." So I sacrificed my son's identity to my husband and to my father. In the midst of the sadness that fills me rises a fierce gladness that my son has taken back his own name.

12

Why Literary Women Break Down

*A*ny minute the Hound of the Baskervilles is going to leap out of that mist," David says.

It's eight in the morning on January second. We're walking past plants I've seen only in California and whose names I've never learned—great spiky blue heads on tall thin stalks, lilies that look like orchids. We squint at the thermometer by the swimming pool. Eighty-three degrees! The air can't be more than forty-five. That explains the Baskerville effect. Shivering, we strip off our sweat suits and hurry into the water. David surfaces.

"It's not the English moors," he says, shaking water from his hair like a Labrador. "It's not even California. It's Shangri-La!"

I swim slowly and painfully. On my last lap I turn on my back. The mist has dissolved in the sun. Gigantic palm trees are waving against a brilliant blue sky. It's probably glorious.

David is sitting blissfully on a stream of bubbles in the

Jacuzzi. "I want you to interpret the dream I had last night," he says as I join him. "Here it is in its entirety. Ready? I'm returning to the public library here in Palo Alto—two enormous apes! I'm leading them by the hand. Or the paw—whatever apes have."

I sputter with laughter. "Are they overdue?"

"I don't know, but they're perfectly docile."

"Are they the two books on American fiction you abandoned when you met me? Maybe they were monkeys on your back."

"And now that I'm writing fiction myself I have them in hand? Not bad!"

After the freedom of the pool, back in our apartment the Stim feels as heavy as one of David's apes. I plug myself in and settle on the bed with a folder of photocopies. As long as I can't sit long enough to write, I'm going to read my way through every word Connie published. What a dreary title: "Ballast Island—A Story of Lake Erie." Must be one of her historical potboilers. No, it's fiction. Elizabeth gets mad at Frederick and sets off across Lake Erie alone in her rowboat. Of course a storm comes up: "It was all Lake Erie against one pair of rounded arms." Those arms are strong enough to steer her boat four miles to Ballast Island. But if she's going to land on its narrow beach and not be swept to her death in the open lake she has to row across the current, against the wind:

> She seized the oars tightly, and, bracing her feet, turned the skiff short to the left, bending double with her effort to force the boat broadside to the wind, across the current. . . . But the well-developed physique, the superabundant vitality and electricity that tormented her in the idleness of peace, gained the victory in this war with the elements, and, panting for breath, with singing noises in her head and blood-spots dancing before her eyes, Elizabeth Pyne beached the

skiff with a last tremendous stroke, and, gaining the higher
ground behind, sank exhausted on the grass.

Nice. Nice. Connie makes me believe in those currents and
winds. And look how she celebrates women's muscle! In her
day a strong woman was a freak. Ladies didn't rescue themselves. This one's no superwoman, though. She's "exhausted
and miserable, and on the verge of hysterics; but of course she
could not have hysterics all alone, no one ever did." She drags
herself around the island until she stumbles on the lighthouse.
"Then she had her hysterics." Very nice. We needed some irony
after the heroics. Now what?

She meets a shapeless woman with yellow eyes, hair, and
skin. "Are you the lighthouse keeper's wife?" Elizabeth asks.

" 'I'm the keeper; there ain't no other that I know of.'

'You live here?'

'Yes.'

'Alone?'

'Yes.'

'Why?'

'Because I want to.' "

A woman lighthouse keeper? She must be the only one in fiction. She calls herself "Miss Jonah" and she fills her lighthouse
with flowers "in boxes, pots, and baskets, on shelves, on the
floor, hanging from the ceiling, and climbing over the plastered
walls." She wades into the water up to her waist to drag Frederick's boat ashore. Then she tells the young lovers, clasped in
each others' arms, "Well, folks, when you get through, we'll go
back to the house. I'm a little damp myself." I love Connie's
prickly spinsters.

David comes in with two cups of coffee and sits on the bed.
"What do you remember about Jonah?" I ask him.

"A lot of swallowing up and vomiting out."

"Not enough. I'll go to the library after my lunch with Mary.
It's only a five-minute walk from Tressider."

In November I could walk an hour without pain. In December my adhesions dragged me back to a half-hour. Then twenty minutes. This morning even with Valium I had trouble with the ten-minute walk to the pool. I'd better get to the library while I still can. Gloomily, I drive onto the Stanford campus and park behind the student center. There's Mary's bike. I can tell it from the dozens parked in front of Tressider Union by its oddly curved high handlebars. From here her trim figure looks like a student's, but when we get close enough to hug I see how pain has marked her face.

"The only drugs that work make me loony," she says as we wait in line for stir-fried vegetables and rice. She's struggled with arthritis since her twenties.

"Do you think there's a conspiracy by the medical establishment to keep women from thinking straight?"

"The worst part for me is knowing that every letter I type is one less letter I can ever type. The joints in my fingers are wearing out."

"Jesus. But you're writing. How are you doing it?"

"I'm dictating," she says. She can barely lift her plate from her tray to the table. "I'm paying a typist ten dollars an hour to transcribe the tapes. Of course I can't afford it on a professor's salary, and it's murdering my style. Some days I'm too depressed to write. I'm never going to get better, Joan. It's just a question of how fast I get worse. Some days—." I start to squeeze her hand, then remember, take hold of her arm gently. "How about you? How are you managing?"

"I haven't figured out how to write at all, except for journals and a few notes on what I'm reading. Lying down, I can only see the one page in my hands."

"You have a laptop computer, don't you?"

"Yes, with a lot of notes in it, but flat on my back I don't have a lap. I've tried resting the machine on my stomach, but even on pillows, it's too heavy for my spine."

"The surgical supply store in town rents all kinds of stuff,"

Mary says. "Maybe they could figure something out for you. Honestly, half the women writers I know are disabled or fighting cancer. We spend most of our time trying to support one another."

I take a mouthful of rice and bean sprouts. " 'Why do literary women break down so?' That's what Connie asked a friend."

"Good question! She thought women broke down more than men?"

"Apparently. She says her friend Frances Hodgson Burnett had 'nervous prostration' every time she finished a book. For six months she couldn't call things by their right names. Connie was completely out of her head when she finished her first novel. When she was finishing her other books, she couldn't find a chair or a bed that felt right or food she could eat. She called it 'mental exhaustion.' "

"I'd call it an anxiety attack."

"It must have been that too. Anxiety that she'd revealed too much of herself. Certainly anxiety about competing with Uncle Fenimore and Henry James."

"At least she wasn't married to them," Mary says. "It takes me six months of agony to write an article that John could polish off in a month. Of course *he* doesn't feel any rivalry between us."

"Neither does David. Neither do I! I've forbidden myself to know that I could ever possibly compete with anyone I love."

Mary picks up her teacup with both hands. "Lots of women hobble themselves to protect their relationships."

"Do you think that's what we're doing?" I ask. "Feminists like us? Settling for sympathy because rivalry is unbearable?"

"But what we want is recognition as equals."

"And to earn that recognition we have to work all the time because our best is never good enough." I lean forward on my elbows. "Mary, do you think our bodies break down because we don't know any other way to control how hard we work?"

"God, I hope not. I don't want to blame the victim. If I think of my arthritis as my own fault, I'll lose what sanity I have left."

"Charlotte's work kept her alive, didn't it?" Mary has been working for years on a biography of the German painter Charlotte Salomon.

"I think so. She painted her way out of despair just in time for the Nazis to murder her."

"What does it say about us, choosing these suicidal women as our subjects?"

Mary looks across the room of packed tables. She pauses a long time. "I don't think I could write about a woman who found it easy to do her work," she says finally. "Not a heroine who blew up trains or rescued people or wrote ten great novels. What would she be a model for? Something I'm never going to be." She turns her tired eyes on me. "Connie and Charlotte—they kept on going and kept on going, right through their despair. They're out there, making space for us."

"Then we'd better figure out some way to tell their stories."

Slowly I walk between terra-cotta buildings with red tile roofs to the larger of Stanford's libraries. I pull out Bibles and commentaries and spread them on a high table next to my notes. What do you know, Connie stood Jonah on his head! Jonah ran from God; Miss Jonah ran from a man. Sailors threw Jonah overboard; Miss Jonah threw herself overboard. She heaved her clothes into a river to make the man think she'd drowned. Jonah falls into the jaws of the whale; Miss Jonah chooses her lighthouse on Ballast Island. "I like it," she says. "It's lonely, but I'm best alone." While Jonah's lamenting, she's filling her lighthouse with flowers. He's passive, she's active. And Henry James says Connie's spirit is singularly conservative?

My right leg buckles. I reach under my shirt and tighten my

brace. My body releases a flood of fluid. It can't be my period. It just finished. What's ahead of me, a life in Pampers?

My wet pants chafe my thighs as I walk slowly out of the library, clutching my notes. Sun-bronzed students jog past and bike around me. A young woman maneuvers her wheelchair expertly past me. I turn and watch her closely. When I finally find my car, I make two wrong turns and end up on the wrong side of the enormous campus.

David's out. I shower and force myself back into the Stim. It makes my lunch rise in my throat. Back to Ballast Island. Frederick's asking Miss Jonah if it isn't dreary and lonely on the island in winter: "God knows it is!" she exclaims. Elizabeth kisses her. "It is so long since any one has kissed me," says Miss Jonah, "so long since any one has called me dear!"

Damn! This independent lighthouse keeper is just another lovesick spinster! What good is she to me? Now she's telling Elizabeth, "It isn't easy to be dead before you've died." Now she's pacing the beach, trying to swallow her misery. She wants to die on her island and be forgotten. "The heart knoweth its own bitterness," she says. Connie said that too, more than once, in her letters. That passionate young oarswoman with broad shoulders like mine turned into that bitter old woman. But Connie is more than the sum of these two women. She's the artist who crafted this stunning story. Did shaping her pain dilute its bitterness? Would writing dilute this bitter new taste in my throat?

I tear off the Stim and drive to the surgical supply store. They have a huge display of incontinence pads. I ignore them. Here's an elaborate gadget that holds a book or papers at any height and at any angle. It's not for rent, only for sale, and it costs seventy-five dollars. I'm not ready to make such a big commitment to disability. They have different kinds of hospital-type bedside tables. The sight of them makes me sick. But one of them tilts to various angles and it has a small metal lip that just might hold my computer. I can rent it by the week. They'll deliver it this afternoon. I drive home along the avenue of royal palms that cuts through the Stanford campus. I'm exhausted and my legs are burning. I figure I've walked a quarter of a mile.

David greets me cheerfully. "The New Jersey realtor just phoned—they've rented our house till September!"

"That's good." I don't care if they've rented it till kingdom come.

David takes a hard look at me. "What's wrong?"

I fall into his arms, sobbing. "I peed in my pants in the library. Even taking Valium I can barely walk. And then I can't read. I can't work lying down, and I have to spend eight hours a day lying in that goddamn Stim! If I can't work, I'm going to lose my mind!"

He leads me to the bedroom and sits me down on the bed. He takes off my shoes and closes the drapes. He finds soothing music on the radio. Brings me two Bufferin and a glass of water. Tucks pillows under my knees and sits beside me, stroking my hair. I hate all this kindness. I hate being the person who needs it. Connie's right. "The heart knoweth its own bitterness."

The doorbell wakes me. It's the man delivering my bedside table. It looks too low. I strap on the Stim and lie down, a huge beached whale. The table hits the top coil. I knew it would. The man raises it to its highest adjustment. Still too low. I bite my lip. Maybe if I lie flatter in the bed? I adjust the pillows and the table clears me by a quarter inch. David brings my laptop computer and rests it against the narrow metal lip of the tilted table. The lip is just wide enough to brace the machine. I can barely see the screen. I shift position. The table jiggles and the hinged lip collapses and the computer slides onto my stomach.

Furiously, I blink back tears. "Maybe we could tape the lip so it stays up," David says. He gets some Band-Aids. They work if

I don't wiggle. He signs the rental receipt and lets the man out while I turn on the computer and stick in the program disk. Instead of a nice blank screen I get an error message. I turn the computer off, wait a minute and try again. Same message. Could the computer have crashed? No. Not today. Hysteria is ballooning in my throat. I swallow it. Think. Think.

"Could the computer be incompatible with the Stim?"

"You're asking *me*?" David's still using a typewriter.

How did I wander into this nightmare world of mad robots? I switch off the Stim, switch on the computer. The computer boots up. I ask it to retrieve a file; it does.

"But the whole point was to write while I'm clocking hours in the Stim!" David shakes his head. My eyes fill. *Think.* Maybe it's just booting up that's the problem. All my disks are backed up. Gingerly I switch on the Stim. Nothing explodes. I type "This is a test this is only a test" and the computer passes the test. "But why is it chiming like that? Every second. It never did that before."

The computer is making audible every volt of electricity pulsing through my body! Sympathetic vibrations between my body and the words I type on the screen. Every word coming straight from my bones. Good.

"It's okay?" David asks. "Great! Maybe you should call the Stim people, though, and make sure the Stim won't damage the computer, or vice versa." He brings me the phone and reads me the 800 number off the Stim monitor. I'm switched from department to department before I find someone who understands what I'm talking about. He laughs.

"That's a new one!" he says. "One woman heard her refrigerator broadcasting the local police dispatches whenever she walked through her kitchen wearing her Spinal Stimulator. They do make some bizarre electronic connections. Your machines won't hurt each other. Just be sure to back up all your work. By the way," he goes on, "I've got your records on my computer screen. You're nearly due to have your monitor printed out and reset."

"I've got the number of someone in San Jose," I say.

"I'd rather see you go to San Francisco."

"It doesn't matter who checks the monitor, does it?"

"They'll check you too," he says. "Go to San Francisco. They've got an outstanding spine center. Your last x rays weren't great."

I call the spine center and make an appointment two weeks away. I call my mother. She's just home from the hospital.

"How are you feeling?"

"The same, the same," she says. "And you?"

"The same," I lie. Maybe she's lying too. "I'm seeing a specialist in San Francisco soon. Maybe I'll ride a cable car!"

"In your condition? Oh, Joan, I wish you wouldn't."

I write "Joan I wish you wouldn't" on the pad of paper in my hand. Around the words I draw a ring of asterisks to match the lights going on in my head. "I wish you wouldn't badger me," she used to say in just this resigned tone of voice. I wish you wouldn't talk back to your father. Or teach while your children are small or divorce Howard or marry David. I wish you wouldn't, but I know you will.

I'm sitting in the Jacuzzi. A woman asks me how long I'm staying in California. "I'm here for a few months recovering from spine surgery," I say.

Why did I say that? I could have said I was here working on a book. I must be getting used to a new identity as a disabled person. I get out of the Jacuzzi. A cloud covers the sun. I want to get back to the apartment for a hot shower, but hurrying, I discover, is a privilege of the able-bodied.

That night I dream I'm in London. I take a wrong turn and find myself lost. I ask someone for directions and he gives me a map marked to show where Leslie is staying. He tells me to phone her. Anxiety flashes through me: something's wrong and she needs help.

I wake wanting to call Leslie but she's on vacation and I don't know where she is. All day I think about her. That evening she phones from Florida. She's been visiting Howard's mother. Early this morning she found her grandmother on the floor, not moving or speaking.

"She's had a small stroke." Her voice is shaky.

"How's she doing?"

"They think she'll be okay." I tell her my dream. "You're psychic!" she says. "Something was very wrong and I sure needed help. I didn't react like a medical student at all. I fumbled around trying to find her doctor, calling my father, looking for her friends—finally I called an ambulance."

"Maybe you're psychic too—arriving the day before she took sick. What if she'd been alone?"

"She's the one who's psychic. Did you know she's a phenomenal gambler? She knows which numbers are going to come up. Probably she had a hunch she was going to get sick."

"And sent you a telepathic message so you came to see her? And then you sent me one, so I dreamed you were in trouble. And I sent you one, so you phoned. But none of us knew we were doing anything at all!"

"Messages like that are probably flying around all the time," Leslie says. "We don't know about them because we don't check. It's funny, I've always known things I don't really know."

"Didn't you catch hell from a physics teacher for leaping to right answers you couldn't explain?"

"She wanted to know how I'd figured out the answer, and I couldn't tell her. I got so mad when she thought I was cheating! But maybe I was."

"You think someone was whispering the answers in your ear?"

216

"That's how it felt."

"I sometimes feel that Connie's putting words in my head. You think we're crazy, hearing voices?"

"I've seen psychotic people who hear voices," Leslie says. "That's different."

"What if they're hearing what's really there, and the rest of us are stuffing our ears with wax?"

"Well, let me know what you hear."

"Maybe I won't have to tell you. Maybe you'll just know."

The next day it's raining. I'm sick of reading, sick of taking notes, sick of myself, sick of David's sympathy. I flip through the files I've brought from New Jersey, pull out one marked "Body." It's full of notes on Connie's rowing and hiking, her appearance and sensuality, her deafness and illnesses. Maybe she can teach me something about putting up with my body. I take the folder to the bed and climb into my Stim.

Here's a letter about some "infernal" pain in her head that made her think she'd be "mad, or dead, before morning." It's February of 1892. In March she'd turn fifty-two. In less than two years she'd be dead. I'm fifty-two now. Where will I be in two years? I heave my thoughts back to Connie. "Neurotic" is the word the English doctor uses for her pain. Connie thinks it's from the artificial eardrums she's been trying, but they're worse than her deafness. "I cannot long stand this sort of pain," she tells her friend Dr. Baldwin. "It is only by constant reading— forced reading—and by sleeping draughts that I get on at all. That sounds rather bad, doesn't it. And probably I don't really mean it. Very likely if the house should take fire, I should be the first to make a desperate effort to escape."

Baldwin would know this was a cry for help. He'd worry about an infection so near the brain. But what could he do? Connie was in Oxford. He was in Florence. Even now it's not a simple trip. You have to take a train to Pisa, a flight to London, another train to Oxford. That's how David and I did it in 1982. Florence in early summer had become a sauna, so we rented a funny house in the old red-light district of Oxford. We must have ridden our bicycles twenty times past the house on Beaumont Street where Connie had lived through such "infernal" pain. I'd never heard of her then.

Last summer, David and I went back to Oxford for a day. I found Connie's house and rang the doorbell. No one answered. A book of old photographs showed that parts of Oxford had hardly changed since Connie lived there.

I look out the window at rain beating flat the blue spiky flowers whose name I still haven't learned. In Oxford, rain would be streaming down the blackened spires of the ancient colleges—Christ Church, Trinity, Worcester. I switch off my Stim, turn on my computer, turn my Stim back on, and watch myself setting off on foot from the Oxford railroad station, the wind tugging at my umbrella.

It's not far to the gray medieval wall that bounds Worcester College. Here's where I turn right onto Beaumont Street. It's clogged with trams. A horse-drawn carriage splashes through a puddle and transfers the cold water to my legs. Number 15 is across from the Ashmolean Museum, one of a row of handsome sandstone houses. It has an elegant doorway with half-columns, a large fanlight, even a broken pediment. Connie's landlady answers my knock.

"I'm a friend of Miss Woolson's," I say.

"You've come at last! I've been terribly concerned about her." She takes me into a long narrow hall that ends at a long narrow garden where trees drip with rain. "Let me have your coat and umbrella. I'll bring tea right up to Miss Woolson's sitting room."

Nervously I walk up the narrow stairway and knock on the door. Connie is kneeling on the rug in front of the fire. She has a game of solitaire spread out on an atlas propped on her knees. Something smells awful. It must be those linseed poultices on the tray beside her. Her weary face is stained with tears.

"The tears are not serious," she says, smiling. "It is only the pain that forces them out. Sometimes, I can even laugh at myself."

Maybe she can, but I can't. I've never seen anyone more forlorn. She takes an ear trumpet from a table and sits in one of a pair of chairs near the fire.

"It is only old friends, you know, who will take the trouble to speak in a trumpet," she says. "But it doesn't matter, since I like so few people. My smile is the basest hypocrisy!"

Her smile looks ironic, not hypocritical. I want to be one of the few people she likes. I want to give her the loving comfort David gives me, but I can't even give her the antibiotic and painkiller and hearing aid she needs.

To reach her trumpet I have to pull my chair so close our knees almost touch. "I hope you'll like the book I brought you," I say carefully into the brass horn. She winces. I must have spoken too loudly. She looks at the book I hand her, with my name printed just below hers on the gold-and-white cover.

"Oh, I always like books," she says, as if my offering this one to her was nothing special. "I have given up trying not to accumulate them! The truth is that they are my companions. Where other people are talking, I must read."

How can I make her respond to this book, to me? I can't. Any more than I could make my mother respond to it, or to me. It was a mistake, coming here.

The landlady carries in a tray of tea and hot buttered scones. I pour the tea and carry a cup across the room to Connie. Unless I'm sitting right beside her talking into the trumpet, I can't talk to her. That's why books have to be her companions. If she sits in a room where people are talking and laughing, all she hears is what the person beside her chooses to repeat into her ear trumpet. For the first time I understand how much she's lost—not just talk but music and theater, the bells of Oxford and the rich music of birds, even the significant rattle of an oncoming tram. My anger softens.

"I understand you're unable to proceed with your next book," she says. "Of course you don't suffer the great drawback of deafness, and the lonely life, that are my lot. But I would not in the least attempt to say that life ought to be easy for you—for the heart knows its own bitterness and cannot always explain it."

Suddenly she gasps. Tears roll down her cheeks and she claps her hand to her left ear. She gestures to a tray that holds a little brown bottle, a glass of water and a spoon. I bring it to her. "Laudanum," she says. "It will put me to sleep, I'm afraid, but it's the only thing that stops this infernal pain."

Drug therapy hasn't improved much. She measures drops into the glass and drains it. I help her to the horsehair sofa and wring out a napkin in the pitcher of warm water on the tea tray. She lets me wash away her tears as if she were my child.

She says softly, "I have a horror of being ill—ill a long time, over here all alone. I don't in the least mind dying, you know, if one could be sure to die, and have it over."

I feel exactly the same way. Death doesn't terrify me. It's not being able to die when you need to that's horrifying. I cover her with the large shawl draped on the back of the sofa, and sit on a stiff chair beside her. The laudanum has relaxed the furrows of pain between her eyes, though their traces remain, like the creases between my mother's eyes when she'd take off her adhesive butterfly. The furrows between Connie's eyes aren't my fault. I didn't put them there by doing things she wishes I wouldn't.

"Why don't you write a different book?" Connie says drowsily. "Something about you and me."

"You wouldn't mind?"

"Having you work out the puzzles of my life, and yours? Joan, I wish you would."

That's what I came to Oxford to hear.

The rain has stopped. I strip off the Stim and go out. Shaggy strips of old bark hang from the lower branches of a eucalyptus tree like the strands of a fright wig. The new wood is perfectly white, like a newborn infant's fingers. The line of trees leads to Oak Creek. It shifts, as I walk slowly along it, from noisy ripples to smooth pools. Every obstacle—round stones, jagged stones, thick reeds—makes the water behave differently. The still pools are boring. What the water does when it's obstructed is what's interesting. Maybe what's interesting about me is what I do when I'm impeded.

Coming back into our building I see a sign: DREAM LECTURE TONIGHT. WILLOW ROOM—7:30. After dinner I tell David I'm going to investigate. "But don't bother missing me. I'll probably be back in fifteen minutes."

The speaker is one Doctor Hillevi Ruumet. She's an attractive woman with curly brown hair, about my age, dressed the way I would dress if I were giving this lecture—tweed jacket, tailored skirt, interesting earrings. The audience is some ten women and two men, most of us in sneakers and sweat suits. Doctor Ruumet tells us she did her doctoral research on dreams, but drifted away from traditional clinical psychology toward Jungian work because she was interested in the way dreams help people grow. What she says about the importance of dreaming for psychological health isn't news. Then she surprises me.

"We can reenter our dreams," she says. "If a child has a nightmare, after you calm her down and hear her out you can suggest she go back and ask the monster what it wants. Perhaps it just wants to play."

221

"I've had dreams where something killed me," a woman says.

"Dreams like that are terrifying," Doctor Ruumet says, "but it helps to realize they mean new beginnings. They tell you you're ready to let some part of yourself die so something new can be born."

I think of Artemis the Hanged One, submitting to death. I think of the eucalyptus trees renewing themselves. They led me to the creek, even to this lecture. Maybe it's a good omen. I could use one. I stand in the back of the room until my legs ache. Then I sit a few minutes until my back hurts. Then I stand some more. I like the way this woman deals with her audience, inviting questions, responding thoughtfully, sometimes wittily. When the lecture is over I introduce myself.

"I wish I were going to be here longer than two months," I tell her. "I've been dreaming furiously for months."

"You must be going through a major transition," she says. "Two months' work on dreams could be fruitful."

"Do you have a couch? I know you're not a Freudian, but I'm recovering from spine surgery and can't sit."

"We could work that out," she says, and gives me her card.

The next afternoon David goes off to play tennis. After days of hanging around the courts looking for partners, all he could turn up was a game of doubles with a man and two women in their eighties. Now he shambles in, half-crawling, imitating his geriatric partners. Then he collapses on the bedroom floor. He isn't acting. "What happened?"

"I don't know," he groans. "I crouched for a low volley and something snapped in my back. I thought I'd been shot."

I climb out of the Stim and get a big bag of peas from the freezer. I wrap it in a dishtowel and drop to my knees so I can slide it under David's back. Then I bring him pillows to put

222

under his head and knees, Bufferin, a glass of water. Ever so graciously.

"Looks to me like an open-and-shut case of spine envy," I tell him.

"But not now, and not here, three thousand miles from our chiropractor!"

The Yellow Pages list dozens of chiropractors. One of them takes x rays and tells David he's made a major mess of his back that will take about a month to heal. So now while I'm lying in my Stim eight hours a day, I have company for fifteen minutes out of every hour while he lies on his frozen peas. A few days later I leave him there while I go to my first appointment with Hillevi Ruumet.

"Tell me about your injury," she says, "but describe it in active terms. Just for a moment imagine it's something you've done rather than something that's happened to you."

It takes me a minute to find the beginning of the thread that's led me here. "I've snapped off the fifth lumbar vertebra in my spine," I say slowly. I hear my words with a therapist's ears. There's another voice in my head, annotating my words. Is it Connie's? *You've disconnected essential parts of yourself,* it says. "My detached vertebra didn't settle in one spot," I go on, choosing my words very carefully. "It kept moving back and forth." *Just like you,* says the voice, *teaching classes, forming committees, organizing demonstrations, giving talks, raising money, writing articles, leading delegations.* "I tried to stabilize myself by putting out bone spurs," I say, "but they crushed my nerves until I couldn't walk." STOP, *you said to yourself. Just stop.* "A surgeon cut away the bone spurs and transplanted bone from my hip to fuse my vertebra to my spine. So far, my spine is not accepting the bone graft." *You hate to accept help, even from yourself.* "My nerves are swollen"—*with your own self-importance: if you don't save the world, who will?*—"and scarred, and shreds of scar tissue have gotten stuck to my bones. They yank and tug

223

and set off spasms in my legs." *You're still attached to that hyper-active life. That attachment is crippling you.*

I'm stunned. "Do you think I'm responsible for what's happened to me?"

"No. We're not responsible for our illnesses. But the body is eloquent nevertheless. Close your eyes. Can you visualize your bone spurs? How do they look?"

"Like the tentacles of a sea anemone. More like an octopus." I watch them grow and sway and surround and crowd and squeeze the nerves that feed my legs. It's like watching the giant squid crush the ship in the old movie version of *Twenty Thousand Leagues Under the Sea*. My chest gets tight.

"Stroke them gently," Hillevi says.

"I can't. They're thrashing around. They make me sick."

"Thank them for trying to help, and tell them their help is no longer necessary."

Gradually their wild waving slows. They droop, they hang limp. I make myself stroke them.

"Your body is not your enemy, Joan. It will do its best for you if you ask it to cooperate. You need to love it—the body you actually have, not the perfect body you wish you had."

I open my eyes and dry my upper lip on my sleeve. "Have you ever known a woman who loved her body?"

"Not many. We have a lot to unlearn."

I see myself stuffed into my mother's size six dress. I see myself waddling through the Stanford library in wet pants. I see Mary's hands. "If I can't heal my body until I learn to love it—"

"For your body to heal, your detached vertebra needs to fuse with the rest of your spine, right? And that will happen when your spine integrates bone transplanted from your hip?" I nod. "There's an amazing resemblance between that process and what Jung calls individuation. To become whole, we have to integrate the rejected parts of ourselves into consciousness."

"That's exactly what I've been trying to do ever since my

back broke down," I say. "So why am I getting worse instead of better?"

"Maybe our business together is to explore those rejected parts and find out why they're not fusing with the rest of yourself."

"But if I'm not responsible for my condition—"

"Your psyche can only do what's doable. Some things aren't. I can never be an opera singer. You couldn't live without kidneys. But your psyche seems to have helped stop you in your tracks. Maybe it can help you get back on a new track."

God, I hope so.

13

The Healthiest Woman
in New Jersey

$\mathcal{W}$e need a picture of your pain," says the receptionist at
Saint Mary's Spine Center. On drawings of the human
body I shade the right groin, right leg, left leg, upper back. Next
page: what relieves the pain? Lying down. What makes the
pain worse? Walking. Standing. Sitting. Swimming. Making
love. Turning over in bed. Cooking. Washing dishes.

The person who filled out this form is crippled.

A fit-looking young woman with a cloud of curly brown hair
breezes in. "Joan Weimer? How're you *doing?*" Her excess
cheeriness says she works with people in depressing circum-
stances. Her name is Samantha and she's a physical therapist
teamed with surgeons here at San Francisco's stellar spine center. "Come on inside and we'll see what you look like. You can
come too, Mr. Weimer, if you want to." I want him to.

"See if you can bend a little to the right."

Cautiously, I drop my right shoulder about three inches. Everything inside me is rusted stuck. "Now to the left." Two inches feels dangerous. "Now bend forward, slowly." I touch my ankles. Nothing to it. "That's great! Now bend backward." Less than an inch and I wince. "Okay, lie on the table and let's see what your range of motion looks like. Keep your knee stiff while I raise your leg." My left leg goes up about two feet and stops. My right leg goes half that far. "They should point to the ceiling," Samantha says. She pushes each leg a few inches higher. Lightning flashes from hip to heel.

The doctor walks in, very tall and thin in his white coat. Without looking at anyone, he shoves my new x rays into a lighted box on the wall. "No more fusion than in the last x rays," he says. "*Five* months post-op? That's not good."

I look at David. No fusion. Another operation. Another year like this one.

"You've had the Spinal Stimulator only two months?"

"The insurance company held it up." My voice trembles.

"Still, you've clocked your full eight hours every day," he says, reading the printout of the Stim box. "You should be a lot further along. How many miles are you walking every day?"

"*Miles*? I can barely walk ten minutes."

"You have to get up to five miles a day. Your bones won't fuse unless you pound them. You need physical therapy, three individual sessions and three group sessions every week. Samantha will set you up with a clinic in San Mateo."

San Mateo is a half hour from Stanford. He's making disability into a full-time job. When am I going to write my book?

"Aren't there physical therapists in Palo Alto?" I ask.

"I'd send you to the San Mateo clinic if you lived two hours away. It's the best in the state, maybe the best in the country. I want one of the directors to treat you herself."

I hear him. I need the best of the best. *I am a mess.*

"In the short run, stretching your adhesions will make you flare—" the doctor says.

227

"Flare?"

"Flare up," says Samantha. "The pain will get worse. It's nerve tissue you'll be stretching. Like when I lifted your leg."

"Here's an order for a bone scan," he says, scrawling on a clipboard. "I'll call you if it's not normal. Be sure you get in your eight hours every day in the Spinal Stim. Here's a prescription for large doses of calcium, and phosphates to help you absorb them, and orders for a blood test after you've taken them two weeks. Call if you have any questions."

He turns to leave. David blocks his path and sticks out his right hand. "Thank you, Doctor. My name is David Weimer. And this is Joan Weimer."

The doctor looks up through his bifocals, obviously startled. "Right. Right." He takes David's hand, glances at me. "Good luck."

When we're outside David says, "I wasn't even sure he knew your name. I just had to get him to look at us once!"

I didn't notice. I don't care. *I'm not fusing.* I'm one of the statistical failures. But I'm the healthiest woman in New Jersey! That's what the internist told me when I got my first complete physical in honor of my fiftieth birthday. I could hike uphill faster and play tennis harder than when I was twenty. What happened to that woman? How did this woman—hobbling slowly along, leaning on her husband's arm—take her place?

"I'm not fusing." My voice is as wobbly as my legs.

"Not yet," David says. He holds me firmly around the shoulders. "But now there's something you can *do* about it!"

He expects me to say I'd go to boot camp, I'd go to Lourdes on my knees, I'd go to hell to get well. *I* expect me to say it, but I don't. I don't believe for a minute that this patchwork of remedies will work. There's much too much the matter with me.

"Do you want to do something else, now that we're in San Francisco?" David asks.

Like what? Museums? Parks? Shops? Films? I can't walk. I can't sit. I can't even speak. I just shake my head. I look down at my body with loathing. *My* body. This body with so much the matter with it is mine. Is *me*. There isn't any me except the one who lives here. And I can't move out. I can't vacate my body like a house I've rented. No more than Maria Luiza's daughter could move out of her cell. I can't even feel the compassion I felt for bodies like hers. All I feel is shame. Shame, and pure hot hatred.

At least I don't have cancer. My cousin Nancy has lymphoma, I learn when I get back to Palo Alto and call my sister with my news. Our cousins Natalie and Jerry and Margie have already died of cancer in their thirties and forties. My ailment won't kill me. But it doesn't protect me from their ailment, either. Outside my window, gardeners are pulling dead leaves away from cyclamen buds that stick up like telescopes from the debris. A baby with my genes is turning in my daughter-in-law's body. But people are not plants. Only the census taker will think my new grandchild replaces my dying cousin.

I phone the Peninsula Spine Education and Treatment Center. They know all about me. They schedule my first six appointments. Drill sergeants have taken over my life. Stretch your adhesions and pound your bones, says Saint Mary's spine team. Turn your shame and hate to love, Hillevi says. Write your book, says Connie. You need me more than ever now.

No, I *don't*! Just leave me alone!

I can tell you a few things about hating your own body, Connie says. That's right, she can. She wrote a fine, bitter story about an ascetic little missionary. I pull the shabby brown book off the shelf. Eight hours still to clock in the Stim. All the useless hours I've spent lying in the thick coils of this revolting snake! All the months ahead.

Take me somewhere else, Connie. Anywhere. With a few

sharp details she drops me into a forlorn mining settlement on the snowbound shores of Lake Superior—the furnace glaring against the dark winter sky, the monotonous tramping of the stamping mills, the blackened stumps, the miners' shanties. Good. That's how things are, all right. But they're not grim enough for Peter the Parson. No firewood for him. He fasts. He scourges himself. His "evil tendency to self-indulgence must and shall be crushed." The girl who loves him asks, "Is it part of your high office to be cold, and hungry—and wretched?" And sexless, but Connie can't say that in 1874. She can make the parson bring forward "his own greatest sorrow with unpitying hand: 'You do not really love me, such a one as I.' "

There it is. *That*'s why he's acting like a medieval monk instead of a Protestant parson. He hates himself because he's positive no one could possibly love him. Connie *must* have understood that from the inside. I'm positive she couldn't accept love any better than the parson could. Not just because she'd seen how love and marriage killed her big sisters, but because she believes she's done something horrible. Anyone who loved her would find out and leave her. Pain was much better. Pain let her feel exalted instead of loathsome.

That's how her parson feels. He marches off to defend a thief from lynching by a mob of enraged miners. "Thou proud, evil body," he says to himself, "I have conquered thee!" Connie adds dryly, "And he had; at least, the body answered not again." The miners stone the parson to death. Her readers protested, called him a martyr. Connie knew he was a suicide.

I adjust my sights from the blackened stumps of the mining camp to the blue and yellow blossoms outside my window. Was that why you jumped out your window, Connie? To destroy a body you hated? I don't believe it. You're no ascetic. You celebrate soft pillows, strong coffee with thick yellow cream, the dense perfume of Florida orange groves. You never pretended to be suffering for the sake of your "high office" as an artist. You distrusted asceticism.

"Self-denial is giving up what one really likes," you said once. "Search for the secret taste of each person, and see if *that* is indulged!" The parson's secret taste was for martyrdom. Maybe that was your secret taste too.

And what is *your* secret taste? Connie asks.

Mine? You think I have some desire, some secret taste that's somehow satisfied by my disability?

Isn't there something you want and don't know you want? she asks.

How the hell should I know? Where would you look for a secret you're keeping from yourself?

I pick up my journal and write down Connie's question. On the opposite page I've recorded a dream. Of course, that's the place to look for secret desires. Everyone in my dreams is me, Hillevi says. So my most secret, most rejected self should be the dream character who's least like me. Last night's dream was ghastly.

I was stopped at a traffic light. A man with a mangy gray beard climbed into the back seat of my car. In the rearview mirror I could see him spooning drugs into his mouth. Another man got into the front seat beside me. He had a gun. I jumped out of the car and they drove away. I stood there, shaking. Safe. Stranded. Furious.

These men can't be me. All right, maybe the guy with the gun, but the derelict? Me in filthy gray clothes, my skin filmed with dirt?

If he's not you, who is he? Connie asks.

Nobody, he answers. I do nothing and I have nothing. No home, no work, no love, no future. I hate people who have something. I hate myself.

He's in my stomach, like hunger. I couldn't be hungry for what *he* has. If I had a secret taste for drugs, I'd be swilling Valium, not flushing it down the toilet. If I yearned to be a parasite, lying in this Stim would be paradise.

Gridlock. I back out and come in at a different angle. What do *you* want, I ask the derelict.

I want your car, he says.

What for?

So you can't drive yourself. It's your *driven self* I'm stealing.

An electric shock zips through me. Has the Stim gone haywire? Maybe this jolt is the "click" Hillevi says you feel when you hit on the meaning of a dream. I twist in my Stim for a box of tissues on the night table. A pile of books crashes onto the floor. A stack of folders starts to tumble after them and I slam my hand on them.

My work. I'm not *driven* about work. I love my work. Without it I'd be living my mother's life. Is this car thief telling me I really want to be "derelict" in my duties? That I want that enough to hold my life up at gunpoint? That's crazy.

A hummingbird is drinking nectar from the yellow flower, its wings a blur.

Perfect image of your old life, Connie says. And now you're every bit as driven by your new inner life as you ever were by human rights or teaching. You're so busy you don't even have time to drive to San Mateo.

You're a fine one to talk, I tell her, with your fourteen-hour work days. Maybe jumping out the window was the only way you could stop driving yourself. No one works that hard for money, not even for art. Your work was your penance for being alive.

And what are you working for? she asks. You think you have to work all the time to justify your right to occupy space on the planet.

What if she's right? What if that derelict won't give back my mobility until I satisfy his taste for aimlessness? What if my bones won't fuse until I fuse him and his desires with the rest of myself? I'll be lying here forever, that's what.

David comes into the bedroom with a big illustrated book in his hands. "Take a look at this statue." He shows me a photograph of an enormous bronze horse springing off the page, ridden by a tiny tense urchin. "It's in the National Archaeological Museum in Athens. Just think, three months from now we'll be seeing it!"

I make a noncommittal noise.

"Yes, David," David says, "won't that be exciting? You and that spine doctor really know how to make a person feel important."

"Give me a day off, will you? I don't always have to respond the way you want me to."

"You could pretend to be interested in what I say."

"I don't *feel* interested right now. I feel *bad*. I have a right to feel bad! Just lay off me!"

David looks startled. He's not nearly as startled as I am, hearing myself blow up at him when he's trying to cheer me up. Now he's going to go off and nurse his bruises until I coax him back. But he's still here. "You're always so responsive, I've come to expect it," he says.

"Well, *stop* expecting it. I don't have to be wonderful all the time. I'm entitled to live on the planet even when I'm not wonderful!"

David laughs. "Okay. I'll go heat up the minestrone for dinner."

He heads for the kitchen and I close my eyes. David must have known it wasn't me talking. That's why he just went to the kitchen instead of to the Arctic Circle. The real me is almost never angry or even impatient with him. How could I be? Our life together has to be wonderful. He paid a terrible price for it. He sacrificed his children to be with me. Our love has to be better than wonderful. It has to be perfect to justify their pain and his pain and my children's pain. Just like my work. My children paid a price for it so I have to love it, the same way I have to love David, perfectly and forever.

You know that's crap, says the derelict.

Wouldn't you rather be real? Connie asks.

233

"Soup's on," David calls.

I drag my Stim to the table, parking the battery on the empty chair beside me. "Maybe you'd better dish up another bowl of soup for Stim."

"It *is* like having a third person living with us," David says. "Smart, but not much of a conversationalist."

I can't believe he's not sore at me. Maybe he doesn't really *want* me to be wonderful all the time.

"Genuflect!"

The command comes not from a black-robed priest but from a thirty-something woman with long red hair and a dancer's body. Robin Strom, a director of the Peninsula Spine Education and Treatment Center, is teaching Back Stabilization Class, Level One.

"Prayers are optional," Robin says, "though a lot of people call on God while they're doing this exercise."

Robin's six students are watching themselves in the mirror that fills one wall of the studio—five women in baggy shirts and pants, one man in red running shorts with muscles bulging everywhere, everyone but me disgustingly young. Three of them are trying to ward off spine surgery, I learned before class, and two are recovering from spinal fusions like mine. But their doctors sent them here just ten weeks after surgery. It's five months since my surgery, and here I am, bones unfused, muscles baggy, flushed with anger. I step onto the blue mat and try to figure out how to genuflect.

The others drop onto one knee and then rise smoothly to their feet. I crash onto one knee and push myself back up with my hands.

"Use your abdominal obliques," Robin says.

"Where are they?" I ask.

"At the sides of your waist. Put your hands there and push your right shoulder down. Feel the muscle at your waist flex?"

"No."

She puts her hands at the sides of my waist. "You're wearing your brace!"

"Shouldn't I be?"

"Not during class. We're building an 'inner corset' of muscle to take its place." I rip off the brace and toss it into a corner. The air feels chilly where the sweaty plastic has been. My torso feels naked. "Now drop your right shoulder. Feel the muscle harden at the side of your waist? Now drop your left shoulder. Are you dropping it? We'll have to work on that side. This time, flex your obliques *before* you genuflect."

I experiment with my shoulders until I think I feel something harden at my waist. Then I sink gracefully to the thick blue mat and rise smoothly to my feet. I'm as thrilled as if I'd done a triple somersault in midair.

For an hour we stretch and squeeze, kneel and stand. Everyone else can reach and bend over and sit and walk without twisting or arching or flexing their spines out of "neutral"—the position in which they have the least pain. Everyone else can lie down without leaving neutral, can genuflect, drop to all fours, slide prone, and roll over like well-trained dogs. For the first time in my life I'm at the bottom of the class, and it's not just because I started two weeks after everyone else. My body is stupid because every one of its cells is resisting what Robin is teaching us. Instead of genuflecting or balancing like a bird-dog or pretending to be a dead bug with my arms and legs stuck up in the air, I want to run away from my body like a mother walking away from a toddler having a tantrum in the supermarket. But I can't run away. I haven't even learned the right way to walk. Besides, I'm the one who wants to pound the floor with my fists and feet.

235

Standing in Hillevi's waiting room, I leaf idly through a copy of yesterday's *New York Times Book Review*. A photograph catches my eye. The face looks familiar. I turn back. It's Connie! It's a review of my anthology! Nobody told me the *Times* was going to review my book. The reviewer admires Connie's "excellent" stories. That's no surprise. It's the photo that rocks me. That middle-aged woman with her hair in a dignified bun—she's *real!* She's not just a voice in my head. She's a historical person. People all over America are looking at her this week. They're going to read her stories. My heart lurches.

"Look," I say when Hillevi opens the door, "look, here's Connie!"

Inside her office I say, "I don't know how to use our time today. I'd love to talk about Connie, and why she worked so hard and why I do. But I've got this huge backlog of dreams"—I wave my dark-red journal at her—"and I've just gotten rotten news about my spine." I sink into her low beige chair.

"Let's see if your body can tell us why you're not fusing. Let it speak in its own voice, as 'I.' "

I'm good at telling my body what to do. Asking its opinion cracks something rusted in me. "I've been trying to stabilize myself by growing bone spurs," I say finally. "That made everything worse. Now the bone graft is trying to stabilize me in a different way. I've never liked stability. It feels like prison. The way my brace feels now." I twist in my chair, twitch my loose shirt over the spare tire the brace creates.

"Maybe you're confusing stability with stagnation. Let's see what's obstructing your fusion. Close your eyes and inhale through your feet. Let the breath come all the way up your body."

Sounds pretty flaky but I'm willing to play along. I pull a

breath up my legs without much trouble. Near my stomach it meets a clam shell, purple and green, hard and brittle.

"Can the breath go around it? Or can you can make it porous so the breath can flow through it?"

I can. It does. It gets as far as my ribs and meets a formless dark mass.

"There's something in my chest. It's that same damned octopus I saw the first time I was here."

"Can you make it change in some way? Maybe its color?"

I can make it turn red, like an octopus I once saw in an aquarium, after someone stirred it with a pole to make it mad. It flails awhile, furiously. I'm damned if I'll stroke it. Slowly it fades to coral, then to pink, then white. It's still tough, but thin enough now so the breath can flow through it.

"Now visualize your spine. What does it look like?"

"Patchy light spots. Dark fissures."

"Let your breath wash them with the warmth and energy of the sun." I try to suck the sun up into my body. Hillevi laughs. "The sun has plenty of energy of its own. You don't have to pull it in. Just let it in."

My fissures fill, my bones bathe in sunlight. I bask in the warmth. But how much time do we have left? I open my eyes. It's four-thirty already. "Your mind can help your bones heal," Hillevi says, "the same way it can give you high blood pressure and allergies and heart attacks."

"But it's impossible for me to learn everything I need to learn in just six weeks before I leave California!" I pull out a list I've made of topics I want to discuss, like an agenda for a committee meeting. "I even had a dream about my frustration. I was trying to leave to meet with you, but some puppies had left their droppings around the house and I had to clean them up first."

"Some of my clients bring their shit to the office," Hillevi says. "You clean yours up before you come."

Back Talk

I howl with laughter. "You're absolutely right! I prepare for our sessions the way I'd prepare for a class."

"That Masculine way of focusing has given you a lot—respect, success, a feeling of control—but you might want to learn a diffuse focus that's part of the Feminine. It's open to impulses it doesn't initiate. It's receptive to possibilities beyond and outside the rational. It's indifferent to clocks and deadlines."

"As a feminist I have a lot of trouble with those categories. In the time we have left, I'd really rather talk about last night's dream."

"Fine," says Hillevi. She thinks I'm ducking.

"I'm in the basement of my sister's house when a gray cat stalks in. She leaps onto my shoulder and rubs her flank against my cheek and I stroke her. Then I remember I'm allergic to cats. I pull the cat off my shoulder, toss her out the door and wash my hands."

"Are you allergic to other animals? Dogs, or horses?"

"No, just cats. Violently."

"I hate to tell you this, but cats ordinarily represent the Feminine. You call this cat 'she.' Why do you suppose your body chose cats to be allergic to?"

I don't want to think I "chose" my allergies any more than I want to think I "chose" my detached vertebra. "I have no idea why I'm allergic to cats, but I can tell you why I'm allergic to the 'Feminine.' " I really didn't want to get into this.

"How do you understand the Feminine?"

"As a sexual stereotype that makes women men's mirrors, or muses, or murderers—anything but complicated human beings working out their own destinies." I gave this speech in Cairo.

"Jung said the Feminine and Masculine were part of the psyches of all women and all men."

"But didn't he say that women's rationality and spirituality and decisiveness were inferior to men's?"

"Yes," Hillevi says, "and that women's intuitive and receptive and nurturant capacities were greater than men's."

"That's essentialism! It says men have individual talents for building bridges and making war and composing music, while women are all alike—all dependent and passive and narcissistic."

"That's the false Feminine."

"Let me tell you the rest of this dream. I'm still in the basement. Now I notice a huge vase of irises and daffodils. I bury my face in them. They're fresh and fragrant. I figure my sister has a reason for keeping them in her basement, but I want to carry them upstairs. I go to pick up the vase but my hands are full of stuff—laundry, books, tennis racquets—and I can't find anywhere to put it down."

"Who is your sister in your inner life?"

"Ruth? My busy, responsible, down-to-earth self, I guess. The dutiful daughter to our mother."

"And what do you associate with these flowers?"

"Early spring. That fresh, cold smell and dazzling color that means the end of winter."

"So they're associated with the earth's annual rebirth."

I see where she's going and I don't like it one bit. "You think my unconscious is telling me to resurrect some 'Feminine' self that my brain knows is a patriarchal construct?"

"You're the one who has to decide what it's telling you. What do you associate with irises?"

"Georgia O'Keeffe. Vulvas. Indecent exposure. I know, I know, the 'Feminine' again. And they fade fast."

"Ephemeral beauty. Lilies of the field that toil not."

"Like my derelict?"

"Maybe the Feminine face of your derelict." She does have a point. "Sometimes we reject the best parts of ourselves," she goes on, "and they have to steal into our lives the way the derelict stole into your car. Your derelict might be a mask for Dionysus."

"I've locked him out, you're saying, the same way I've kept the flowers in the basement."

"Your dreams are saying you're ready to let him break in, and you're ready to stroke the cat and bring the flowers upstairs."

I'm wary. This stuff about some lost "Feminine" self sounds like that psychiatrist telling me that because I was a woman it was neurotic for me to want a Ph.D. Hillevi's not saying that. She has her own Ph.D. She's one of the smartest people I've ever met. But I don't trust this diffuse receptivity she's talking about. All you have to do to get walked over is get diffuse and receptive.

"You might want to buy a few irises and some daffodils," she says. "Don't analyze them. Just live with them. See what they have to tell you."

The flower stand has daffodils and irises. I bring them home and stick them in a glass and take a good look at them. Words rev up in me like a motorcycle. Maybe I can shut them up if I draw the flowers. The daffodil is open. It's all unfolded, all visible, thrusting its stamens at me. Blatant. Two of the irises are stiff green shafts with dark purple heads. Boring. One iris is starting to open. Yellow tongues are thrusting up from its violet petals. I draw that one, doze off, look again. The tongues are more erect now. Delicate white lines are streaking from the yellow centers like the pulses of orgasm. I love it.

Then words barge in and spoil everything. These very sexy, very feminine petals are blooming right out of those stiff masculine stalks. Those softly curled petals unfolding their mysteries are Salome and her dance of the seven veils, Scheherazade weaving fictions to save her life—femininity as seduction, as manipulation, as performance, as power play, as desperation. If this is the Feminine, it can damn well stay in the basement!

Freud's brainwashed me. Those shafts could just as well be my own backbone. Women aren't spineless. Granted, some of our spines are more solid than others, but they're ours. I want to look at these flowers without preconceptions. All day I watch

240

them loosen, open, unfold. By evening, they've faded from violet to lavender. Their edges curl. The delicate spokes are hard, firm grooves and ridges. But dark petals are still wrapped around the shaft. Their edges are sharply defined but their color and shape are still mysterious. Will they open before the flower dies?

I want all my petals to open before I die. Not to die with petals furled like my cousins dead or dying in their forties. "Unused the life in them," Tillie Olsen says of people stunted by disease or poverty or ignorance. I want to use all the life in me, every volt. But was I more alive racing across a tennis court than I am now, watching and waiting and listening?

In the morning the daffodil's edges are crisp and brown. The petals still wrapped around the iris stalks are dry and crumbly. Unlived the life in them. Not everything can open.

14

Meeting Miss Grief

S leep dumps me in a huge high-tech shopping mall, all glass and chrome and lights and free-floating flights of stairs. A man runs down the steps, stark naked, playing a white accordion. It's David! Has he lost his mind? I run through the mall begging people to help me find him. Police are everywhere, and reporters. Maybe David's some kind of terrorist, living a violent life I don't know anything about. I race up and down the open staircases, in and out of stores and cafés, desperate to find him before the police do.

I wake up panting and sobbing. Those red numbers, that must be a clock. That square is the outline of a window. This must be David sleeping peacefully beside me. How did he get back here? I strip off my sodden pajamas and wrap myself around him. When I wake again, he's gone. Sunlight is filtering through the blinds onto the tumbled bed, but the night's terror drifts through it like atoms of dust. I write the dream in my journal. Now it's a story. That feels better. I know what to do with a text. That accordion, now, that could stand for any art form. And chasing after an artist—that's what I do every day! I really would do anything to save Connie from her terrible death. And she may have been as mad as my naked musician.

Was she? I pull the blankets up under my chin. Henry James thought so. But that was after she killed herself. Before that he's telling friends she's *the gentlest and kindest of women,* the *admirable friend* who lets him rest on her *infinite charity.* Then he hears she's dead. He mourns the loss of his *intimate friend.* Then he hears how she died. He's devastated. He collapses. He tortures himself imagining her *lonely unassisted suffering.* It was *insane* of her not to answer his letters or to send for Dr. Baldwin. Her influenza must have turned her *general depression* into *delirious insanity.* She must have suffered *some sudden explosion of latent brain-disease.* Now that he thinks of it, he realizes her *melancholia* was *chronic.* Her temperament was always *exquisitely morbid and tragically sensitive.* She was *never wholly sane.*

Was he making her crazy so he wouldn't feel her death was his fault? He knew he'd exploited her, and then evaded her because she mirrored too well the "disappointment and depression of my own existence."

I'll take a walk along Oak Creek. I stick my legs in my sweat pants, but they throb and tremble as if I really had been running all night. Thinking about craziness hasn't been enough to dissolve the craziness of my dream. I drag my Stim into the living room, thwarting the brat who's trying to bang it against the walls and throw it on the floor. I'll take another look at "Miss Grief," Connie's story about a woman writer whose eccentricities and intense "melancholia" seem like insanity to the narrator. The story came out just when Henry James was sweeping Connie off her feet in Florence in the spring of 1880. I arrange myself in my machine and both of us on the sofa with the book. My stomach settles. Words are just the thing for acid indigestion of the psyche.

And these sentences are so beautifully crafted that they give me a nearly sensual pleasure. Connie's narrator is a rich young bachelor who's smugly satisfied with his success as the author of "delightful little studies of society." Then "Miss Grief" appears, an emaciated woman writer who won't leave him alone.

"Grief has not so far visited me here," says the narrator, "and she shall not now."

That sentence is about *me*. It's about how I was until my spine collapsed. I watch the words glimmer on the page. A hundred years ago, Connie wrote a story about my obsession with her, the suffering woman artist who brought grief to my door.

I pull a blanket off the sofa back to cover myself. I'm not really like Connie's narrator. He tried to drive Miss Grief away and I leapt to meet her. He failed to find a publisher for her work and I succeeded. He's so oblivious to her poverty that he let her starve to death, and I'd do anything I could to save her life. I'm nothing like that sanctimonious self-serving twerp.

Now another line is pulsing on the page. "Vampires!" says the aunt of Miss Grief. She means the narrator and the rest of the male literary establishment. "Vampires! you take her ideas and fatten on them, and leave her to starve!" The Stim weighs on my stomach like an accordion. What am I doing right this minute if not fattening on Connie's ideas? I use her the same way he uses Miss Grief—"as a memento of my own good fortune, for which I should continually give thanks." I may be disabled, I tell myself, but lucky me, I'm not "exquisitely morbid and tragically sensitive," lucky me, I'm not starving to death or dying of lymphoma. I'm not even in a wheelchair. It's disgusting to give thanks because other people suffer more than I do. I want the world to be fair.

No, I don't. If the world were fair, I'd be living in a wheelchair. I don't want to be Miss Grief.

. . .

That evening I tell Hillevi about the mad accordionist in my dream.

"Is there some part of yourself you're terrified of losing?"

Oh God. Her hundred-and-eighty-degree turns give me vertigo. "You mean it's myself I'm chasing?"

"The most terrifying encounters are always with the self. Could this accordionist be a composite portrait of your own creative self?"

I slouch lower in the low beige chair. "I suppose I would see that self as naked and crazy," I say slowly. "Crazy to expose myself in public, crazier to think I could be a real artist."

"Maybe your accordionist isn't crazy or criminal. Maybe he's just a free spirit. His creativity is revolutionary. It's volcanic. It might erupt, like that furious toddler in you."

"What am I supposed to *do* about him?"

"Just live with him. Scratch his head from time to time. A dream is a dispatch from your journey toward wholeness. It's about accepting or resisting the dark sides of yourself."

"Resist is right!"

"But you're *not* resisting the accordionist. You're chasing him. What's terrifying is the threat of losing him. You're ready to integrate him into yourself. That's probably why he appears as the person closest to you—David. And maybe that's why he appears as male—because you've excluded this part of yourself so long, it feels Other."

My head hurts from spinning. My back hurts from sitting. "I'm caught between old selves and new ones," I complain, "and every one of them's inept."

"Jung said individuation's not for everyone," Hillevi says, standing up. How can she look so unrumpled? "It's much easier to stick with the capable person you were than to make room for these clumsy, undeveloped parts of yourself. Becoming whole always feels like a comedown."

I take the elevator to the basement instead of the lobby. I wander the streets looking for my car. Driving home I get lost.

The next day's mail brings a letter from my department chair at Drew. I check the postmark to see what planet it was mailed from. I study the logo. It's the clock tower over Brothers College. I see myself checking my watch against that clock as I hurry across the courtyard to class. It's like watching an old home movie. In the envelope is a note: everyone hopes I'm healing well and enjoying California. Also next fall's teaching schedule. I'm down for the American novel, a course in women's literary traditions, and a graduate seminar on Whitman and Dickinson. Who does he think is going to teach those courses? Even if I could resurrect the professor I used to be, I wouldn't trust her. She'd start in again chairing meetings and teaching classes and meeting students for intense conversations in the snack bar. She'd send the derelict and the mad musician diving back underground. I don't want them down there making trouble.

It's Saturday morning, my turn to call Sharon.

"How am I? Frustrated!" I tell her. "Every time I have to genuflect it feels like being forced to say, 'Thy will be done.' I've always wanted *my* will to be done."

"It must make you so damned mad to know that all your will and all your discipline aren't enough to heal your spine."

"You said it. I have to force myself to swallow these disgusting phosphates, and to lie around in my Stim for eight hours every day. And now I'm in back school three hours a week, and I'm spending three more hours on Robin's table. I have to swim twenty minutes every day and walk until I can do five miles a day and practice my exercises an hour every night. And then

I'm seeing Hillevi twice a week. I'm getting nowhere with my book. All my time's going into repairs!"

"I wish I could send one of my patients to Hillevi," Sharon says. "That suicidal man I told you about says he's going to kill himself to punish me for not being a good enough therapist."

"To make you sorry for the way you treated him?"

"Right. I try to remember his hate is just transference, but it sure feels personal."

"Do you know the old song about a child who's going to eat worms and die to make everyone sorry? No? I used to sing it for company while my father played the piano and everyone laughed."

"Sing it for me. It might help me with that patient."

"Anything for you, Sharon. Ready?

> They always always pick on me,
> They never never let me be.
> I'm so sad and lonely, that I could cry,
> Feel so—something, something—
> That I could die—"

Out of nowhere tears erupt. Sobs rattle the cables on the Stim.

"Oh, Joan," says Sharon softly. "It was a sad and lonely little girl who sang that song." I can feel her arms around me.

"I don't like her." I'm sniffling.

"I do! She had to bury her sadness so she could survive, but it's safe for you to start unpacking that box. You're a grown-up now."

"I feel about eight years old."

"That old? I've been three all week."

Miss Grief has finally visited me here. Not as a solitary spinster or melancholic genius but as a lonely child. She's come to meet

247

the sad child in me. It's that fat little girl with skinny braids wrapped around her head who sits with Connie in the front bedroom watching her sister Emma die. It's me in my ugly brown oxfords holding Connie's hand while she says good-bye to her dying sister Georgie. I follow Connie home from the funeral. We wander around the house, picking up books and putting them down. We look at photos of Emma and Georgie draped with black crepe. We know the way to be loved is to be dead. If we weren't afraid it would hurt too much to die, we'd eat those worms right now.

I must have been a child haunted by death. I don't remember myself that way, but why else would I be so absorbed by the deaths of the Woolson children? Death itself never touched me. I knew there was a war far away in Europe, where mothers and fathers and even children died, but there were no deaths in my house. Except one. My grandfather's. Sam lived with us after Grandma Rose died. In the pocket of his navy wool overcoat there was always a surprise for me—a tiny live turtle, or a pink celluloid doll, or a package of gum. He'd settle at his card table and yell "Service!" and all the children would jump to see who could be first to bring him his slippers and his cards, who could strike the match for his cigar, who'd bring him a scissors so he could cut and fold the joker of the deck into a perfect sleigh. In the morning before anyone else was awake I'd climb into his bed and he'd tell me how the three little pigs put on their little red riding hoods and went into the forest to meet Goldilocks. He'd let me ride horsie on his hard round stomach. I'd cuddle up to his big warm body.

Then early one morning when I was six my mother came into my bed and held me in her arms and told me that Sam was dead. He hadn't been sick. He'd been testifying in court and passed out and died before anyone could save him. I must have cried, but I don't remember that. What I remember is thinking I mustn't cry. That would make my mother even sadder. When she left my room I got up and found a piece of lined notebook paper and a pencil and wrote "Sam died today December 6 1943." I got up and I wrote it down, and that's what I still do with loss.

Loss! When Sam died I lost the only grown-up who wasn't afraid or angry and thought I was fine just the way I was. I mourned without letting anyone see and then I put up a wall of words around my heart. Since Sam left me I haven't been able to mourn for anyone real. Instead I mourn for children I never knew, for little Annie and Julie and Gertrude, for lovely Emma and Georgie, for Connie. It's my own dead self I've been mourning, the self who could feel her own pain.

"Your body's strong," Robin says, "and it learns fast."

Today I could "stick-em-up" and be a "bird-dog" and a "bridge" and even genuflect without shaking. Now I'm lying in a blue paper gown on Robin's table. She holds my left knee against her body and slowly rotates my hip in its socket. Everything slides smoothly. Then she tries the same thing with my right knee. I gasp. She rotates my hip clockwise and counterclockwise and tears run down my face without asking permission. When she's done she hands me a towel without comment. Tears must be normal here. "Okay, loop the towel over one foot. Now straighten your knee. That's it. Now pull on the towel and slowly tug your leg up to a forty-five degree angle. Keep your foot parallel to the ceiling."

The left foot is willing. The right foot is not. Not. Not. The tears run again.

"Add that stretch to your daily exercise routine. Thirty seconds each leg, three times, twice a day. Once you stretch out those adhesions they won't send your leg muscles into spasm, and you'll be able to walk longer distances and your bone graft should start to fuse. Honest. Now turn over on your stomach and I'll work on those muscles."

She digs her fingers into my legs and I think of general anesthesia. "You accept pain well," she says.

"Do I have a choice?"

"People differ a lot in how much they can take. As much as they differ in taking responsibility for their own healing."

"Sometimes I think—Robin, could you ease off just a little?—sometimes I think this injury is doing me a favor. It made me stop what I was doing."

"An illness did that for me," Robin says. "We'd just gotten this clinic going, and I was working sixty hours a week when an ovarian cyst burst. It filled my body with blood. Not a very subtle message."

"Something about being a woman?"

"A Jungian analyst had been telling me I was trying to exclude the Feminine. She said I had to be focused and active every waking minute because I was afraid if I stopped for a minute I'd wind up like my mother."

"Have you been reading my journal?"

"You too? The first time I saw what I was doing to myself was when that cyst burst and I found myself lying on a gurney in the emergency room doing the payroll!"

"Why were you doing that?"

"It was payday, and no one else could write the checks. In case I died, I wanted to make sure everyone got paid. When I didn't die—but came close enough, and spent months convalescing—I finally realized I want more from life, however much life I have, than work. I want an intimate relationship. I want a child. I'm thirty-five. I don't have forever. That's what my blood was saying. Loudly."

Her blood, my spine. "Have you really changed your life?"

"After such a loud wake-up call, even I could see how narrow my path had become."

Robin's fingers are teaching me the exact path of the nerves in my legs. I see them as roads, as highways on a map. As lifelines. It was something wise in me that squeezed those paths narrower and narrower. Made it impossible to ignore the pain of strangling myself. Not just my legs, my *self*. It took major surgery to widen those paths. Some vital force is flowing through me for the first time in years. It hurts like hell.

I tell Robin what I've just seen.

"Did you see how the light in the room got brighter just then?" she asks. I didn't. "I always see that when someone has an epiphany."

Robin turns me over and starts working over the fronts of my legs. It's slightly less awful than her work on the backs. "Do you think pain produces understanding?" I ask.

"I don't know. Maybe receptivity does."

"I dreamed last week about someone who had that kind of openness." If Robin's working with a Jungian, I can tell her about a dream. "She was a very big black woman in a hospital gown like this one I'm wearing now. She was sitting in a chair with her legs apart and her gown open. Her breasts were large and they had the most astonishing nipples—brilliant red like the liquid core of an active volcano."

"Sounds like you met the dark goddess."

"I think of her as the Volcano Goddess. I can see lava pouring out of those craters and spreading around me in a pool. Rippling red and gold, beautiful but deadly. But there was another side of her, too. Projected on the wall like some kind of x ray I saw her breasts glowing and pulsing like a great white cloud."

"Volcanoes destroy what was there," Robin says, "and create something new."

"Pretty drastic transformation—like having your body fill with blood." Robin hands me a towel and helps me sit up. When I get off the table my knees wobble. She grabs my elbow. "How do you suppose I wound up in California, in your office and on your table?" I ask while I pull off the sweaty paper gown and dry myself. "The odds against it must be a million to one."

"Synchronicity," Robin says.

I stick my aching legs into my sweat pants. "What's that?"

"Meaningful coincidence. When the student is ready the teacher appears. Synchronistic events tell you you're on the right path."

I pull on my turtleneck. I'm trembling, maybe with cold after so much sweating, or from Robin's assault on my nerves. Or from pure excitement.

I stumble to my car. I manage to find the freeway. Synchronicity. That would explain why people turn up at the very moment I'm ready for them, or when we're ready for each other. David. Connie. Sharon. Hillevi. Robin. Not accidents. Synchronicity. What does it say about the world?

Moving my foot from the brake to the accelerator takes conscious effort. I switch on the car radio. A solo trumpet goes through my body as if Robin had turned it into a sieve. Tears fill my eyes. I know this music but I don't remember where I've heard it before. On the second refrain I realize I've marched to it for twenty years at Drew commencements. This melody has played while I've stood under huge oak trees as part of an aisle of black-gowned faculty through which our students walk. I've saluted students who had wept in my office while they told me that their sister just attempted suicide, or that their mother has terminal cancer, or that their best friend died in a car crash, or that they've just had an abortion—healthy-looking, fresh-faced students who look as if nothing worse than a flat tire had ever dimmed their lives. I've stood there and saluted the students who came to my office when they'd finally written a stunning poem or won a Woodrow Wilson fellowship or broken through their fear to organize an alliance of gay, lesbian and bisexual students. Some came with champagne because my letter of recommendation helped them get into law school, and some came back after law school to tell me they'd decided to defend civil liberties instead of huge corporations. Most of them I'll never see again. My ties to them are another kind of lifeline. My tears say it's important. They don't tell me how to do that work without narrowing my own path.

Now the freeway is passing between soft green hills. Yesterday I got a letter from my academic assistant, Colleen, with her wonderful eccentric haircut, long on one side and short on the other. Colleen made photocopies of Henry James's letters for me, took the train to Washington with me to lobby against the *Contra* war, cooked black-bean soup for me after my surgery. Now she writes that she can't finish her honors thesis. She finds herself staring out of windows thinking how much she hates life's demands of her. She doesn't understand what's gone wrong.

I'm just beginning to understand it myself. I've set a dangerous example. I'll write and tell her she doesn't have to justify her right to occupy space on the planet. I'll tell her I think it's a great idea for her to go to Ireland and wait on tables and look at the heather and the peat bogs and the rainbows.

The sky ahead of me is misty. Just above the green hills it's a soft dove gray, but higher it's pearly and broken with patches of bright white. These patches brighten and dim, pulsing with energy. Never in my life have I seen a sky do this. I watch, transfixed. I could swim through those silvery clouds to that throbbing light. It rocks me in armless arms, massages every inch of my body to the rhythm of its great heartbeat.

A horn blares. I'm headed straight into one of those green valleys. I stop the car on the shoulder. I'm shaking. Not because I might have killed myself. Because the sky is an exact, perfect replica of the wall in my dream. The breasts of the Volcano Goddess are glowing and pulsing in the sky. The sky is performing my dream right now right in front of my eyes.

Words speak themselves in my head. Transfiguration. Miracle. Lunacy. Is anyone else looking at the sky? Does it mean anything to anyone else? Traffic streams past. No one else is parked on the shoulder. The sky is still throbbing, a dance in white and gray. The whole world is mist, I think, that just parted to reveal this radiance pulsing behind it.

I'm not imagining it. It's still happening. Something is sending me a sign. I've been given a tremendous gift. But from whom? From some force so vast and so wise that I might conceivably say to it, "Thy will be done"? I'm drenched. I ease the car back onto the highway. No person as new at life as I am should be allowed to drive.

15

Nightmare Doubles

arch twelfth dawns sunny. My birthday. Today I've lived as many years as Connie had when she took her life. Soon I'll be older than she ever lived to be, living days and hours she tossed away like an apple core.

I slide out of bed without disturbing David and go out to walk along Oak Creek. This morning currents from opposite sides of the little stream are meeting in the center and fusing in a feathery *V*. It looks so effortless, this meeting of ripples in a new design, a simple, symmetrical response to the shape of the banks. The muddy bank is slippery. I look down for a stone to stand on and notice the fuchsia *V*s on my boots. There were *V*s on Connie's boots in my first dream about her! Where are all these arrows pointing?

I walk back to the apartment, full of the question but strangely indifferent to the answer. David is sitting on the sofa in his bathrobe, reading the paper. He pulls me onto his lap.

"Happy birthday, sweetheart. How does your new maturity feel?"

"Like utter ignorance," I say. "Like I'm still in Miss Greenleaf's class learning long division."

"Maybe you're getting younger instead of older."

"I'm sick of the fifth grade! Every time I see Robin she shows me something else I'm doing that destabilizes my back. Every time I see Hillevi I meet some other part of me that's undeveloped or twisted. I'm fifty-three years old, for God's sake! Aren't I ever going to be okay as I am?"

"You're okay with me," David says.

I pull myself out of his lap. "That helps." But not enough.

Night after night I dream about Connie. I find her mother's diaries but wake up before I can read them. I find a large folio of Connie's letters but before I can read them I have to do my laundry, and before I finish the washing I wake up. One night Connie takes me to a Catholic church, and the next night I find her lost writings in a Catholic church. I take the book to a library but before I can read it I wake up. Cheated. Baffled.

"A Catholic church is a funny place for a Jew like me to look for an Episcopalian like Connie," I tell Hillevi.

"Maybe your search for Connie is a search for a spiritual home," she says.

"What a strange idea! But it moves me, somehow."

"Take the feeling into your body," Hillevi says. "Where is it?"

It's between my throat and my heart. It's a streaky sunset, spreading red and coral and pink across my chest. It's a much gentler glow than the Volcano Goddess's fiery nipples, a much warmer embrace than her misty reflection in the sky. It's a place I'd like to stay.

. . .

After back class I strap on my brace. It feels funny. I ask Robin to watch me walk in it and without it.

"It's molded wrong," she says finally. "Extension is right for most people, but with spondylolisthesis, your neutral position is flexed. The brace feels odd now because your neutral position is beginning to feel natural."

"Could my brace be *causing* my pain?"

"Could be. Take it to a surgical supply store and ask them to remold it while you stand in neutral."

I go home and call the store that rented me the bedside table. They tell me to come in and see Earl at two o'clock but Earl isn't there at two o'clock. At four Earl is there but he doesn't know anything about molding braces like this, I should come back tomorrow when the orthotist is in. The orthotist has never seen a brace like mine. I should take it back where I got it. Look, I say, holding on to my temper with both hands, I got it in New Jersey. Don't you have a heater for softening plastic insets like this? Great, you soften it and I'll stand the way I'm supposed to stand and you just press it to conform to my back, okay? The orthotist wants to talk to my surgeon and I say if the surgeon knew anything about this he'd have ordered the brace molded the right way to begin with. Finally he does what I ask.

I walk out of the store and around the block to my car and my legs don't hurt. I walk around another block. I'm not imagining it. My legs don't hurt! I want to grab people passing me on the street and tell them, "I can walk just like you!" That's what Dave said when he finally emerged from his body cast as a scrawny two-year-old. I wept then. I weep now.

But by the time I get home I'm outraged. "Can you believe this?" I ask David. "All these months my bones haven't been fusing because I haven't been pounding them because it hurt too much to walk—all this time my brace was *causing* the pain! It was keeping me from healing!"

I take my temper for another walk. I circle all the gardens of our huge apartment complex without hearing anything from my legs. It's a miracle. I need someone to thank, but who? Robin, obviously, but how did my body get to her clinic? Pulled there by a long chain of unlikely events. Dragged there against my will. I resisted going to San Francisco, resisted going to San Mateo. I always want *my* will to be done, I told Sharon, but look what happened when it wasn't! So whose will *was* being done? Whoever staged my dream in the sky? Maybe. But it took my will too. I had to force that furious toddler to live in "neutral" and bully that poor orthotist into remolding my brace. I walk to the creek and study the currents. Show me, I say. Show me how my will and another will might flow together. How reason and mystery might merge in a *V*.

Someone is opening and closing doors downstairs. It's the middle of the night, I'm alone in the house. I try to get up to phone the police but panic paralyzes me. The sounds get louder and bolder.

I wake up with damp sheets wrapped around my neck. Finally my heart slows down. I am sick to death of this dream. As a child I'd wake up from it trying to scream for my mother but I couldn't make a sound. Two months ago at my mother's apartment I dreamed it. Dreamed it in the hospital two months before that. Either I lie frozen or I race around trying to lock windows and doors, and I always wake up before I find out if the men are going to kidnap or rape or torture or kill me.

The house is my self. The intruder is my father. I figured that out in my first psychology course. So why am I still having these dreams? I turn my pillow over. Then I stifle a groan. I know everyone in my dreams is me. Those intruders are me. More buried selves clamoring for attention. But I'm paying attention!

"What do I do about these guys?" I ask Hillevi.

"Ask them in. Before you go to sleep ask your Dreammaker to bring them back so you can ask them what they want."

Sure, Hillevi. Whatever you say.

Maybe Connie can teach me how to deal with my dark doubles. I discovered hers by chance one snowy day in Cleveland. I was looking for a reel of microfilm in the rows of ivory filing cabinets in the Western Reserve Historical Society when I saw a box labeled "Letters Belonging to Constance Mather Bishop." I knew who she was—the little girl Connie's devoted nephew had named after her. Strange, this box wasn't indexed with the rest of the family papers. Idly, I rigged the reel on the microfilm reader. All the letters were from Connie or about Connie and all of them were shocking. That must be why they'd been separated from the rest of the family papers in their respectable gray acid-free boxes. Maybe I didn't find them by chance. Maybe it was synchronicity. Maybe Connie wanted me to find them and led me there.

Most of the letters were about her brother, Charly. I knew about him because Hannah makes a huge fuss about his birth in her memoirs. A son after eight daughters! A scrawny, sickly boy, but a boy. But the family genealogies never included him, so I figured he'd died in infancy. The letters I was cranking through the microfilm viewer, though, showed that Charly had lived plenty long enough to make a mess of his life and a misery of Connie's. The family had good reasons for erasing him. I copied the letters. I pull them out now.

Connie is writing her nephew about the *terrifying telegrams* and *dreadful letters* she's been getting from Charly. He seemed to her *completely broken in mind and body.* She was living in *a state of constant trouble and dread* because her mother's *whole happiness—even her life, I might almost say, depends and always has depended upon how Charly is, and how he feels. I spend my whole time trying to keep her well and comfortable; but it is of no use if she thinks Charly is in trouble.*

I can hear Connie choking on her bitterness. There she is, pushing forty, stuck in the South tending her mother while

Charly tours Europe, tries Chicago, settles in California. There she is writing herself into breakdowns to support her mother, and who does her mother care about? Who does her life depend on? Charly! The lad who ran for his life when his father died, who never writes except to dun Connie for money. And now Connie discovers that his terrifying symptoms are *the result of morphine.*

She turned half a dozen plots around prodigal sons and brothers like Charly. Some of them are such convincing drunks I'd bet a dollar Charly drank, too. Someone always adores them "as the prodigal is often so dearly loved by the woman whose heart is pierced the most deeply by his excesses—his mother." She's a woman who "rejoiced in sons; daughters would never have been important to her." Flat out, Connie admits she never had a chance with her mother. But why was she so devastated when her rival died?

The shock of Charly's death made her ill for three months, "made me suffer more than I have ever suffered in my life." He was only thirty-six, but she hadn't seen him for fifteen years. I don't understand why his death should make her suffer more than the deaths of the big sisters who'd mothered her, more than the death of the father who adored and understood her, more than the death of the mother whose love she could never win. Was it the diary he left that showed "suffering so piteous that it broke my heart"? If you led me to those letters, Connie, help me understand what you want me to know.

Jupiter Lights. Connie's one bad novel. The heroine shoots a violent alcoholic who's her brother once removed and then suffers the agonies of the damned. Eve had to shoot Ferdie. He was coming after his wife and son with a knife. You'd think the wife would be grateful, but instead she attacks Eve: "Here you are alive, and *Ferdie* dead! He was a great deal more splendid than you are, he was so handsome and so young! And yet there he is, down in the ground; and *you* walking about here!"

Those words come straight from hell. Connie must have

heard them every time her mother looked at her: why aren't you dead and your six splendid sisters alive? Connie wished she *was* dead. When Charly was born and Hannah drowned him in adoration Connie wished *he* was dead. When he died she felt like a murderer. I know she did. It's what Eve feels. Where? Loose pages tumble around the bed. Here. Eve believes she should be "imprisoned for life—hanged. How people would shrink from her if they knew! Cain, where is thy brother? And the Lord set a mark upon Cain, lest any finding him should kill him. Would it come to this, that she should be forced at last to take her own life, in order to be free from the horror of murder?"

Oh my God. It *did* come to that. The pages crumple in my hands. That's what Connie wanted me to understand. That's why she led me to those letters. Someone had to know. She killed herself when she was my age because she couldn't live another day with the killer who lived inside her. That's her terrible secret. That's why she couldn't let anyone love her.

How had it felt, wanting Charly dead? Once I stabbed my sister with a scissors. She'd stabbed me to the heart by saying I was "too young to know" some secret she had with our brother. For months I was sick with guilt. But it wasn't just guilt that made Connie sick. It was loss. A necessary part of herself died with Charly. He was brilliant and demanding and irresponsible and destructive. She couldn't let herself be like him any more than I could let myself be a derelict or a volcano. But she needed his free spirit to be alive somewhere in the world.

I tear off my Stim and sit on the side of the bed staring out the dark window. Connie was braver than I am. She faced her nightmare double, lived with him every day. My criminal selves are still locked in my dreams. I look up at Vicki's Dream-Catcher tacked over the bed and say out loud, "I want to meet this man who's been after me all my life and find out what he wants. Do you hear me? I mean it! I want to meet him *tonight!*"

I go to sleep and docile as a lamb I dream that someone is pounding violently at the door of a shack where I'm living. He's going to knock the door down if I don't let him in. With my heart pounding as loud as his fist I open the door. I know what a momentous act this is. A furious man is standing there, his fist raised to pound again. I step back and let him in. He doesn't throttle me. He just sits down quietly at the kitchen table. He tells me how unhappy he is that I've rejected him. I'm sorry, I say, I've tried but I just can't love you. He gets up and leaves. I close the door behind him.

I wake up flabbergasted. I've told myself what to dream and how to behave in a dream? It's shocking. It's like seeing a dream performed in the sky. What happened to my nice neat categories—conscious and unconscious, outer and inner, the world and myself? All scrambled together like the white and yolk of an egg. The material and spiritual worlds merging like the currents in Oak Creek.

Maybe I'm not just pretending that mind can heal matter, not just imagining that spirit can speak to spirit. Maybe that's actually happening. Maybe there's no frontier between what Hawthorne called the Imaginary and the Actual. Maybe I studied Hawthorne without knowing why, and goddesses without knowing why, so that ten, twenty years later I'd be ready to understand that dreams are as real as physical therapy and Connie's presence is as real as my dreams.

I go for a swim. Twenty laps don't bring me to my senses, but they don't hurt my legs either.

Six-thirty the next morning Mark calls: Lauren Alev Randall-Myers was born at eleven-thirty last night! She's big and healthy with long, thin fingers like Norma's and spiky black hair. Norma had a terrible labor and then another cesarean. Mark sounds exhausted. We are both full of tears. I long to be there. I want all my children and grandchildren right here with me right now. The desire sharpens to pain. Why didn't I want this closeness when my children were small and wanted me? I taught them to play by themselves so I could write essays about parents and children in literature. Now I could be such a wonderful mother! I'm not in so much of a hurry now. I'd listen to their stories and tell them mine and sing them songs and bake them oatmeal cookies. I did those things. But now I'd be all there while I did them, not half-thinking about the papers I had to grade or the meetings I had to organize. Now I'd watch my children become themselves with the same respect that I watch the currents flowing in Oak Creek.

Dave calls. "I'm beginning to understand why I was so obsessed by that abandoned puppy I found in the old city of Jerusalem," he says. "I wouldn't leave until I found someone to take it in. That puppy was me."

Leslie arrives in Palo Alto. She takes in the flowers and the swimming pools, tosses her down jacket on the sofa and says, "Tough life you guys have! Cleveland has five inches of dirty snow."

We take a tray to the little table on the patio and she soaks up the sun the way her bagel soaks up honey.

"Geriatrics is depressing," she says, spreading peanut butter on top of the honey. "I like obstetrics much better."

She knows more about these mysteries than her own mother does. That's humbling. "I can see why you'd like the beginning of life, not the end."

"Death isn't so bad," she says. "It's the getting there."

"Sometime I want to ask you about Connie's dying," I say. "About her symptoms." David goes inside. He breaks out in a rash when I mention Connie's name.

"Differential diagnosis of a woman who's been dead a hundred years?" Leslie says. "Sounds like fun. Let's do it now."

"You really want to? Okay. Her doctor said she had a mild

case of influenza, but I found a letter by the woman who came to look after her, and she says Connie was having horrible pain in her bowels and vomiting bile. Does that sound like flu?"

"Vomiting bile is caused by a couple of things," Leslie says. "Got a piece of paper?" She draws me a dreadful diagram that shows exactly how gallstones or an intestinal blockage or pancreatitis would produce Connie's symptoms.

"They're serious illnesses?"

"Any one of them could kill you. They're all extremely painful. They'd have been hard to treat a hundred years ago."

So Connie's dive out her window may have been her only alternative to a prolonged, excruciating death. I never thought of that. It changes things. "Tell me something else. Do the symptoms of drug withdrawal match the symptoms of flu?"

"Some of them do." She scrawls a quick list.

"What about restlessness and anxiety and insomnia?"

"They're symptoms of drug withdrawal. I don't associate them with flu. You think she was addicted?"

"To laudanum, yes. She told her doctor she *must* have the large doses of laudanum she was accustomed to taking, but he said she was so weak they'd kill her."

"He was right," Leslie says. "If she was going through withdrawal on top of everything else, it would have been ghastly."

"I think she knew exactly how ghastly it would get. Her brother had told her." Can I ask her this? I can. "Have you ever thought of killing yourself?"

"No."

"Neither have I. I love being alive. But I can imagine wanting to die. Whatever death is, it can't be worse than living with unbearable pain and no hope of relief. I hate the way Connie died, crashing out of that window. It horrifies me. But if I were in her place I'd have done what she did. If there was no one to help me die I'd have killed myself. It shocks me to hear myself say that."

"It doesn't shock me," Leslie says. "Lots of things are worse than death."

"Could you help someone die?"

"If they had no hope of recovery and were suffering and wanted to die? Doctors do it all the time. They don't talk about it, but they do it."

"Could you do it for me?"

She looks at me. "I'm not so tough, Mom. You're not just some patient of mine. It would be awful."

"But if you knew I wanted it, and the alternative was terrible?" I shouldn't push her like this. I can't stop myself.

"Yes."

"Good. Thank you." I get up and put my arms around her. I'll never have to die like Connie. "That's a better birthday present even than the beautiful teapot you brought me." I didn't know there was this weight on my heart until it lifted. "Want to go for a swim?" I want my whole body to feel this lightness.

The next day is brilliant and warm.

"Let's go to San Francisco and play all day!" I say.

"Can your legs handle the hills?" Leslie asks.

"If they can't we'll sit and watch the fish in the aquarium, or we'll sit in the teahouse at Golden Gate Park."

David says we need the day by ourselves. I figure he also needs the day to himself. Leslie drives north through the green hills and I point out the spot where the sky performed my dream. I expect a noncommittal "Mmm hmm."

Instead she says, "Did I ever tell you I walked on fire?" I stare at her. My arms get bumpy. "It was at the Women's Peace Camp at Seneca Falls last summer. I went with my friend Michelle—you met her in Cleveland, remember, the neuroscientist?" I do remember her—a large, reposeful black woman. She looks a lot like my Volcano Goddess. "There was a long ritual to prepare us for an action against the missile base, and at the end of it some of the women walked over burning coals. You can imagine how skeptical we two scientific types were, but we watched other women do it and then we did it too!"

Leslie always lived two lives. She'd do whatever was expected of her—feed the cats, do her homework, practice the flute—and *then* she'd rig a pully from an enormous tree and go flying out over a gorge. Years later Dave or Mark would tell me about her stunts. I wish she'd called me up the minute she came home from Seneca Falls to tell me she'd walked on fire.

"What was it like, doing that?"

"Amazing. Now when someone says I can't do something, I tell myself 'I walked on fire!' and go ahead and do it. Like the bumblebee who doesn't know it's aerodynamically impossible for him to fly so he just does it."

I laugh and put my hand on her leg. Through her jeans I feel the hard muscles of this down-to-earth young doctor-in-training who walked on fire. "You're braver about fire than I am," I tell her. "My Volcano Goddess scares the hell out of me. To get that soft, misty vapor you have to accept the red-hot rocks and the gas and the molten lava. What if she turned all that power against me?"

"Maybe she has other options," Leslie says. "She could just keep her power contained." Like Leslie herself. "People have all kinds of power they don't know they have. They can die when they don't want to live and they can stay alive until someone comes they want to say good-bye to. There's so much stuff no one understands, like *déjà vu* and walking on fire. It just goes ahead and happens whether anyone understands it or not."

"Like the bumblebee."

We find a parking space near Golden Gate Park and walk under blooming cherry trees to the tea garden. The waitress brings green tea and almond cookies.

"I didn't know you had this mystical streak in you," I say as we watch carp swimming by. "I thought you were a skeptic."

"I think I'm getting skeptical of what I thought I knew. I've been thinking about souls lately. Wondering where new souls come from, and if there are enough to go around. It's an odd subject, isn't it? But I've been thinking about it."

So our minds have been moving along the same paths. A gift, learning that. Connie's gift.

We stroll through the Japanese gardens and climb over Japanese bridges and my legs don't say a word. In blazing sunshine we walk up and down the San Francisco hills, buy giant calzone and eat them as we walk, make up names for vegetables we've never seen before, gawk at a man with a giant parrot on his shoulder, giggle. A month ago I went straight home from San Francisco because my legs hurt too much to walk or stand or sit. A miracle, doing all this today without pain. No less a miracle than Leslie's walk on fire.

I leave her at the bus station with a long hug and drive back down the peninsula to San Mateo, where Robin digs into my nerves and sends both my legs into such fierce spasms she has to cool them on an icepack.

"Sorry," she says, "it was too much after all that walking. Go home and ice some more. This is just a flare."

We're packing up to leave California.

"It's crazy to be leaving now," I tell Hillevi. "What if the Volcano Goddess erupts while I'm six thousand miles away?"

"If she does, just draw the eruption, or dance it or write it," Hillevi says. "You'll be all right because you have ways of expressing it. And you know she's there. You won't fall into the crater by mistake."

"I have moments of bravado when I want her lava to race down the mountainside and burn away my old self. All my underbrush."

"You don't have to burn away your old self. It will just die off as new growth comes up."

Back Talk

. . .

I'm not ready, I'm not ready. Everything is happening too fast.

O'Hare is the biggest airport I've ever seen. I ride a beeping cart from one gate to another. David has taken one plane to visit his children in Minneapolis and I'm taking a different plane to visit my children in Moline. I walk off the plane and see standing beside Mark a platinum-blond child in a red jacket who looks exactly the way Mark did at two. Brendon breaks out of this time exposure and races toward me like a cannonball. I genuflect and hold out my arms and catch his wiry little body against my chest and nuzzle my face against his cool smooth cheek. I hug Mark's solid belly and kiss his dark curly beard. We pile into his battered blue Volkswagen with one white fender and one brown door.

"It's doing things the hard way, isn't it, having babies while you're still in school?" I say. "Of course I did it that way too. Maybe for us it was the only way. If it weren't for these babies, you might still be changing tires."

"That wasn't so bad. You screw on a tire, it stays that way."

"As distinct from putting a clean diaper on a baby."

"Exactly."

He pulls up at the little green house they've rented for a pittance because the area is so depressed. Norma hugs me to breasts heavy with milk.

"Come meet your granddaughter," she says. In the center of their big bed Lauren lies bundled like a papoose.

"Can I pick her up?"

"Of course!"

But I can't. My upper back won't let me. Norma two weeks after a cesarean section is more agile than I am six months after my surgery. She puts the baby in my arms. Lauren fits snugly in the crook of my left arm exactly as her father did. I whisper my welcome to this new person mysteriously connected to me. She nuzzles at my breast. Norma laughs and takes the baby and settles in the rocking chair, humming to Lauren as she nurses.

I find Mark in the basement loading diapers into the washer. Brendon is making roads with Mark's sacred socket set. "You let him play with your tools? What a nice daddy!"

"Sometimes. Lots of times I'm impatient and mean and want to run away so *I* can be the kid."

"Shucks. Human like the rest of us." I hand Brendon a wrench and something stabs me between the shoulder blades. "Can you do anything for my upper back?" Without hesitating Mark puts his fingers on the vertebrae that burn. "How did you know which ones hurt?"

"I asked the Maker and Source. I'm surprised it got through. I'm not a very clear channel these days." He tests the strength of my right arm while he touches different places on my spine. "Brendon! Where's my activator?"

Brendon produces a little gadget with a rubber plunger and Mark nudges two vertebrae into different places. The pain stops as if he'd flipped a switch.

The next day Brendon does my "bird-dog" and "stick-em-up" and "dead-bug" exercises with me. He takes me outside to show me his dead bugs, to make me listen to the birds and to the vacuum cleaner roaring across the street. He gets tired. "I need a hug," he says. I hold him. Nothing competes for my attention. Mark had to compete with the urgent agenda of a twenty-four-year-old woman. It's not the absence of responsibility that makes grandparenting better than parenting, I decide. It's lack of conflict.

Every night I dream about babies. One night I'm giving birth, another night I'm taking care of dozens of tiny babies, stacked in a drawer like pieces of chalk. I dream I find a healthy baby girl aban-

doned in the woods. I want to adopt her, but a lawyer says I can't until I know who she is.

Norma has mastitis. When Mark goes to school I tell her to rest with the heating pad. I'm Earth Mother. I change Lauren's diapers and I change Brendon's diapers and then I change Lauren's diapers again. I make macaroni and cheese and wash the pots and give Brendon a bath and sterilize bottles for Lauren's drinking water and try to comfort Brendon when Norma is nursing. In quiet intervals Norma and I talk about feminism and spirituality and politics. Even then I feel trapped in the relentless domestic rhythms. My back is killing me.

I gaze out the window at the scraggly back yards. Probably it's raining like this in London, where we're heading next. It can rain like this in Rome, too, pour for weeks while all your chairs huddle in front of the radiators shrouded in wet laundry. But when I was living there, because all my children were grown up, I'd walk out on my wet underwear and go look at the Madonnas in the Vatican. Some Earth Mother! If I were mothering small children now, I'd be every bit as impatient and restless as I was thirty years ago. I could never be satisfied with the "little piece of quiet" Mark knew mothers need. It's not real babies I want to adopt. It's that abandoned baby in my dream. It's my newborn self, wailing for empty hours and quiet spaces to grow in.

At breakfast Mark says, "There's a look on your face I know so well. What have I done to annoy you?"

"Nothing! It's raining and my body hurts. It has nothing to do with you. Did you really grow up believing whatever bothered me was your fault?"

"Maybe all kids do."

"I'm sure I yelled at you when something else was bothering me."

"I do that to Brendon. Norma's patience amazes me. I can see how it's made Brendon secure in places I'm not." He gets up and pours himself another bowl of cereal. "Sometimes I find myself wishing my own mother had been able to give me that." There's no anger on his face. Just sadness.

"You couldn't possibly wish that more than I do." My eyes are full.

"You gave me a lot of other things."

"Nothing that matters as much."

Mark bends to kiss me as he leaves for school. I hold on for a moment to his thick beard. I couldn't give him what I didn't have any more than my mother and father could give me what they didn't have, or their parents could give them what *they* didn't have. The universality of the equation doesn't make it any less hateful.

Brendon is sitting on the kitchen floor playing with the plastic gears I brought him and singing to himself. Norma is crooning to Lauren. I put the cereal boxes back in the cabinets. This is a happy house. Sometimes Norma is hard on Mark and sometimes Mark ignores Norma and they both have too much work and we can't send them enough money to make life easy, but still this house is happy. The house where Mark grew up was often full of shouts and tears. The house where I grew up bulged with my parents' misery. The strong storm windows my father manufactured could barely keep that unhappiness from exploding all over the street.

I collect the glasses and bowls from the kitchen table and run water into the dishpan. The hot water makes my face flush. Even my mother's hot flashes were *my* fault. All my parents' illnesses and all their unhappiness was all my fault, which is why Mark thought what bothered me was his fault.

I couldn't stop doing the things that made my mother swallow phenobarbital and my father swallow bicarbonate of soda by the boxful until it killed him. I couldn't stop hurting them but I couldn't stand their pain either. As soon as I could I ran away and looked for ways to relieve other people's misery—people in Newark and Vietnam and Egypt and Brazil and Nicaragua and El Salvador. My parents' pain stretched all over the globe. Now I'm holding on to the pain in the Woolson family. I don't want it inside me, or I'll be trapped in misery forever like my parents, but I want it right next to me. It belongs to the little girl who wanted to eat worms and die. It connects her to the suffering human race.

That must be why I teach about pain and choose a tormented woman as my soul mate and write about suffering people in developing countries. I work all the time because I have to make amends for failing to make my parents happy, and for bringing unhappiness into my children's lives. For failing to save Connie's life. For failing to end all the suffering in the world.

In the bedroom Lauren wails. Brendon looks up. "The baby is crying," he reports, "but I'm okay!"

"You sure are," I tell him, "but I'm not. I need a hug." He jumps up and squeezes me tight around the neck.

I used to hug my mother that way. She wasn't always severe. The moments I remember are the ones I need for the story I tell myself about my life. For years I saw myself as the bad daughter of a good mother. Now I see myself as the rejected daughter of a jealous mother. Neither story is the truth. It's not my real mother I'm remembering, not the complicated person who happened to be my mother. What if my own children forget how I rocked them and read to them, how I encouraged them to explore, how I made them laugh? What if all they remember is my hardness and meanness and impatience?

Dr. Frederick is out of town, so his associate sticks my San Francisco x rays and today's new x rays into lighted boxes on the

272

wall. He stands silent, looking from one to the other, hands on hips, for what seems like five minutes.

"Is it bad?" I finally ask.

"It's phenomenal! You're ninety, maybe ninety-five percent fused. Are you sure these last films were taken six weeks ago?"

"Aren't they dated?" I sound rational but my whole body is vibrating with the news.

"They are, but it's hard to believe what I'm seeing—from next to no fusion to nearly solid fusion in six weeks? What have you been doing?"

Succinctly—because his freight-train manner hasn't changed since my surgery six months ago—I tell him: Stim. Megadoses of calcium. Phosphates. Torture sessions with Robin, whose seven-page report I hand him. Muscle building. Swimming. Walking. Remolding my brace. I continue the list silently. Bathing my bones in the power of the sun. Watching the waters in Oak Creek. Recognizing my dream goddess in the sky. Finding my selves in Connie.

"You're nearly well," he says.

My heart lurches. Not disabled! No more surgery! "Even though my back and legs still hurt?"

"You'll have pain until you're a hundred percent fused. Start weaning yourself from the brace. Wear it only when you're out walking, but keep using the Stim until you have x rays that show you're solidly fused. Six more weeks should do it." His hand is on the doorknob of the examining room.

"Would you thank Dr. Frederick for me?"

"Sure."

He'll forget. It doesn't matter. I'll write Dr. Frederick from London. I stand at the receptionist's deck writing a check, my hand shaking. I can have my old life back—if I still want it.

16

Not Everything Can Open

The president of the College for Psychic Studies can see me at three o'clock. Walking there and back will meet my daily quota, four miles. I'm pounding my bones into London's streets, ignoring aches and pains, leaning into the April wind as I push for the finish line. David's in Munich. If he were here, or Hillevi, or Sharon, I wouldn't be walking down Queen's Gate now to get psychic advice. But the night David left I had a dream that scared me silly. Not my lifelong dream of a dangerous man coming to get me. I haven't dreamed that since the night I opened the door and let him in.

It was a woman scaring me, a Gypsy sitting with her legs wide apart, her skirt stretched like a table. "Can you tell me how to find Connie?" I asked. "Jump out the window," she said. "Not me! Not on your life!" "Then take her hand," she said. A hand reached down and grasped my hand and pulled me through the roof and swooped me around the stars. I looked down and saw the earth webbed with lines like a map of airline routes, connecting everything with everything else. I looked up to see who was holding my hand, but the face was turned away from me.

All day I kept remembering a story Henry James wrote about a woman's ghost luring a man to suicide. If Connie's trying that on me I want to know. That's why I'm finally taking the advice of a friend who's been urging me to visit the College of Psychic Studies. Very respectable place, she assures me. Almost as old as the Society for Psychical Research, whose heavy volumes Connie studied. The president of the College gives excellent counsel. We'll see.

The beige and blue bricks of the Victoria and Albert Museum are behind me. I cross Cromwell Road and hurry down Queensberry Place. Number 16 has a shiny black door with a polished brass knob. Behind the door must be cobwebs and crones cackling in corners. Behind the door is in fact a library with books rising to a twelve-foot-high ceiling, rolling ladders, people reading in leather chairs. A receptionist tells me the president will see me now. On the landing of the gray-carpeted steps is a pretty, white-haired woman in her late sixties wearing a well-tailored skirt and shirt.

"I'm Brenda Marshall," she says. Her voice is low, her hand-shake firm. Her office looks the way the office of the president of a small college should look—books, files, plants, upholstered chairs. No cobwebs. Not even a crystal ball.

"Thank you for giving me this time," I say as I sit down. "I'm troubled by my relationship with a nineteenth-century woman writer I've been studying for several years."

"What is her name?"

"Constance Fenimore Woolson." I relish the sound of those syllables in this building.

"What sort of relationship do you have with her?"

"Too many sorts. Sometimes she helps me learn her secrets.

Other times she confronts me. Once I thought she gave me a good hard hit in the head!"

"What brought that on?" She settles an embroidered cushion behind her back.

"My son had asked me why I'd chosen Connie rather than some other writer, and I said that probably any of a number of writers would have done as well. The minute the words were out of my mouth, something bopped me right here, above my right ear. I imagined she'd punched me for insulting her."

"I've been nudged in that way."

"By someone who's dead?"

"By a spirit, yes. More than once."

"She gave me a bigger bop last night. I believe she killed herself, nearly a hundred years ago, by jumping out of her window in Venice. Last night in a dream someone told me that the way to find her was to jump out the window."

"Common sense is just as important in invisible matters as it is in visible ones," says Mrs. Marshall firmly. "Don't let her possess you. Exercise your free will." Her mild blue eyes are shooting sparks. "It doesn't surprise me that a person who committed suicide would still be focused on an incarnate being. Such people often die in a state of shame or remorse. Lacking physical bodies, they have fewer options for working through their problems."

That's not so different from what Hillevi told me. Suicide can be a healthy impulse gone wrong, she said, a desire to kill a part of the self that really does need to die so something else can grow. It's a terrible mistake to kill the body you need for that transformation.

"You think she might want something from me? A hundred years after her death?"

"Discarnate spirits do need healing," says Mrs. Marshall in her measured voice. "Some of them get stuck. Some violent types make trouble among the living."

276

"Connie was never violent to anyone but herself."

"She may need you to help her learn something she failed to learn in life."

"Should I consult a medium?"

"I wouldn't. Receiving and transmitting are both very difficult. You two are communicating remarkably well. A third person would only get in the way."

"Can you suggest books for me to read?"

"I'd suggest you *not* read. Respect your experience."

"But I'm so at sea here!"

"Perhaps one article—do you know the novels of Rosamond Lehmann? She wrote about the suicide of a close friend. We have the article in the library downstairs."

She accepts my thanks and sees me out. The librarian promptly finds me the article and I sit down with it in a big leather chair. It seems that Lehmann's dead daughter Sally looked up her mother's dead friend and sent her a report through a medium. He "bitterly regretted this mistake" of killing himself at the peak of his career, Sally said. He couldn't "forgive himself for failing to carry out the mission he undertook." It's hard to copy these words into my notebook. My right hand has gone to sleep. Sally tells her mother to think of her friend "with all the intensity you can muster. See him actually taking his God-given life." Oh, I've done that. I've watched Connie crash to her death again and again and again. Felt every bone crack. "Feel for him as a mother." Yes, as a mother and a sister and a lover and a child. I've done that too. But then you should let all that pain go. "Take him into your garden and try to make him laugh again; that would be a real healing treatment."

I pay for a photocopy of the article and add a five-pound donation to the College. It's hard to fish the bill out of my wallet with these pins and needles in my hand. The polished brass doorknob shoots electricity from my palm to my armpit. I look

277

carefully at the knob, but it looks ordinary enough. Shaking out my hand, I walk down Queensberry Place and wait at the light at Cromwell Road. Suicide may have been Connie's mistake but my mistake has been holding on to her pain for so long. I did it because I began this journey to meet Miss Grief knowing more about her grief than my own. Studying her pain is helping me find mine, but maybe it's hurting her.

I'll take her for a walk in Kensington Gardens. She must often have approached them from this side, walking with Henry James from his rooms in De Vere Gardens. My left hand is cold and my right hand is hot and still tingling. It feels like someone is holding it. I smile. Today Connie's walking with *me*.

We pass under the elaborate wrought-iron swirls of the Queen's Gate. Nannies are pushing baby carriages, silver-haired women are talking earnestly together on benches, gardeners are weeding. No one is looking at me strangely. We stop under a blossoming cherry tree in the Flower Walk, its branches bobbing with noisy birds. How could you jump out of a world with all this in it, Connie? She tugs me toward the Round Pond. On the concrete rim seven ducklings are sunbathing in a heap like a gray feather cushion. I don't want to be overheard talking to Connie, so I say to a woman standing there, "Aren't they funny?"

The woman smiles, shrugs, says painfully, "I—do not—speak English."

"*Parla italiano?*" I guess.

"*Si!*"

The woman tells me she's here from Rome visiting her son. I haven't spoken Italian for three years, but nouns and verbs and prepositions flow out of my mouth. She hasn't heard about the exhibition on Pompeii just up the street at the Accademia Italiana, so I give her directions and a big *arrivederci*. My Italian wasn't this good when I was speaking it every day. Connie's Italian was flawless.

We head for the white statue of a youthful Queen Victoria and skirt Kensington Palace. Such a disappointing palace—just a heap of red brick. I never cared for it, Connie says. Let's walk by Alice James's house on our way home. We turn down Argyll Road and stop in front of number 41. This is where Alice worked at what she called "the hardest job of all . . . to get myself dead." The bay window seems to bulge with her effort. I gave England one more year after Alice died, Connie says. Alice hoped Henry would turn to me once she was off his hands. He didn't. He just wanted to be my "con-frere." My brother writer. That's how he signed himself in the volume of Shelley's poems he gave me. I told him I'd be his "admiring aunt." To be that I didn't need to live under gray English skies and pay English prices. I moved to Venice. You know the rest.

Workmen are gutting Alice's house. They let us teeter over boards and drainage pipes and look straight up from the basement through the missing ceilings to the third floor. I'm glad to see them rip the pain out of that house, Connie says. We walk down the hill and I go into the Safeway to buy food I like that David doesn't. While he's eating Munich *bratwurst* I'll have salmon and a huge head of cauliflower that I'll sauté with a lethal quantity of garlic and eat all week. Does Connie like garlic? She seems not to have come into the store with me. Walking down the street to our apartment, there's nothing in my hand but the loop of the plastic grocery bag. I wonder where she went.

I cook quickly and eat slowly, browsing through *Time Out* for something I want to see that David wouldn't. There's a rave review for a play called *Massa*, about a real-life Victorian poet who married his servant. I'm reading the last paragraph when a tingle zips from my right palm up through my chest and down to my left palm. What is this, some bizarre disease? Connie reviewed a novel on the same subject as the play—*That Lass o'Lowrie's*, it was called. I think I'll go see it.

The theater is four rows of seats in an airless room over a pub in Camden Town. My hands distract me from the dialogue of the "pit-brow lassies" shoveling coal ten feet away from me. Blackout. Lights on. Now the poet and his friends are coming home from an evening at the theater. On the table five feet away from me he slaps down a playbill for *That Lass o'Lowrie's*. Volts race through me. I grip my seat to keep from leaping onto the stage. Now the characters are arguing about the same class issues Connie wrote about in her review. I sit on my hands. I don't know if she helped me speak Italian, but I'm positive she's dragged me all the way up here to Camden Town.

At home I have my hands under cold running water when David calls. "I got into the office where Hitler and Chamberlain and Mussolini agreed to sell Czechoslavakia down the river! It was just an ordinary room, wood paneled, but it gave me the creeps." I tell him about my hands. "I can see you perfectly," he says. "Your hair is frizzled by electricity and your body's painted blue."

"That must be my aura you're seeing," I say.

"You don't think you're having a heart attack or something?"

"No, I'm just full to bursting and totally drained. Exhilarated and exhausted, all at the same time."

"Should I come home?"

"No. I think this stuff waited to happen until I was alone. I wouldn't miss it for anything."

I climb into bed. "Connie," I say out loud, "would you please let go of my hands now? I need some rest!"

The next thing I know the sun is shining and my hands are quiet. No dreams. I'm spooning Earl Grey tea into the teapot when I remember the dream that sent me to see Brenda Marshall. Someone pulled me through the roof by my right hand. The same hand Connie was holding yesterday. Suddenly a shock races up my right arm through my chest and down my left arm. I drop the spoon. My body's become a truth detector. Or do I zing when I'm *wrong*?

I pull on my sweat suit and start my dead-bug stick-em-up routine. This isn't the first time a dream's confronted me in daylight. But it's one thing to see your dream pulsing away in the sky. It's something else to have it zipping through your body. I genuflect. Whose will is being done here? I'll exercise mine, the way Mrs. Marshall told me to, by taking my walk in Holland Park. I'm a little afraid of Kensington Gardens. Peacocks are rattling their tails at peahens who have perfected indifference. Leaning on the fence, I ponder the connections between my dream life and the world of beaks and feathers I used to think was the only real one.

I leave the park by the Duchess of Bedford's Walk so I can walk home by way of Argyll Road. Dust and clatter rise from number 41. Right here Alice James lived her painful life to the end. Her friend Katherine Loring had a lethal dose ready if she wanted it, but she never did. They found that hypnosis eased not only the pain of her cancer but also the "moral discords and nervous horrors" that "sear the soul, so I go no longer in dread." That's what Alice wrote on the last day of her life. There was no one to hypnotize Connie, no one to give her an easy death if hypnosis failed.

She did prepare her friends for her death. "If I live, and live here," she wrote in November, "I may write a little volume not about Venice, but on the islands of the lagoons. But I may neither live, nor live here." She warned her editor at *Harper's* that she was "profoundly discouraged," that she would "do very little more." Not because she'd lost her powers; she knew what they were: "If I could go into a convent, (where I didn't have to confess, nor rise before daylight for icy matins), I think I could write three or four novels better than any I have yet done. But there are no worldly convents. So I'll write my new effusions on another star, and send them back to you by telepathy."

A shock rides its course from hand to hand. I clutch the low black gate in front of Alice's house. Connie knew! Even before she died she knew she'd send her words back by telepathy: It took her nearly a century to find a receiver. If only I'd been alive when she needed me. I could have provided that worldly convent. I could rent a floor of a palazzo looking out on a Venetian canal, and fill its balcony with pots of cyclamen. I'd protect her from distractions and shield her from worry. She'd have a great Late Phase like Henry James. She'd earn a place like his in the canon.

Imagine David in a *ménage à trois!* He's wildly jealous now of the way Connie soaks up my time and attention. And do I really want to be Mother Superior of Connie's worldly convent? My attention span as Earth Mother was pretty short. And how would it feel to live with her immense talent? I'd be paralyzed. Silenced, erased. I couldn't bear it. Not even to save her life.

I ride the creaky elevator to our flat and flop across the bed to read over again the words Connie wrote just a month before her death. On Christmas Eve she tells her childhood friend Belle Washburn, "if at any time you should hear that I have gone, I want you to know beforehand that my end was peace, and even joy at the release." She wasn't ill when she wrote that letter. That afternoon she'd walked for two hours with her dog along the Adriatic beach and watched "the sharp peaks of the Dolomites . . . riding along through immeasurable space, they are the outer edge of our star, they cut through the air as they fly. They are the rim of the world." Already she was seeing our warm earth as a cold star, already she was flying with the mountains through the icy air. "I should like to turn into a peak when I die," she says, "to be a beautiful purple mountain, which would please the tired sad eyes of thousands of human beings for ages." People can look to her if they want to. She's not looking to the hills or anywhere else for help. She wants "nothing to do with the eternal sorrow and despair of poor human beings."

It's too late to call her back. She's made up her mind to die. Not because she has an excruciating illness or because she dreads an addict's death like Charly's but because she's ready. For decades she's imagined women falling from cliffs and lighthouses and parapets and bridges. Now she's going to open her shutters and hurl herself out. I accept her death. I have to. But I can't stand the way she dies.

I want to change it. I could take the next plane to Milan, the fast train to Venice, the vaporetto up the Grand Canal to the San Gregorio district, the stairs to Connie's rooms on the second floor of the Casa Semitecolo.

A small black puppy leaps on me with growls and bared teeth. Tello races ahead of me into the sitting room. There's Connie's carved walnut table from Florence, her own china and silver arranged in glass-fronted cabinets, shelves and shelves of books.

The puppy dashes into Connie's bedroom and jumps onto the bed beside her. My approach is cautious. Her head shifts restlessly on the pillows, her breath comes fast and shallow. I take her hand and she opens her eyes. She knows me.

"For a long time my daily prayer has been that I may not live to be old," she says, as if we were in the middle of a conversation. Which I suppose we are. "Well, I don't know anyone so old as I am now!"

"I'm just as old as you are," I say.

"You'll never be as old as I am. I've been trying to imagine my body fading gently out of life, but it's too stubborn. Perhaps if the suggestion came from you—"

"Is that really what you want?"

"That window is the 'open door.' " Her voice is firm, though she's so weak she can barely turn her head. "I'll walk through it if I have to. But I'd much rather not. You could help me think myself dead."

"You'd have to believe I could do it," I say.

" 'All things are possible to him that believeth.' "

"Jesus meant restoring life. He didn't mean dying."

"He said *all* things.' "

If she has any lingering desire to live, I tell myself, my suggestion will have no power. I pull her favorite yellow chair next to her bed. To sit in it feels like sitting in her lap. I want to sit in her lap, be her child and have her comfort me. A wave of longing nearly suffocates me.

"If you would like to have it, I'd like you to have my stand-up desk," she says.

I can't trust my voice to tell her how much I would like it. But she knows. I take off my necklace with its silver circle like an empty womb, a good talisman for two menopausal women. I let it swing above Connie's head and tell her to gaze at it. You are feeling drowsy, I say. Your eyes are growing heavy. I sound like a parody of a platform mesmerist. You want only to go to sleep, I tell her. You couldn't lift your arm if you wanted to, but you don't want to. Your eyes grow heavier and heavier. When you can't hold them open a moment longer, go ahead and close them. Are you ready to turn into a mountain peak?

"Yes."

"Are you ready to ride through space? To cut through the air as you fly along the rim of the world?"

"Yes," she says.

I want to ask if she's really sure she's ready to go, but I don't want to interfere with the suggestion that she is. "Whenever you're ready, you can begin to become that beautiful purple mountain. Whenever you're ready, you can let go of life. You can rest. Rest. Rest. Rest."

The creases of pain between her eyes and around her mouth are fading. I close my own eyes and tell myself to rest. Not forever, just long enough to lend her my subjective power.

Pale daylight is seeping through the drapes. I've slept for hours. And Connie? She hasn't moved. Light shallow breaths touch my hand as I hold it near her face. Her face is peaceful and beautiful. Finally she opens her eyes. She's returning from very far away. But she is returning.

"How do you feel?" I ask.

"Rested," she says. "But disappointed."

"Maybe there were negative suggestions in the room." If there were negative suggestions, they came from me. I don't want her to die.

Connie looks at me and says, "You don't want me to die."

So our telepathy works. "No. Are you feeling better?"

"I don't want to feel better," she says. And then, very deliberately, "I don't want to feel anything ever again."

She means it. I light a lamp and go to the dining room where I know the nurse keeps the laudanum. I choose the pink porcelain cup from the cabinet. I pour into it several ounces of the liquid. Then like an alcoholic trying to hide her habit I pour an equal amount of water into the bottle. That's as far as I can go to protect myself from the legal consequences of euthanasia. About the moral consequences my conscience is oddly silent.

Connie reaches out her hand for the cup. My eyes ask her if she's sure. Her gaze holds mine steadily. It was me wavering before, not her. She drains the cup. I sit beside her on the bed and she settles into my arms. Soon she's asleep. And then I feel a change. Her body feels heavier. Whatever animated it has gone. Something seems to have risen. I feel for her pulse, and find none. Gently, I put her down on her pillows. Her face is full of peace, even of joy. I pull back the drapes, pull in the large framed panes, push out the heavy slatted shutters. Sunshine streams in. This is the open door. Connie is joining the mountains.

Hard sobs rack my chest. But down in the narrow courtyard below me there is no white heap moaning *"freddo."* There will be no police inquiries. Henry James will miss the searing grief that deepened his soul and quickened his Late Phase. No Late Phase for Connie either. Not everything can open.

My hands are quiet.

Back Talk

. . .

Ed essa da martiro e da essilo venne a questa pace: and from martyrdom and from exile she came to this peace. Those are the words
William James chose for the urn that held his sister's ashes.
Connie was exiled even more completely than Alice from her
country and from her own desires. But if she was a martyr to
her history and to the irreconcilable claims of her own nature,
she managed to turn that martyrdom to art. That's what matters now.

EPILOGUE

avid meets my plane in Athens and we take the bus to Delphi. I want to find the spring where the Pythia drank, and the sacred chasm where she sat on her tripod, breathing smoke from burning laurel leaves and letting the god's prophecies enter her empty womb. The priestesses had to be women past the age for childbearing. I may not have the sibyl's gifts, but at least I'm the right age for the job.

We get to the sanctuary very late in the afternoon. It's vast and baffling. I can't find the chasm. Italian schoolchildren race up and down the terraces carved in the mountainside, screaming to one another. The next morning I wake very early and go out on our balcony. The green mountain under me slopes sharply before it slides gently into the Gulf of Corinth. Each range of mountains across the Gulf floats up through the dawn a different color. David comes out and puts his arm around me. Now I'm seeing with his eyes as well as my own. It's still wonderful but it's different.

We decide to look for the ancient pilgrims' path before the other tourists wake up. All we hear is our footsteps and bird calls. Beyond the sanctuary we find a path leading down to a terrace full of fallen stones. Three Doric columns from a little round temple to Gaia are all that's left of the great goddess that Apollo overthrew. Poppies and buttercups push up around the fallen blocks of white marble. David goes off to photograph a rock face where greenery burgeons from millimeters of soil, and I follow a stream that leads to a deep gorge. It may not be the sacred Castalian spring where ancient pilgrims purified themselves, but it feels like a sacred place. I kneel and wash my hands and wrists, my neck and lips. My eyes fill. These aren't tears of grief or even anger. They're about recognition.

Mother Gaia, here I am. Here you are. Rock-bottom reality, old as the hills. My body's astonishing power of renewal is a tiny mirror of yours. Teach me to be a Pythia—a woman whose womb is no longer a place to shelter babies but a channel for truth, a woman who dares to inhale the burning laurel leaves and say how things are and must be.

This is the first time I've prayed since Cantor Rosbach died.

From Athens we fly to Iraklion. On our way to the Archaeological Museum we walk through an outdoor market, ducking skinned rabbits and enormous livers hanging from hooks. I'm still shuddering when we reach the cool museum. I stand in front of two small faience statues of the Snake Goddess. A huge snake twines around the ears and breasts and belly of the larger figure. The smaller one holds a snake in each of her outstretched arms. Then I notice her nipples. They're bright red. They're the same fiery red as the nipples of the Volcano Goddess in my dream.

I hug myself, trying to keep my pounding heart from cracking open my chest. This red-nippled goddess presided over human destiny three or four thousand years before she appeared in my dream. So my dreams connect me not just with the California sky but with an ancient religion that revered a power and wisdom it saw as Feminine. I gaze and gaze at her, trembling. She brought me to this island formed of volcanoes and all but destroyed by them. She's showing me how creation and destruction twine together like the snake coiling itself around her belly and breasts and ears.

I leave David looking at bulls' masks and walk out of the museum porous as a fishnet and invulnerable as a tank. I step over broken paving stones, dodge motor scooters. This must be how it feels to be in a state of grace. I want to immerse myself in some ritual way.

There's a pool on the roof of our hotel. I push off into the long glide of the breaststroke, excruciating the last time I tried it a month ago. A few tentative strokes feel fine. A lap feels wonderful. I swim lap after lap. I know in my bones it's over. I'm strong as ever—stronger than I was before these months of exercises. I'm not going to have to learn to live horizontally, or live limited by pain. At least not yet, not from this injury. I've shed the skin of this year of disability. In my new skin I am shiny and vulnerable and stunningly alive.

Each lap I dedicate to one of the people who helped me heal. The surgeons, the physical therapists, the Jungian analyst who opened my dreams. The friends who held me in the net of their love. My father for my stubbornness. My mother for my ability to laugh. My grandfather for my conviction that life is good. My great-grandparents for leaving Russia for a country where I'd get the best of treatment. My children for their wisdom and forgiveness. David for seeing me through every hour of this long year. This morning he told me that he woke in the night thinking "Joan's healed." And Connie. For helping me retrieve my fractured parts and start to fuse them into myself. Connie who has helped me heal though she could never heal herself.

For the first time in over a year I dress without my brace. My body feels extravagantly free and alarmingly vulnerable. What if one of those motor scooters runs into me? Stopping to look in the window of a jewelry shop, I try to cover my rear by grasping one wrist in the other hand behind my back. I see only one thing in the crowded window—a ring shaped like a serpent uncoiling, a narrow strip of gold. I have to feel it on my finger. It fits perfectly. But could I stand to wear it? It would look down my finger at every word I write. It could strike at any word that wavers from the truth, hissing like the volcano in my dream. It would demand that I keep shedding old skins. Demand that I hang upside down and submit to the deaths that precede new life.

The coils of the snake on my right hand mirror the thick twisted gold of the wedding band on my left. I think of Connie's diamond ring that I wanted so badly to feel on my finger. If I buy this ring I'll be marrying the Snake Goddess. Would that be infidelity to David? Or to the Judaism I haven't practiced but would never renounce? I don't feel divinity emanating from the Goddess, under any of her thousand names, any more than from Jehovah or Allah. It's all one force. One Unity, Dave says. One Maker and Source, Mark calls it. The cause of things that happen even though they're impossible, according to Leslie. To connect with that force I need to see the most intimate parts of my female self as tiny images of the sacred. I need a reminder that the immeasurable force that creates and destroys is also intimate enough to send signals to me. That it exists inside me. The serpent is as good a reminder as any.

The ring costs eleven thousand drachmas, the jeweler says. You can have it for ten. Ten? I can't pay more than eight. Eight is fine, he says before I've made up my mind that I'm brave enough to wear this ring. Walking out of the store I feel some force flowing from the ring into my body. It doesn't buzz or tingle but it's there. I run the fingers of my left hand over the serpent's coils, stroking her. Under the hot afternoon sun I'm shivering.

David lets me into our hotel room. He's wrapping an apple in a plastic bag and securing it with two rubber bands.

"I can understand why you wrap shampoo that way," I say. "It can leak. But an apple?"

"Does everyone have to be just like you? Do you have to supervise every move I make? This insatiable need of yours to control—" His face is red. He's shouting. Anger flares up in me and subsides. He's right. I want to be in charge after a long year of dependency. Abruptly he stops yelling and plants himself right in front of me. "But I love you so goddamn much!"

We stand frozen for a long moment. Then we both burst out laughing. We fall into each other's arms. When we pull back I see his eyes are swimming too.

That night I dream I discover an important carving on a marble fragment. I fully expect to see that stone when we go to Knossos, the home of the red-nippled Snake Goddesses. If the carving is there, I don't find it. The next day we drive through fertile valleys between rocky crags where a volcano hiccuped millennia ago. We walk around a jumble of stones that used to be a provincial palace. The heat keeps us moving from one patch of shade to the next. And there, on the walls of rooms used for rituals thirty-five hundred years ago, I find simple signs carved as deeply and crudely as graffiti. What is this, I ask David—a trident? Or is it a three-branched menorah? Or maybe a cross with the arms turned up at the ends? And look at this cross with its four ends sprouting into *V*s. Is it a tree of life? A person sprouting into a tree? A person hung from a tree? Before Christ, before Moses, these symbols meant something to the people who carved them here.

I can feel the yearnings in the hands that carved these images. It streams from these stones into some part of me whose name I haven't learned. The deeply carved lines whisper something about transformation, about a yearning so strong for the renewal of life that it accepts the sacrifice of what already lives.

I hate sacrifice. I like addition, not subtraction.

Here in Crete people leapt and somersaulted between the horns of bulls without knowing if the bulls would be sacrificed or if they would. They danced with the knowledge that life continues only on the sacrifice of other life. You can't get away from it, not even if you eat only vegetables and tie rags around your feet. But you can dance between the horns of the dilemma—that loss and renewal are inseparable, two sides of the sacred double axe that cuts both ways. That I have had to sacrifice illusions to receive Connie's gift, a gift shaped by her destruction of herself.

Pruning encourages new growth. Vineyards bear lavishly after lava scrapes a mountain bare. The sacrifice of my active life was only temporary, I think as I fall asleep that night. It did me the tremendous favor of taking me out of life without killing me. The life that was unused in me was the part that could wait and watch and discover that I live in a vibrating web of connection. That web connects dreams to the world, the living to the dead, and the living to each other. We are forever tearing it. Now that I know I live in a cosmos and not a chaos, I have to try to mend the gaps I can see.

I dream that I'm wandering out of a bookstore into a garden of bare trees. One tall tree has been trimmed into a V. Such drastic pruning! It must have been diseased or hit by lightning. Still, it has an odd grace. Four creamy blossoms bloom just below the V. Pruned by loss, strengthened by grafts, it's blooming out of season.

ACKNOWLEDGMENTS

*D*avid Weimer insisted I could find the voice to write about the experience this book describes. Every page, sentence, and word received the benefit of his wisdom.

My children, David, Mark and Leslie, helped me think over our lives together but refused to censor what I wrote about them. My stepchildren, Mark and Joan Weimer, Brit and Judy Weimer, Calvin and Noelle Weimer Roso, prayed for my recovery long before I understood that prayer could do any good. My mother, brother and sister helped me remember. Sharon Blessum taught me loving friendship.

Eve Merriam gave me the courage to write what I thought was an unpublishable book. I wish she had lived to see it in print. Vanessa Ochs showed me how to cut out a third of my first draft and get the "raw" into what was left. Mary Felstiner passed every thought and sentence through her laser mind and loving heart. Daniel Harris pointed me toward nineteenth-

293

century spiritualism and asked penetrating questions about an earlier version of this book.

My editor Olga Seham saw a gleam in five hundred pages of earlier thrashings, and asked the hard questions that helped me write the best book that was in me. Malaga Baldi has been an ideally tough agent and warm friend.

Grace Paley gave me astute comments on Chapter 7 and helped me remember that political activism is a form of pleasure. Many friends and colleagues commented on all or parts of the manuscript, or helped me think through its themes: Jacqueline Berke, Sharon Blessum, Janet Burstein, Pearl Charles, Vicki Christensen, Suzanne Gardinier, Georgia Heard, Janet Larson, Janet Neipris, Chantal Rosas-Cobian, Mira Stillman, Jerry Stillman, Cheryl Torsney, Barbara Wright. Kathryn Kimball shared the journal she kept after her own spine surgery.

Woolson's descendants James and Beverly Woolson, Molly Mather Anderson, and Henry S.F. Cooper, Jr. were generous with their knowledge of family history and warmly hospitable to me.

Librarians at the Western Reserve Historical Society and the New York State Historical Association were particularly patient, as were Signore Morbidelli, director of the Protestant Cemetery in Rome and Josie Cook, head of Interlibrary Loan at Drew University Library. Kathleen Reich, Rollins College archivist, was an enthusiastic and resourceful ally.

Adriana Greci-Green found Casa Semitecolo in Venice and photographed the windows from which Woolson fell to her death, proving to my satisfaction that the fall could not have been an accident. Paul Arnold photographed old photos of Woolson and her family.

Drew University provided and repaired my indispensable computer; allowed me to postpone my sabbatical leave until the end of my disability leave; funded my travel to archives in Winter Park, Cooperstown, and Cleveland; gave me a Faculty

Acknowledgments

Research Grant in 1990 and 1991, and a leave of absence for all of 1992 on short notice. Dean Paolo Cucchi was unfailingly supportive of my work. A number of student assistants made photocopies, checked footnotes, and talked over Woolson's fiction with me: Jean Scully, Colleen Dube, and David von Schlichten were most enthusiastic. Students in my classes in nineteenth-century American literature gave me new ideas about Woolson's fiction; students in my Nonfiction Writing Workshop in the fall of 1991 showed me that Woolson's power to haunt was not confined to me. Professors Sally Rackley and Bob Fenstermacher helped me avoid gaffes when I strayed from my own discipline.

Dr. Robert Morrison, Dr. Kim Sommer, Dr. Jim Zuckerman, physical therapists Robin Strom and Elizabeth Buchanan, Jungian analysts Dr. Hillevi Ruumet and Dr. Diana Beach—these healers, along with everyone else named here, have my deep admiration and gratitude.

NOTES

1

p.11: biography of her aunt: Clare Benedict, *Constance Fenimore Woolson,* Vol. II of *Five Generations (1785–1932)* (London: privately printed, 1930, 1932). Hereafter referred to as Benedict.

p.13: "didn't make her do things she didn't want to do": original letter is in the Benedict Library, Protestant Cemetery, Rome.

p.14: "astute . . . rivalled Henry James's.": Van Wyck Brooks, *The Dream of Arcadia: American Writers and Artists in Italy 1760–1915* (New York: Dutton, 1958), pp. 194–95.

p.15: "enrage myself . . . hate's very enlivening.": CFW letter to Katharine P. Loring, 19 September [1890]; Loring Papers, Beverly [Mass.] Historical Society.

p.15: Matthew Arnold . . . longing for death.: Matthew Arnold, *Essays in Criticism* (Leipzig: Bernhard Tauchnitz, 1887), vol. 2, pp. 139–40; "Thoreau" in James Russell Lowell's *My Study Windows* (Boston: Houghton Mifflin, 1886), p.

204; *An Author's Love: Being the Unpublished Letters of Prosper Mérimée's "Inconnue"* (London: Macmillan, 1889), vol. 2, p. 195; all in Rollins College Archives.

p.17: "debris . . . cool-enfolding death.": Walt Whitman, "When Lilacs Last in the Dooryard Bloom'd."

p.18: "crape-veil'd women . . . through the night": Whitman, *Ibid.*

p.20: "And when, it may be . . . Depart.": *The Teaching of Epictetus: Being the 'Encheiridion of Epictetus,' with Selections from the 'Dissertations' and 'Fragments,'* trans. and ed. T. W. Rolleston (London: Walter Scott, 1888), p. 135.

p.20: "the open door . . . wholesome life impossible.": Epictetus, p. 200.

2

pp.31–32: "the only working hypothesis . . . T. J. Hudson.": CFW letter to Dr. William Wilberforce Baldwin, 20 July 1893; Morgan Library.

pp.34–35: "Deny the power . . . life of the body": Thomas J. Hudson, *The Laws of Psychic Phenomena* (London: G. P. Putnam, 1893), pp. 203, 123, 285.

p.36: " 'knows things he didn't' . . . You see what I am.' ": Henry James, *The Ambassadors* (1903), (London: Bodley Head, 1970), pp. 37, 40, 42.

p.38: "call spirits . . . call for them?": *Henry IV, Part One,* III:1, 53–55.

3

p.54: *"He would have grown . . . I've become."*: Quoted in *Fathers: Reflections by Daughters,* ed. Ursula Owen (New York: Pantheon, 1985), p. 231.

4

p.59:   *"Remember what it was . . .* to make amends.": Joan Didion, *Slouching Toward Bethlehem* (New York: Farrar, Straus and Giroux, 1965); rpt. in *Eight Modern Essayists*, Fifth Edition, ed. William Smart (New York: St. Martin's Press, 1990), pp. 234, 237.

5

pp.86–87:   "Sitting on the floor . . . which were people.": Virginia Woolf, *To the Lighthouse* (New York: Harcourt, Brace and World, 1927), pp. 78–80.

6

p.90:   "I went to the woods . . . Living is so dear.": Henry David Thoreau, *Walden, Or Life in the Woods* (1854), *The Norton Anthology of American Literature*, ed. Baym et al. Third Edition, vol. 1 (New York: 1989), pp. 1682–83.

p.95:   "with the nerves . . . keeps me there.": letter to Linda Guilford, n.d., quoted Benedict II: 41.

p.95:   "I am called . . . rest at noon.": letter to Sam Mather, 22 August 1887; Mather Family Papers, Western Reserve Historical Society.

p.96:   "from five in the morning . . . aches to the shoulder.": letter to Henry James, 30 August 1882; *Henry James: Letters*, ed. Leon Edel, vol. 3 (Cambridge, Mass: Harvard University Press, 1974–84), p. 544.

p.96:   "beautiful regular profile . . . almost cold, manner.": CFW letter quoted Benedict II: 185.

p.97:   "occasion . . . the first draft.": letter to Henry James, 30 August 1882; *Henry James: Letters*, vol. 3, p. 544.

p.98:   "Rising early in the morning . . . at nine.": CFW, "The Haunted Lake," *Harper's New Monthly Magazine* XLIV (Dec. 1871), 20–30; rpt. Benedict I: 49–57; p. 56.

p.98:   "walking up and down . . . silent train of thought. . . .": "Haunted Lake," Benedict I: 57.

p.99:   "could not alter . . . on the same day.": CFW letter to Henry James, 30 August 1882. *Henry James: Letters,* vol. 3, p. 544.

p.99:   "I do'nt think . . . hating that salmon).": CFW letter to Henry James, 12 February 1882, in *Henry James: Letters,* vol. 3, p. 529.

p.107:   "in rapt attention . . . low, cultivated voice.": Linda Guilford, "Notes in Memory of Miss Woolson," Western Reserve Historical Society.

p.107:   "flush of pleasure . . . characteristic essays": Linda Guilford, *The Story of a Cleveland School from 1848 to 1881* (Cambridge: John Wilson, 1890), pp. 76–77.

pp.107–8:   "literary talent . . . lovely dress!": Benedict I: 292 n.

7

p.118:   "habit of studying . . . swept along in the train": "Jeannette," in *Castle Nowhere: Lake-Country Sketches* (Boston: Osgood, 1875), pp. 154, 175.

pp.118–19: "slender form . . . thrilled my own heart.": "Wilhelmena," in *Castle Nowhere,* pp. 285, 300.

p.119:   "a cold observer . . . that moved them. . . .": "Ethan Brand" in *Hawthorne: Selected Tales and Sketches,* ed. Hyatt Waggoner (New York: Holt, 1970), p. 375.

p.120:   "Powers of observation . . . monstrous detachment.": introduction to Gordimer's *Selected Stories* (New York: Penguin, 1976), p. 12.

pp.123–24: "Solitary pedestrian" . . . "sufferings will be forgotten.": "In the Cotton Country" (1876), in *Women Artists, Women Exiles: "Miss Grief" and Other Stories by Constance Fenimore Woolson,* ed. Joan Weimer (Rutgers University Press: 1988), pp. 135–38, 147–48.

p.125:   "intercourse with the world.": Preface to *Twice-Told Tales* in Waggoner, p. 587.

8

p.132:   "lost her reason.": Benedict I: 42.
p.148:   "It is a hard thing . . . obstacle existed.": Benedict I: 67n.
p.148:   "quick consumption": Benedict I: 77.
pp.148–49: "there was no possible use . . . at the head in *every* line.": Benedict III: 334n.

10

p.176:   "marry an inferior . . . adjuncts of the lady.": CFW's review of Mrs. Burnett's *That Lass o'Lowrie's*, Contributor's Club, *Atlantic Monthly* XL (Sept. 1877), 365–66.
p.176:   Lady Elinor Eglantine St. Clair: "From Mrs. Woolson's Journal," in Benedict I: 121; "Lady Han" from Hannah Woolson's Commonplace Book in New York State Historical Association, Cooperstown.
p.176:   "Mrs. Van-Something . . . the lower classes.": CFW letter to Paul Hamilton Hayne, All Saints Day, 1876; Duke University Library.
p.180:   "well and strong . . . in our lives": "Raspberry Island. Told to me by Dora," *Harper's New Monthly Magazine* LV (Oct. 1877), 737–45.
p.180:   "a visitor . . . no matter where you find it": in Benedict I: 323.
p.183:   You must have had a fine time . . . how can you?: CFW letter to Edmund Clarence Stedman, 1 October 1876; Edmund Clarence Stedman Papers, Rare Book and Manuscript Library, Butler Library, Columbia University.

11

p.195:   "Not all of them will love you, whichever way you choose": Adrienne Rich, quoted in Carolyn G. Heilbrun, *Writing a Woman's Life* (New York: Norton, 1988), p. 129.
p.197:   "To imagine a man spending his life . . . moment never comes.": Benedict II: 145–46.
p.197:   "Imagine a man . . . obtained by them.": Benedict II: 135.

pp.197–98: "deepest charm . . . try as I may to think so.": CFW letter to Henry James, 7 May 1883, in *Henry James: Letters,* vol. 3, p. 551.

p.198: "to whom nothing . . . light of her use.": "The Beast in the Jungle" (1903) in *The Complete Stories of Henry James— 1900–1903,* vol. 11, ed. Leon Edel (London: Rupert Hart-Davis, 1964), pp. 401–402.

12

pp.207–212: "It was all Lake Erie . . . heart knoweth its own bitterness.": "Ballast Island: A Story of Lake Erie," *Appleton's Journal* (28 June, 1873), 833–39.

p.210: "Why do literary women break down so?" CFW letter to Stedman, 23 July 1876.

p.210: " 'nervous prostration' . . . 'mental exhaustion.' ": CFW letter to Stedman of 14 March, 1879; letters to Sam Mather of 22 Jan. 1887 and 16 October 1889.

p.211: singularly conservative?: Henry James, "Miss Woolson" (1887) in *Women Artists, Women Exiles,* p. 271.

p.217: "infernal . . . desperate effort to escape.": CFW letter to Dr. William Wilberforce Baldwin, 5 February 1892; Morgan Library.

p.219: "The tears are not serious . . . laugh at myself.": CFW letter to Sam Mather, 8 February 1892.

p.219: "It is only . . . in a trumpet": CFW letter to Sam Mather, 20 May 1892.

p.219: "I like . . . basest hypocrisy!": CFW letter to Henry James, 30 August 1882; *Henry James: Letters,* vol. 3, p. 544.

p.219: "I have given up . . . I must read.": undated CFW letter to Flora Mather, Benedict II: 52.

p.220: "great drawback . . . cannot always explain it.": CFW letter to Dr. Baldwin, 20 July 1893.

p.220: "I have a horror . . . have it over.": CFW letter to Henry James, 7 May 1883; *Henry James: Letters,* vol. 3, p. 551.

13

p.230:   "evil tendency . . . body answered not again.": "Peter the Parson" in *Castle Nowhere*, pp. 99–135.

p.231:   "Self-denial . . . is indulged!": Benedict 2: 110.

p.241:   "Unused the life in them": Tillie Olsen, *Tell Me a Riddle* (New York: Dell, 1960), p. 99.

14

p.243:   *gentlest and kindest . . . never wholly sane.*: italicized words are quoted from *Henry James: Letters*, vol. 4, pp. 460–64.

p.243:   "disappointment and depression of my own existence.": *Henry James: Letters*, vol. 3, xv.

p.244:   "delightful little studies . . . continually give thanks.": "Miss Grief" (1880) in *Women Artists, Women Exiles*, pp. 248–69.

15

pp.259–60: *terrifying telegrams . . . the result of morphine.*: Italicized words quoted from letters belonging to Constance Mather Bishop: WRHS Drawer 34.3.

p.260:   "as the prodigal is often so dearly loved . . . would never have been important to her": *Jupiter Lights* (New York: Harper & Bros., 1889), pp. 222–23.

p.260:   "made me suffer . . . broke my heart": CFW letter to Sam Mather, 16 January 1884.

p.260:   "Here you are alive . . . about here!": *Jupiter Lights*, p. 316.

p.261:   "imprisoned for life . . . horror of murder?": *Jupiter Lights*, pp. 160–61.

p.264:   "letter by the woman . . . vomiting bile"; "She *must* have . . . so weak they'd kill her.": Molly Mather Anderson papers.

p.277:   "bitterly regretted . . . healing treatment.": Rosamund Lehmann, "Bereavement: with an Account of a Suicide," *Light,* Summer 1979, 64–66.

p.279:   "the hardest job of all . . . to get myself dead.": *The Diary of Alice James,* ed. Leon Edel (New York: Penguin, 1982), p. 211.

p.279:   Volume of Shelley's poems inscribed by James to Woolson is in Benedict Library at Protestant Cemetery, Rome.

p.279:   "admiring aunt.": CFW letter to James, 12 February 1882, in *Henry James: Letters,* vol. 3, p. 529.

p.281:   "moral discords . . . no longer in dread.": Alice James, *Diary,* p. 232.

p.281:   "If I live . . . back to you by telepathy.": CFW letters quoted by Henry Mills Alden, "Constance Fenimore Woolson," *Harper's Weekly* 38 (3 February 1894), 113–14.

p.282:   "If at any time . . . joy at the release.": Benedict II: 393.

p.282:   "the sharp peaks . . . poor human beings.": Benedict II: 411. Original in Rollins College Archive.

p.283:   "For a long time . . . not live to be old": letter to Sam Mather, 23 November 1893; "I don't know anyone . . . as I am now!": letter to Sam Mather, 16 January 1884.

p.286:   *Ed essa . . . questa pace":* quoted by Edel in "A Portrait of Alice James," *Diary,* pp. 21–22.

About the Author

JOAN WEIMER is professor of English at Drew University. She is the editor of *Women Artists, Women Exiles: "Miss Grief" and Other Stories by Constance Fenimore Woolson*, and co-editor of *Literature of America*. Her work has appeared in *North American Review*, *Anima*, and *Legacy*, and won the John H. McGinnis Award for nonfiction from the *Southwest Review*.

About the Type

The text of this book was set in Palatino, designed
by the German typographer Herman Zapf. It was
named after the Renaissance calligrapher Giovan-
battista Palatino. Zapf designed it between 1948–
1952, and it was his first typeface to be introduced
in America. It is a face of unusual elegance.